2—
1982

# ADULT LEARNING IN YOUR CLASSROOM

## The best of TRAINING Magazine's strategies and techniques for managers and trainers

D0730905

Compiled from articles that have been published in

**TRAINING**
THE MAGAZINE OF HUMAN RESOURCES DEVELOPMENT

**LAKEWOOD BOOKS**
**50 South Ninth St.**
**Minneapolis, MN 55402**
**(612) 333-0471**

**Editor:** *Philip G. Jones*
**Compiled by:** *Linda M. Standke*
**Design:** *Audrey Kupers*

**With special thanks to:** *Chernah Coblentz, Nick Elsener, Todd Heimarck, Carol Kennedy, Sharon Proskin, Reg Sandland and Wanda Stephenson*

*TRAINING Magazine's purpose is to recognize and serve the special needs of training professionals and managers responsible for developing their organizations' human resources. Because the management of learning in an organization is more function than job title, TRAINING's more than 190,000 monthly readers include training and development managers and practitioners, mid- and upper-level executives, personnel directors, sales and marketing managers, audiovisual professionals, university professors and school superintendents, and hospital-based education directors. In short, TRAINING is written for everyone who manages the learning of others, and is responsible for applying everything we know about adult learning, motivation and performance to make people more effective on the job.*

*TRAINING, The Magazine of Human Resources Development (USPS 414-190), ISSN 0095-5892, is published monthly by Lakewood Publications, Inc. Thomas J. Nammacher, chairman; James P. Secord, president; Philip G. Jones, Michael C. Miller, vice presidents. Lakewood also publishes Airport Services Management; Potentials In Marketing; Recreation, Sports and Leisure and business books.*

*Contents of this book copyrighted © 1982 by Lakewood Publications, Minneapolis, MN 55402. All rights reserved. No part of this publication may be reproduced, stored in a retrieval system, or transmitted, in any form or by any means, electronic, mechanical, photocopying, recording, or otherwise, without the prior written permission of the publisher. Printed in the United States of America.*

*ISBN 0-943210-00-3*

# Table of contents

# Insuring back-on-the-job performance 3

# Understanding the adult learner 4

Make sure your trainees
want to learn what you
have to teach

# Motivating and managing learning in the classroom

by J. B. Cornwell

"**H**ow can I motivate my students?" "What can I do about students who don't want to learn?" "How can I show students the value of my objectives so they want to learn?"

Sound familiar? Those questions and variations on them are among those most frequently asked by classroom teachers/trainers seeking to become more effective.

Unfortunately, there are no simple answers. Students are human beings. Because of their individuality, no technique will stimulate all of them— even in the unlikely event that your presentation is ideally suited to them all.

But there is at least one way to ensure that students will want to learn what you offer and will invest considerable effort doing so.

Let's assume, though, that, in the planning session, you have accurately identified the performance needs of your students and have formulated specific objectives that describe performances the students will agree they don't have.

**Learner assessment**

Think about the experiences you have had with good salesmen. No, not the con artists who made you feel you'd been had. I mean those who sold you something you really wanted and made sure it fit your needs. Many car and insurance salesmen fit that description. When you finish this paragraph, put the book down, close your eyes, and relive the whole experience. Then come back.

One of the things that first-rate salesman did was find out what our needs were. The car salesman asked questions about the size of the family, how much driving we do, how much money we wanted to spend and some questions about our attitudes toward cars. Then he checked his conclusions with a statement-question sort of like this one:

Well, let's see now. You've got one six-year-old, you live a block from work but you take long, driving vacations and you tow an 18-foot ski-boat. It seems to me that comfort and prestige are more important to you than price and economy. Is that correct? Okay, then I think our Superdynamic Flowmobile V12 Formal Sedan with towing package, stereo, power dimmer switch, and robot remote gas pump detector would fit the bill. Have you looked it over? Would you like to test drive it?

Do you see what he was up to? Doesn't it seem likely that he was testing what he knew about you, what he thought he knew about you and the conclusions he drew from that *before* he started filling out a sales contract? As a matter of fact, you probably responded by correcting some wrong assumptions he made. For example: "No, actually reliability and low maintenance costs are very important to me. What do you have in a six-cylinder, standard-shift, two-door sedan?"

When did the salesman start getting your full cooperation? Wasn't it when he offered you a car with the features *you* wanted, that met your needs the way *you* saw those needs? That's what I thought.

When, then, do you suppose a teacher is likely to get full cooperation from learners? I suggest it will be when the learners agree that the objectives fit what they see themselves as needing.

If we thoroughly analyzed the needs of our learner population in the early stages of the design of our presentation, we would have a reasonably accurate set of assumptions about what they want and why. However, even if that analysis of a generalized population includes asking direct, to-the-point questions about what the learners want and why, we must establish— verbally— the connection between self-perceived needs and our product.

For example, imagine yourself in either role in the following situation. You are about two hours into a presentation on behavioral objectives:

**Presenter:** Karen, from watching you these past few minutes, I've decided that you're bored to tears with this program. Am I reading you correctly? But I assumed that, with your new job in training nurses' aides, you'd be really turned on by behavioral objectives.

**Karen:** Oh, I *was* turned on— until the program started. It's just not what I expected. I don't see how it relates to my situation. Behavioral objectives may be useful for training production workers and technicians, but my problems are different. I'm dealing mainly with attitudes.

**P:** What had you expected to learn?

**K:** I expected to learn how to do a better job of changing attitudes. What I'm getting is how to set objectives for and evaluate skills.

**P:** How do you determine whether or not you've changed attitudes?

**K:** That's pretty intangible. I have to go on gut feeling and on feedback from the nurses and patients.

**P:** You said you came here to learn how to do a better job of changing attitudes. Assuming you went back and did a better job, how would you know? What evidence would convince you that you were doing a better job?

**K:** Well...I don't know.

**P:** Does this seem logical to you: Attitudes describe how people feel about things? What they do and say is evidence of how they feel. The only indicators we have of what people feel is what they say and do—in other words their behavior. Do you agree so far?

**K:** To tell you the truth, I never thought of it that way. But yes, that makes sense.

**P:** Well, suppose you nailed down some observable behaviors that are acceptable evidence of the attitudes you are trying to produce. Would that make it easier to measure how well you are doing?

K: It sure would! Writing behavioral objectives that describe those behaviors would be the first step toward improving my course. I guess I had the cart before the pony. Could you go back over the key points on describing conditions?

If the presenter had begun by establishing the connection between Karen's perception of what she needed and the objectives of the program, Karen wouldn't have been bored two hours later. All too often, "Karens" leave our presentations feeling frustrated. How, then, do we establish this connection? How do we get the learners to agree that we perceive their needs accurately?

Here are a couple of helpful approaches:

1. **Presenter:** As I understand it, everyone here is a new instructor. Is that right?
   **Learners:** (a murmur of assent, some affirmative nods)
   **P:** Okay, our survey indicated that most new instructors felt they needed to be able to tell how well they had done. In other words, a method to measure how good they are. Does that seem desirable to you?
   **L:** (another murmur of assent)

2. **Presenter:** The title of this presentation is "Writing Behavioral Objectives." Behavioral objectives specify what we are going to achieve so that, when we are finished, we can accurately measure what we have achieved. Now, I would like you to tell me how this subject might fit your situations and what you would like to get out of today's session. Why don't you start out, Mike?

In both cases, a climate is established for serving the learner. (Of course, we must adjust the presentation to accommodate any real needs that we had perceived inaccurately.) We have probably successfully accomplished this step in the opening of our presentation if, after the presentation, the learners answer "Absolutely yes" to the question, "Did the presenter accurately perceive what you wanted from the presentation?"

### Commitment to objectives

Let's return to our professional salesman for a moment. Do you recall what he did after you agreed on what you wanted and needed? Did he give you a detailed description of his prod-

uct, its features and benefits? Actually, that's the next step in a traditional sales presentation: after the salesman has "qualified" his prospect (clarified what the prospect wants and needs and received the prospect's agreement about it), he describes the product in detail.

We should do something similar. We'll describe our product in detail, or state our behavioral objectives and the things that will happen during the presentation.

If we work from notes, our notes at this point will tell us to state the objectives—"After this presentation you will do such and such, under such and such conditions, to such and such standard"— and describe the presentation— "To accomplish this, we will do the following...."

Is it now clear to the learners what the objectives of the presentation are? What evidence convinces you of that?

Have you ever heard this little ditty? *I know I said what I thought I said.*

---

**LEARNER ASSESSMENT (SAMPLE)**

**PROGRAM**

The purpose of this questionnaire is to provide the presenter of this program with insights into your current skills in knowledge or about the subject. By knowing what new skills and knowledge you would like to get from the program, what personal goals you are pursuing that this program can contribute to, and some personal characteristics about yourself, the presenter will be better able to serve your needs in the presentation.

This form will be held in the strictest confidence and will be destroyed after the program.

Name_____ Age_____ Gender_____

Years of formal education_____ Title of current position_____

Briefly describe the responsibilities of your current position.

How do you expect the results of this program to improve your life and career?

What is the most important thing you expect to get out of this program?

How long have you been working in the type of job you now have?

Complete the following sentences.

I hope that this program will_____

I hope that this program will not_____

---

**LEARNING CONTRACT (SAMPLE)**

In the matter of the training course, _____, objectives and outline attached, and in consideration of the expense and effort invested in making this course available to me, I agree to do the following:
1. Appear in the classroom at the scheduled time(s).
2. Be alert and in as good physical and mental condition as possible.
3. Give my undivided attention to the presentations and projects scheduled.
4. Complete all projects assigned according to scheduled completion times.
5. Achieve the objectives listed on the attached.

Signed, _____ date _____
    Student

In consideration of the above, I agree to devote my full attention and energy to assisting _____ and other students enrolled in this course in achieving the objectives listed on the attached.

Signed, _____
    Instructor

*I know you heard what you thought you heard. The problem is: You didn't hear what I said.*

The point is, you heard my words, but you didn't hear my meaning. Let me try different words: Listeners don't always understand the speaker's words the way the speaker intends them. The only sure way we have of confirming understanding is to have our meanings fed back to us.

Are you still convinced that your learners understood the objectives? How will you convince yourself?

You might ask some of them to explain how they will apply the objectives to their jobs. You can watch the others for nonverbal feedback to see if they agree.

Once the learners clearly understand what the objectives are, we must be sure that these are also the learners' objectives. Just because they agree that we understand their needs, doesn't mean that they automatically agree that our solutions to those needs are worth the effort. The car salesman doesn't assume that we will buy his car just because we agree that we want and need a new car.

The question we must now answer for the learners is: What do I have to do to get it? (Remember asking the salesman how much the car cost? Is there any chance that you would have signed the sales contract before you knew?) What the learners have to do is cooperate during the presentation. So tell them what is going to happen and how—and get some feedback.

Now it's time to close the deal. When salesmen use that term, they mean getting the prospect to commit himself or herself to a contract. What the learners will do is give an overt (outward) sign that they are going to pursue the same objectives that you are during the presentation. The overt sign may be a nod of the head or a statement, such as "Yes, that's a worthwhile objective that will help me get where I want to be. I'm going to put forth the required effort to achieve it."

To the casual observer, the closing of the contract may be too subtle to notice. It may be just a casual transaction, like this:

**Presenter:** Well, that's our objective, and that's how we plan to achieve it. It will require your cooperation and effort. Can I count on that?

**Learners:** (Heads nod. But one learner stares blankly at the presenter.)

**P:** Do you need time to think it over, Sam?

**S:** Not at all. I just didn't think it mattered whether I wanted to cooperate or not, and I was wondering why you bothered to ask. No one ever asked before.

**P:** How do you feel about being asked this time?

**S:** I'm not sure. I don't know whether you're trying to avoid wasting your time on learners who don't want to put forth any effort or avoid wasting my time on things I don't want to learn badly enough to work at.

**P:** Would you accept both reasons, plus the fact that having made a conscious, outward commitment increases the probability that you actually will work at it?

**S:** Hmm. Maybe that's manipulation and maybe not. Either way, my desire is in motion; let's go.

Okay, so that wasn't such a casual transaction. But would have been had Sam just nodded, or if the presenter hadn't read his nonverbal feedback. Learners don't always respond exactly as we would like them to. What would you do if a learner says, "No. I don't think it's worth the effort"? Tell him to get his keester out of your classroom?

Well, we might do that, but it's not our classroom. It's theirs, the learners'. I'm there to fill their needs. I'd ask the learner how much effort it *is* worth. I don't think it's likely that a student would say "None." But if he did, I'd ask him what he proposes to do during the presentation. I'd also give the rest of the learners a chance to offer their comments.

Once we've closed the contract with the learners for mutual effort toward achieving the objectives, we are ready to begin the planned learning experiences.

At this point, we've completed the opening of our presentation. The strategy and sequencing of the opening are the same as in the classical sales presentation:

1. *Qualify the learner.* Get agreement from the learners that you accurately perceive their goals and needs.

2. *Describe the features, benefits and price of the product.* Describe the objectives of the presentation and the things that will happen during it. Get feedback to confirm their understanding.

3. *Close the contract.* The purpose of the first two steps is to get a valid contract. Get an overt commitment from the learners to work at achieving the objectives.

You have probably opened your presentation effectively if, after the presentation, your learners answer "Absolutely yes" to these questions:

1. Did the presenter accurately perceive what you wanted from the presentation?
2. Were the objectives clear to you from the beginning of the presentation?
3. Has the presentation provided you with solutions to your real needs?

### Suggested exercises for trainers/presenters

For one presentation you make:

1. Have all your learners complete a learner-assessment form that you design or a variation on the same learner assessment sheet in this article. Or, if you cannot directly collect learner perceptions of their needs, list those needs as you perceive them.

2. List learner needs that will be served by your presentation.

3. Opposite each need listed, enter one or more objectives of the presentation that will serve that need.

4. Write down your plan for getting agreement from your learners that their needs have been accurately assessed and that the objectives will solve those needs.

5. Write down your plan for establishing that the learners understand what the objectives are and what will happen during the presentation.

6. Write down your plan for getting commitment from the learners to invest effort toward the objectives.

7. Use your plan the next time you make that presentation. If you have decided to ask for a written contract from your learners, use the sample learning contract provided here or some variation on it. **T**

# Why do we want trainee involvement?

by Martin M. Broadwell

A couple of things often give the new classroom instructor the feeling of "losing control": turning the group loose for a discussion and breaking the group up into some kind of subgroup assignment. But we know that an instructor has to be truly exceptional to reach learning goals without actively involving the students. This raises a number of questions: What kind of involvement do we try for? Is just any kind of involvement good? Is it the involvement that causes the learning? What are some of the ways of getting useful involvement?

## Why involvement?

Considerable argument is offered both for and against involvement. Many experienced trainers who advocate it claim it makes a course more interesting and helps numb the "pain" of learning. No doubt about it, the involved student may find an otherwise dull course more interesting. Involvement seems to make time go faster and relieves the boredom of a monotone lecture. It forces students to concentrate on the subject at hand. But involvement based on this premise is incorporated to overcome something negative. Instead, it should be built into the design *of our training program* to accomplish something positive.

Other instructors try to add a respectable amount of participation to a classroom setting in the form of showing a few slides or a movie or occasionally using an easel and chalkboard. This, they believe, adds credence to the classroom activity. Because it is expected and because all the "right" books suggest it, they dutifully—and mechanically—try to get the group involved by using often uninspired tools and techniques.

Some instructors rely on involvement to fill up class time when they run short of material. With no particular objective in mind, they decide to toss out a couple of discussion questions and make a subgroup assignment that will keep students busy. They might try to justify their "efforts" by saying that the students "always like this exercise" or "this question really ties them in knots." But this hardly represents the use of involvement as a learning tool.

## The best design

Basically, the only reason for generating meaningful involvement is that it *can be* the best teaching method available to accomplish the learning goals we're seeking. This reason applies to any technique we use—anytime. And it should govern our approach to all course designs.

Involvement itself is certainly not synonymous with successful teaching; nor is just any kind of involvement guaranteed to be satisfactory. When we feel the urge to add involvement, we shouldn't satisfy that urge by, say, arbitrarily assigning a role play. We should assign role play only when that type of involvement is most likely to elucidate a certain point we need to reach a certain, *specified* objective. The same reasoning should dictate the use of other techniques, too.

## Added benefits

In addition to being a good technique for reaching an objective, involvement gives us a chance to get feedback from students, feedback that is related directly to the goal we're striving for in the activity itself. If we're doing a role play to teach salespeople how to close a sale, we receive feedback in precisely the areas we're concerned with. By hearing the efforts to overcome objections or close the sale, we know where the trainees' strengths and weaknesses are in the subject we're teaching.

Furthermore, the feedback produced by the involvement usually is transmitted back to the students, too. In the example above, the sales trainees can see how their approaches work (or don't work) and can make any necessary improvements. They don't need an instructor to tell them what's wrong with their presentations, especially if they've seen themselves role play on a videotape.

Feedback through involvement also allows us to measure the success of our objectives, especially those we hoped to attain at the end of a class period. Any kind of involvement will have students doing something, saying something, working on something that is the result of things that have been taught in class. By simply observing the involved and participating students, we can match what we see against what we wanted to see (our objectives) and decide whether or not we've met our goals.

## What kinds of involvement?

Involvement is, simply, any kind of student activity that is observable. (We'll avoid the obvious fallacy in this definition—the case where students are *mentally* involved." In its simplest form, it's a student answering "yes" or "no" to a question or writing an answer in a blank. In its most complex form, it might be a student doing individualized instruction with virtually no aid from the teacher.

The best way to stimulate involvement activities early in the teaching game is to pick those that provide some kind of built-in controls for the teacher. An example of a controlled involvement activity would be a subgroup assignment with rigid restrictions. Such activities may sound fixed, inflexible, and unimaginative—and they are. But they should be, because the novice instructor usually isn't ready to allow much latitude. That will come. First, the instructor must learn to handle the involvement technique itself.

Having each student make lists of reasons, name two problems, or give one written solution to a problem are other ways of stimulating involvement. We can have the students teach a portion of the material, especially in an area where one of the students is an experienced resource person. We can have them work on forms or find things in manuals. There are good, practical forms of involvement. If they are chosen because they are the best for the student at *this time* to *this subject*, they probably will be successful. If they're viewed as a means of getting through the training day as quickly and painlessly as possible, they may still be as successful. But obviously not for the right reasons.

One problem with involvement: It is easy to get caught up in the *doing* of it, without considering the *purpose* behind it. Therefore, the instructor, be he novice or old hand, always ought to ask, "Is this really a *meaningful* activity?" Excessive reliance on involvement techniques presents another problem—using them just because it's easy to do so. Adult learners need a reason for doing things in class. Many will play our game for just so long before asking themselves, "Why are we doing this?" Naturally, they aren't happy with the answer: "Don't worry, you'll see it all clearly a little later." A little later, we may find ourselves with fewer and less capable students. And for good reason. ∎

Reprinted from TRAINING, May 1977

Wallflowers and motor-mouths can change

# Stimulating and managing participation in class

by J. B. Cornwell

How can I get learners to ask questions and participate in classroom discussions? What can I do about wallflowers who won't speak up? How can I control that "motormouth" so that other learners can participate and I can stay on schedule? These questions represent one of the eternal challenges to the classroom presenter. I'd like to explore that challenge and offer some practical solutions. But, first, let's consider some why's.

## Why have participation? Why not lecture?

It would be inaccurate to say that adults cannot learn at all from listening to lectures. But it's certainly true that we are more likely to learn—and learn more—from what we say and do in guided discussion than from what we hear in lectures. Evidence is abundant, as a matter of fact, that if we can't participate in learning, many of us actually nod off.

Most experts agree that all adult learning is self-directed. As adults, we want to test, to try out new ideas and concepts, which we accept only after some sort of validation exercise. We have taken control of our own lives and aren't as pliable as we were as children. If that's so, then why do some learners resist participating?

I once asked a trainee why he didn't speak up in class very often, and he replied, "Mainly because I don't want to look foolish. But also because I don't have much to add to what others have to say. I don't want to waste class time just saying that I agree with someone." "You don't have any

questions?," I asked. "Oh, yes. But if I'm patient, someone else usually asks them." "Why do you think you may look foolish if you speak up?," I persisted. "I guess it's always been that way. If I ask a question, someone puts me down. If I say what I think, I may be ridiculed. I don't need that. I'm not as smart as a lot of people, and I don't have their way with words. Why should I stick my neck out?"

Apparently, this individual had been "trained" to believe that speaking up is more likely to result in his being embarrassed than rewarded. He also felt that his ideas weren't of value to the group and that even valuable ideas must be well-articulated to be acceptable.

Obviously, teachers and trainers in this person's past had inadvertently fostered this unfortunate non-participation. As a result, entrenched habits would have to be unlearned and a whole new set of experiences collected before this trainee could voluntarily participate in discussions or ask spontaneous questions.

On the other hand, many learners are so anxious to participate that it is as much of a challenge to limit them to their share of time as it is to get others to open up and say what's on their minds.

## Why do some learners want to talk all the time?

It seems to me that the learner who tends to dominate conversation is usually an alert, aggressive, confident person who likes attention. Frankly, I tend to be such a type when I'm in a learner role. I think that's because I'm also a trainer, and I feel I should help the presenter. But it's

also because I like to be noticed. My past experiences have caused me to believe that participating brings rewards— recognition and respect, as well as new knowledge—rather than punishing embarrassment. I think that most over-participators are seeking both recognition and knowledge.

It's important to note that it's irrelevant whether nonparticipators and over-participators have accurate self-perceptions. What is important is what we *believe* to be true and how that affects our participation in the classroom.

As I see it, then, there are three major categories of learners:

1. The typical learner, who wants to participate in order to learn more. Our only problem here is keeping the door open for participation and keeping the discussion aimed at the objectives of the session.

2. The non- or under-participator, who may be inhibited for any one or any combination of reasons.

3. The over-participator, who is probably seeking to show off a little as well as to participate for better understanding.

Typical learners are not going to participate just because they want to. They are going to evaluate the learning environment to decide if a particular session demands participation or a look-and-listen attitude. They may not do this consciously, but they do it.

Key words in describing a learning environment are *formality* and *focus*. A formal room arrangement— seats lined up in neat rows facing the front, a podium for the speaker to keep notes on (and hide behind), a raised platform at the front, screens and easels clustered by the podium— usually says "lecture." Most, if not all, the features of a formal environment tend to focus attention at all times on the presenter and, therefore, inhibit participation.

On the other hand, with a totally informal environment—no podium or platform, chairs arranged around tables, visual-aid paraphernalia scattered about— there is no one central point of focus created by the physical characteristics of the room.

In the formal environment, each learner has plenty of opportunity to feel alone. He is only one of many focusing attention on the presenter. And if he decides to ask a question or offer a comment, he must wrest attention away from the presenter and go "on stage" in front of all those people— a very threatening prospect to a shy person. But if he's seated at a table with three to five other people, he'll feel less alone and will be able to converse with them to gain some support for his idea or question.

Obviously, the climate influences how much anxiety a learner feels about the possible punishing results of speaking to the group. In both verbal and non-verbal messages to the learners, the presenter establishes this climate early on. As the presentation proceeds, the presenter either will reinforce that initial climate or cancel it.

The most obvious way for you, the trainer, to initiate a participative climate is to come right out and say that you planned for the session to be a group discussion. Say that you want people to question the ideas and concepts you will introduce and ask them to relate each idea to a problem or situation on the job or relate an experience that shows the idea in action.

Many presenters ask learners to describe problems to which they seek answers during the session. This approach initiates a participative climate and gives each learner a chance to try participating.

How the presenter responds to those initial participations will set the climate for the rest of the session. If he or she is warm and receptive to these inputs, participation will continue. But if he or she is cool, argumentive, unresponsive or in any other way fails to reward participation, he or she probably will end up doing the rest of the talking.

Here's how some learners I interviewed described trainers who successfully stimulated participation:

• "She says, 'Yes. Say more about that,' and nods her head and says, 'Right, right, and how do you feel about that?' I guess she just invites us

to talk and then keeps us talking. Most important, she listens to what we say and shows respect for our ideas as well as our feelings."

• "His sessions sound like a cross between interview and a counseling session with a 'shrink.' He doesn't offer a single fact or opinion of his own. Instead, he gets us to talk about the subject by offering provocative comments, stories and questions. Finally, he summarizes what we've said."

• "She walks over to you and watches you intently while you are talking, at close range, as though just the two of you were having a conversation. She leans toward you while she nods and says 'yes' or 'right.' Sometimes, she even puts her hand on your shoulder or arm as though she

were reassuring or protecting you."

• "He reaches toward us with his hand open and palm up. Sometimes he beckons with it as though asking us to keep talking. He signals to the one who's talking and keeps the others from butting in."

Many trainers believe that, in groups of more than 20, participation is not practical. Perhaps wide-open, free-flowing participation isn't, but I think that limited participation is possible and just as beneficial as in smaller groups. Participation in a large class should be limited to small-group discussions, with each table or group of four to six discussing and deciding upon an issue. Then a spokesperson for the group can present their ideas to the larger group. Thus, each learner is involved in the learning— testing understanding,

getting feedback and making adjustments— just as though he had interacted directly with the presenter.

So much for the basics. Now let's see how those problem learners, the wallflower and the motormouth, can become more productive participants.

The wallflower is a learner who resists participating. Whether this non-participator actually has been trained to keep quiet or simply is a shy person, he or she is more likely to speak up when the threat of embarrassment is nonexistent. As the presenter, you can reduce this threat in several ways. Watch the trainee's face to see if it registers clear understanding of what is going on before asking him or her a question. And always ask questions with no "wrong" answers; after another learner has said something concise and accurate, ask the wallflower if he or she agrees. Always express approval of inputs, particularly those offered by wallflowers. Remember, you have two kinds of learning going on: the objectives of the session plus the spontaneous participation of all learners.

The motormouth is a learner who over-participates, usually from a simple case of aggressiveness and/or excessive enthusiasm. Here, there's always a risk that an adversary relationship will develop between the motormouth and the presenter. This begins when the presenter ridicules the learner or his or her ideas. Even though the other learners usually lose patience with the motormouth before the presenter does, they usually resent the presenter berating or belittling *any* of their colleagues. When that happens, the climate collapses. The savvy trainer might ask other learners to comment on motormouth's input. If those inputs interfere with the success of the session, someone eventually will say so.

A more subtle technique is to use some body language on motormouth. Move about the room so that you do not directly face him or her, and, at the same time, use some of the techniques already discussed to draw other learners out. If that doesn't throttle the motor down to an acceptable level, try holding out your palm at him or her in the classic policeman's "stop" signal when he or she tries to interrupt.

Obviously, I haven't offered any pat answers to complex problems here. Nor did I intend to. My intention has been, rather, to describe and discuss the types of learners and learning environments all trainers eventually will encounter and to emphasize the importance of spontaneous, productive participation. **T**

| HELPING TRAINEES PARTICIPATE: KEEP THE OTHER GUYS TALKING | | |
| --- | --- | --- |
| Leader Statement | Leader Attitude | Leader "message" to group |
| I see. Yes, yes. | Neither agree nor disagree; noncommital but positive | I'm interested in what you're saying. |
| In other words, you think... If I understand you correctly, your decision would be... | Be sure you understand what he means. | I've listened, I understand, I have the facts. |
| You feel that... You are upset about... | Be sure you understand how he feels. | I've listened; I understand how you feel; your feelings are important. |
| The group seems to feel that... The key ideas you have expressed seem to be... | Summarize group contributions. | This is what you have expressed; it is important. |

Trainees often acquire new
patterns of behavior by
watching the trainer

# The trainer as a behavior model

by Bernard L. Rosenbaum
and Barbara Baker

You have the best intentions in your desire to motivate people to learn. So you study adult-learning principles and build into your training experiential exercises in order to encourage self-directed learning. But when you conduct the training session, participants don't accomplish the learning objectives to the degree that you expected. Perhaps that's because *your behavior* in the actual interpersonal situation of teaching didn't support your intentions.

There *are* specific trainer behaviors that support adult-learning principles and that help you, the trainer, accomplish your training objectives while building the participants' self-esteem. In Managerial Grid language, this is 9,9 training (maximum concern for the participant and maximum concern for learning), and it is highly motivating to the learner. These trainer behaviors are soundly based on five principles of motivation that apply to all areas of interpersonal communication. And because they are behaviors, they can be demonstrated, taught and applied in a way that no theory can. Once your training philosophy and intentions support your teaching behavior, you'll become both effective and believable.

When you think about your own experiences as a participant in a training session, you probably find that you often can remember more about the instructor than you can about course content. Behaviors modeled by an instructor can have a powerful impact on group and individual performance. Participants are likely to discount the quality and usefulness of course content when instructor behavior erodes participant self-esteem. Particularly in training courses that teach *motivation*, the trainer must be *motivating*. Instructor behavior that is at odds with course content produces feelings of discomfort within a student, which he or she tries to relieve by discounting the quality and relevance of course content and by engaging in other defense mechanisms that restrict learning.

## Five trainer behaviors that increase motivation to learn

**1 Maintain and enhance the self-esteem of participants.** For most participants, the motivation to learn can be increased by creating a classroom environment that boosts the participants' confidence in their own ability to learn. Research has demonstrated that people are motivated to learn at a level consistent with their perceptions of self-competency. By maintaining and, when possible, enhancing the self-esteem of participants, the instructor creates a classroom environment that boosts students' confidence in their ability to perform. The motivation to learn is thereby increased.

Research clearly supports this conclusion. Individuals who are told they are incompetent to achieve a specific goal or task will perform worse than those who are told they are competent to achieve the task goals. And individuals and groups of low self-esteem are less likely to achieve goals they have set for themselves than individuals of high self-esteem. The more failures a person has, the less the person will aspire to in the future and the less the person will be motivated to obtain. As a matter of fact, there is a significant positive relationship between self-concept of ability and grade-point average.*

Fortunately, there are specific trainer behaviors that do maintain or even enhance the self-esteem of participants. The trainer who is aware of these would do the following:

• Listens to ideas.
• Praise ideas of participants.
• Acknowledge participants' ideas.
• Turn questions back to the group.
• Write down participants' ideas on a flip-chart.
• Refer back to previous comments by using the speaker's name.
• Point out positive behaviors and their effect.
• Reinforce group compliments of an individual and elaborate upon them.
• Ask for examples from the group's own experience.
• Share his or her own experiences.
• Admit to being wrong.
• Avoid arguments and making "right" and "wrong" judgments.
• Show enjoyment of the class.
• Spend additional time with people during breaks and before and after class.
• Focus on the learners' concerns rather than on his or her own preoccupations.
• Express confidence in the group.
• Ask questions that the learner probably can answer.
• Give complete reasons for directions.
• Share information.
• Keep notes and live up to follow-up commitments.
• Give constructive feedback and build behaviors through positive reinforcement.
• Begin sessions on time.

**2 Focus on participants' behavior and not on personality or attitude.** When an instructor focuses on the personality traits of a participant, the odds of eroding the participant's self-esteem are increased. One way to improve classroom communications is to focus on specifics and behaviors rather than on personality, attitude or subjective interpretations. The instructor who says, "I'd like you to pay special attention to this," is not modeling this principle as effectively as the instructor who says, "I'd like you to take notes." "You're not being cooperative" and "You don't seem to have a very positive attitude" can be replaced with "You haven't handed in the last two assignments on time." Partici-

*A. Korman, *Industrial and Organizational Psychology* (Englewood Cliffs, NJ: Prentice Hall, 1971), chapter 3.

pants respond more productively when their behavior is discussed than when references are made to their personality or attitudes.

The following suggestions should help you concentrate on behavior, instead of drawing attention to more personal attributes.

- Ask for specific examples.
- Use examples when presenting an idea.
- Ask, "How so?" or "How would you say it?"
- Rather than solicit general comments, ask participants to demonstrate their points of view.
- Ask for evidence. When participants offer praise or criticism, don't accept generalities. Press for specifics.
- When offering praise, explain why.

**3** Actively listen to show understanding. Active listening is a communications technique that enables trainers to establish rapport with participants and stimulate open and frank expression of feeling. It aids the trainer in clarifying participant comments and enables the participant to be heard and understood. In active listening, the trainer accepts what is being said without making any value judgments, clarifies the feelings being expressed and reflects this back to the participant.

In the following instances, active listening is particularly important. When a participant makes an emotional statement— "I don't see how we're supposed to get our work done and also attend this class,"— you might respond by saying, "You're feeling stretched pretty thin and are worried about getting your job done." When a participant is being uncooperative, you might say, "You're bored and think this course is a waste of time and not really relevant to getting your job done." And when a participant doesn't seem to understand what you or what another participant has said, your comment might be: "You're a bit confused and uncertain about John's point-of-view."

Other times when active listening responses would be appropriate are:

- When participants keep changing the issue being discussed.
- When a participant is rambling or grandstanding.
- When a participant's remark is important to the group's learning.
- When a participant disagrees with a suggested procedure.

- When a participant is being supportive.

**4** Use reinforcement to shape learning. Participant behaviors that are rewarded tend to be repeated and strengthened. Unlike some other consequences of a behavior (e.g., punishment), positive reinforcement is not accompanied by negative side effects. Skillful trainers are able to identify and reward small units of learning and gradually build that learning into the desired outcome. Trainers who rely on overt and/or covert forms of punishment to induce learning tend to generate a defensive reaction that minimizes transference of the training from the classroom to the job.

Reinforcing learning is a three-step process. First, identify the specific, observable behavior that facilitates the learning process (e.g., answering a question, asking a question, participating in an exercise, completing an assignment).

Next, explain what helpful effect that behavior had on the learning process for the participant and for others (e.g., the question helped to clarify an issue, the participation in a role play allowed everyone to learn more).

And finally, indicate your positive feelings about the behavior (e.g., "I really appreciate your comments, thanks for helping me out").

And remember these hints, which serve as verbal and silent reinforcers to your participants.

- Refer back to a participant's ideas or examples.
- Use people's names whenever possible.
- Nod your head when you agree.
- If a particularly cogent remark is made, don't repeat it to make it "yours."
- When a participant's comments or responses are only partially correct, acknowledge the accurate elements before correcting what's wrong.
- Paraphrase or write on flip-charts in the participant's words rather than your own.

Keep in mind that while the learning is in the acquisition stage, it is difficult to overdo specific and sincere positive reinforcement.

**5** Set goals and follow-up dates and maintain communications. Set training goals that are challenging,

but achievable, measurable and accompanied by specific deadlines. Well-stated, measurable training goals are effective in improving learning. A growing body of research has demonstrated the motivational properties of goals. Moderately difficult and specific goals lead to higher level of performance than do no goals at all or "do your best" goals.

- "Contract" for specific, on-the-job applications of learning.
- Set specific follow-up dates with participants.
- Clearly indicate what level of proficiency you expect and by when.
- Periodically report on progress toward the goal.
- Keep trust and credibility high by maintaining your follow-up dates.
- Evaluate movement toward the goal against established reference points.

## Teaching effective behaviors to trainers

As we've pointed out, trainees often can acquire new patterns of behavior by watching the performance of the trainer. They can abstract common features from a trainer's behavior and transfer them to the job. This is particularly true when the trainer is highly competent, has considerable status and has some influence over resources the trainee desires. That's why certain line managers can make highly effective trainers.

Behavior modeling is a powerful way to provide trainers with skills that facilitate learning. Videotapes are constructed to show trainers successfully teaching others. These tapes (behavior models) show specific trainer behaviors in a variety of situations and problems. Trainers view the models; identify with the situations, which represent their own experiences; rehearse the modeled behaviors under the coaching of a "master trainer"; and are able to transfer the skills to their next training class. This process necessitates spacing the training sessions so that trainers can apply newly learned skills between training sessions.

We believe that it is essential for trainers in Supervisory Skills Training (SST) programs to be able to model everything they are teaching. After all, a significant difference between training that is transferred to the job and training that remains in the classroom is the effectiveness of the trainer as a behavior model. **T**

How you begin your training session determines whether you have trainees or just warm bodies in the class

# Making the most of the first 20 minutes of your training

by Don M. Ricks

The instant a training course begins, a roomful of relaxed, talkative adults is suddenly transformed into dutiful pupils. A mere hint that "it's time to begin" can trigger deadly silence, as faces assume attentive expressions and pens are poised expectantly over notebooks. The instructor's stomach lurches uneasily. He has successfully welcomed people at the door, shaken hands, caught names, passed out jokes and strokes; he has, in fact, established credibility as a Human Being. Now he must prove himself, according to the group's expectations, as a Teacher.

This is a promising moment. Regardless of how long the course will last, the trainees can achieve their highest l.v.p.s. (learning volume per second) during the next 20 minutes. Now is the instructor's chance to mold them into a group of active, working learners. Every face in the room says, "I'm ready—start talking." And the temptation to do just that is tremendous. Yet if those first 20 minutes are devoted solely to instructor talk, they may be wasted; worse yet, they may inadvertently lock both the instructor and the group into a nonproductive learning relationship.

Let's look at a typical opening process and the effects it creates. After a joke or two (the participant's reaction: *These instructors always begin with something humorous to try to loosen us up.*) and an uncomfortable round of self-introductions, the instructor attempts to establish the credibility and importance of the course. *(Why does he think I signed up in the first place?)* Then comes an elaborate explanation of the objectives

and methods of the program. *(Okay, okay, let's get on with it.)*

As attention begins to lag, the instructor tries to create some interaction by inviting questions. *(My gawd, he expects me to ask him something!)* Failing that, he tries asking *them* some questions. *(The course hasn't even started yet. How am I supposed to know what he wants me to say?)* When someone does venture a query, the instructor pounces on it as an excuse for a detailed explanation of several related points. *(All I wanted was a "yes" or "no.")* Beginning to panic, he assures the group that the course will be very interesting. *(Oh yeah. When?!)*

## A class community

By now class members have solidified. They have assumed avoidance postures, waiting for something to happen that will resuscitate them. In a desperate attempt, the instructor shifts to a more dramatic, and louder, style. *(What happened?)* A contrived joke may bring a couple of chuckles ...and several blank looks. *(Was I supposed to laugh at something?)*

Now the instructor, having delivered his introductory remarks but failing to establish rapport, is stuck. He can only proceed with the instructional material, hoping to loosen up the class along the way. The magic words — "Well then, let's get to work"—spark a flurry of movement, a scraping of chairs. Again the pens are poised, ready to take notes.

What has this instructor accomplished during the first crucial 20 minutes? He has conveyed to the course participants that they will play Pupil to his Teacher for the duration.

Pupil is a role they assume effortlessly; each has had from 12 to 20 years preparing for the part. As for him, the easiest thing to be, when standing in front of a group, is a Teacher. So both are forced into compulsive behaviors. He is authoritative, patient, and wise. They are passive, compliant, and dependent. He makes lists on the chalkboard, tosses out humorous comments, and speaks important words. They laugh appreciatively and write down everything. If he's a Good Teacher, they will be impressed by how much *he* knows about the subject.

The problem with such introductory lectures is not that they cover the wrong materials but that they happen at all. In fact, an instructor should not have time to lecture at the beginning of the course. There are too many other worthwhile things to do. Here are four that should rate high priority with all trainers:

1. Neutralize the incipient Teacher-Pupil relationship.
2. Begin to form a class community.
3. Encourage trainees to discover and start to correct any nonproductive learning agendas they may have.
4. Encourage them to formulate definite in-course and post-course objectives for themselves.

The potential Teacher-Pupil relationship has to be disrupted immediately, even before it has begun to function. The canny instructor will use the opening as a time to start reacting to his students, not vice versa. By creating opportunities for the trainees to talk, he can validate their own knowledge and experience, their own potentialities for contributing to the course. He should remember that, at this point, it is more important for people to *feel* right than to *be* right. So he should treat contributions and responses as opportunities for showing approval, not as excuses for displaying his own abilities to correct or explain.

Unless the group is very large, the instructor should make eye contact with, and direct at least one comment or question to, every individual in the room. Thus he will avoid having some people wait for "something to happen to me." And he will prevent that uneasy feeling, a couple of days down the road, of discovering a stranger in the course, someone he hadn't noticed before.

The instructor can also start building a class community immediately. During the first 20 minutes, everyone should make direct eye contact with, talk with, and even touch at least half

Reprinted from TRAINING, August 1977

a dozen other group members. They should also be made to move at least once. Their first instinct was to claim a territory and establish a defensive perimeter; but if they leave their seats and relate to their neighbors on neutral territory, "block party" style, they will be better prepared to work together.

By seating people in small groups of five or six and by briefly addressing each group as a separate entity, the instructor can accomplish a great deal. People will begin to like members of a manageable social unit within which a lone individual can exert influence. Moreover, they will speak up more freely, because they will feel supported by their own team; in confronting the authority personified by the teacher, they will feel they have allies.

A few minutes of personal agenda work at the beginning of a course can produce a marked improvement in the post-course performance results. Trainers can safely assume that everyone in the room is there for the wrong reasons. Some people bring *irrelevant* agendas: "Sue got sick, so I'm sitting in for her"; "Now that I've finally signed up for this course, maybe my boss will get off my back." Others come with *inappropriate* agendas: "I'm here to evaluate this course for use by others"; "I want to find out what I've been doing wrong"; "According to the outline, this course touches on one or two of the topics I'm interested in." And far too many attend with seemingly reasonable, but *non-functional*, agendas: "I'm here to learn the course content" (not "to improve my performance"). "I'll *try* to improve" (not "*will* improve"). "After I look at the whole program, I'll pick out and learn the parts that are directly relevant to my situation."

So an instructor can use a brief agenda exercise to make people aware of their subliminal reasons for attending the course. Here again, the temptation to talk—or, rather, to preach—is strong. But by helping adults discover a) that they may have come into the course with a nonproductive mental set, and b) that more positive alternatives exist, an instructor can indirectly shift attitudes.

## Post-course objectives

Establishing an explicit sense of individual objectives is a critical function of the introduction. Most people have two generalized objectives when they enter the training room. First, they want to *perform well* (i.e., make "correct" responses) in the course. Second, they intend to *learn the materials* (i.e., the concepts and information) they assume the instructor will cover. Usually they have only a vague notion of post-course objectives. They know that what they will learn should help them do a better job—but in some uncertain way and at some undefined future time.

Not only are these objectives too general, they may be counterproductive. In a course which is intended to improve performance rather than increase knowledge, the trainee determined to "can the content" will frustrate both himself and the instructor. He who thinks his purpose is to "do well" will expend his energies trying to figure out the correct answers rather than adopting more effective ways of performing.

The instructor should therefore prepare for the transition from the training room back into the "real world" on the first, not the last, day of the course. Moreover, he should emphasize that the course consists of what *the students do*, not of what the instructor does. Again, questioning is the most effective technique. Something as simple as, "Which should be better—the last letter you wrote before the course or the first one you will write afterward?," can initiate dialogue. Students will discover that their objective in the course should be to change how they write, not just to learn about good writing, and that the real proof of their performance will be a demonstrable improvement in the documents they later produce on the job.

Ostensibly, a course opening serves to introduce trainees to the instructor and to outline the course's content. Actually, such an introduction contradicts two principle premises of modern training: that trainees themselves are the active agents in their own learning processes, and that the instructor should serve as a well-informed guide, not a talking textbook. The instructor's initial task then should be to bring people to a point where: 1) they can work together comfortably in an unfamiliar environment, 2) they will draw freely upon the special resources the instructor provides, and 3) they have set some positive goals to achieve.

The objectives and techniques of the course introduction, therefore, should be the most carefully planned and executed of the whole program. Technique, of course, is not nearly as important as attitude or the role function the instructor brings to the training room. If an instructor considers himself an expert, the group will treat him as an expert depending upon him to make the training happen. But if the trainer sees himself as assisting others in accomplishing their learning goals, the trainees will be better able to work in cooperation with him. Similarly, the instructor who enters the room expecting to enjoy the trainees—not hoping to *persuade* them to enjoy him—will discover that establishing rapport and getting results are easy, even pleasurable, tasks. **T**

Your course introduction is the most important part of the training. If it isn't well planned, your trainees will tune you out—wasting both your time and theirs.

Protect the ego—theirs and yours—when
your class has varying levels of experience

# Dealing with age and experience differences

by Martin M. Broadwell

Perhaps few things plague the training director and the classroom like the presence of experienced employees sitting next to those who are brand new, either on the job or with the organization. There are some solutions but you may have to change your traditional teaching methods to get the best results.

Remember the first public speaking class you were ever in? One of the first things you were told was "know your audience." This is equally good advice for the instructor: "Know your students!" Just because you have people of different age groups or with different years of experience does not—*in itself*—mean that there is a difference in knowledge or skills level among your trainees. One of the things that bothers me a great deal is to be conducting some management or supervisory training (whatever the difference is) and have some old-timer say, "I've heard all that before." I've finally found the appropriate response to that. I simply ask (smiling all the time), "Great, are you suggesting that you've not only *heard* all this but that you're also *doing all of it* now?" I have yet to hear anyone say that they are, in fact, practicing all the things I'm trying to get across, though I suspect there are some who think they are, but are afraid to come out and admit it with peers (who know better) right there in the room. You might also request that the "hearer of it all before" help out with practical examples whenever possible. In other words, enlist the help of the experi-

enced person as a means of selling your own points, and as a means of at least neutralizing any opposition.

This, then, is one of the basic rules of handling the variance: Use the experience to your advantage, rather than have it used against you to your disadvantage. This means sometimes catering to these experienced people in ways your own ego might not like. You may have to give them recognition, ask their opinion, give them talk-time when you'd rather not, and avoid cutting them down when you'd like to. For consolation, remember that these people who do have experience carry a lot of weight with those who don't, and the newer employee may take their word over yours. If this is the case, it's best to have the words *agreeing rather than disagreeing*.

## Protect the Ego

The experienced supervisor or skilled employee probably feels somewhat out of place in the classroom with the newer employees. In a way, it's a put-down to be there. It's sometimes shattering to find that the organization thinks he needs training in areas where he's been working for a long time, and then to discover that he's in a class with a bunch of wet-behind-the-ears beginners. One of the problems for the instructor is that this assault on the ego may promote some frustrations which exhibit themselves in behavior that is undesirable to the instructor. Herein lies the secret to successfully using these people: Protect their egos, not your own. In their frustrations, they may challenge you.

Take the challenge, but in an adult way, trying to find the empirical proofs for what you are saying, not by drawing your sword and trying to cut the person down with an "I told you so!"

If the person is wrong, make the let-down easy, firm, and pleasant. If the person is right, make the thank-you sincere, and the experience a *learning* experience for the whole class. Be careful, though, not to carry this ego satisfaction too far. You can't devote the entire class period to just keeping the egos salved. You have to get in some learning, too. This takes some skill at observation, and it takes some admission that you may not be very good at observation—especially in the early stages of the class meetings.

Let's take an example. You start the class and immediately get a challenge from an older or more experienced student. You debate hurriedly in your mind and decide that this person may become a problem if you don't get him on your side in a hurry. You give the person some attention early in the session. This works well for you, because the students comment, you're looking for participation, and all this is working well. Soon, there is another challenge from this same employee/student, and again you respond in a way to build up the person, giving satisfaction, allowing for discussion, agreeing where you can. Again, there is a challenge from this same person. By now, you're probably feeling dominated by this person who has successfully challenged and won on several occasions, and you would like to hear from the others, who seem to be holding back. A monster is beginning to take shape, and you don't know whether to kill it, run from it, or feed it.

You must set some standards on how much interruption you'll tolerate, how much participation you want from others, then use your teaching skills to meet these standards. This doesn't mean you should go back to putting down the student. It does mean that at some point the student must conform to the rules and procedures of the classroom.

Remember, you reinforced this early participation, diagreement, knowledge-sharing, and the student was responding to your encouragement. It would be improper if you now embarrassed him. The easiest thing to do is withdraw reinforcement. When the person speaks out, listen to him, but don't enter into a discussion about it. If it's a question, hear it out, decide if it is pertinent. If so, then answer it, or reflect it to *someone else*. If it's not pertinent, then say something like, "That's interesting and something to think about later. Right now, we've got to deal with...", and go on with your agenda. An extreme procedure is to look at the employee, listen, but not respond at all...just go on to the next point. It's a bit frustrating, but not necessarily embarrassing, if you don't dwell on the looking and listening too long. There's always the alternative of, "We can talk about that after class, if you like."

### New People Have Ego, Too

Most of these techniques are designed to protect the older, experienced students. But what about the younger ones? Obviously, they have rights and feelings, too, and you should be equally concerned about them. You should find out what they know, what they don't know, what they need to know, how they feel about being in the class with older employees, what pressures they feel, and what they think about why the organization sent them to this course with the older, more experienced employees. Again, your power of observation comes into play, and you must be equally careful not to move too fast, or draw conclusions too quickly.

These employees are apt to be conscious that they're not as experienced as their co-students. They won't be able to answer the questions as readily, nor be willing to answer them even if they think they know the

answers. Again, you must be willing to change your traditional teaching methods. You might even confront the class with the question, "How can we handle this inequity in distribution of experience and knowledge?" You may have to create a makeshift lesson plan right there in the class. Try asking for volunteers to teach certain material in an "aide" capacity. Or you can give some quick knowledge tests to find out

---

**Your own ego might not like these techniques, but they can help resolve this age-old classroom problem.**

---

who can handle what material. This isn't a threat, it's just a quick means of helping out the students and using their resources.

Another technique is to allow the trainees to move at their own pace, if possible. If you know ahead of time that you're going to have a level difference, you can design with this self-pacing in mind. Otherwise, you

can do some of it right in the class. "Those of you who feel you have a working knowledge of this may want to move on to the next step." Or, "Those of you who feel comfortable with this material can be of assistance in helping the others in small-group work." This technique shows consideration for the newer employees, gives them the advantage of the resources in the room, and still deals favorably with the older egos.

Finally, we should protect these less experienced employees by teaching to them at their level, rather than aiming over their heads just because there are a few more experienced people in the class. Some of us have a tendency to talk to one person if we don't watch ourselves. We ask a question, get an immediate answer from one of the students, go on for a while, ask another question, get the correct response from the same student, and before we know it, the rest of the students are sitting around wondering what they're doing in the class in the first place!

We should work on systems that get feedback from all the students; we should respond to the questions of the newer students in meaningful ways. At the same time, when one of the newer employees comes up with a right answer, by all means we should reinforce this immediately and sincerely. If we do, we'll soon have them all working together toward the same objective, helping each other and us, too, in getting to that goal. **T**

Real listening requires
three sets of ears,
each specially trained

# Learning to listen to trainees

by Ron Zemke

If you're like most trainers, you place a high value on your ability to communicate. For every 20 minutes you spend holding forth in the classroom, you spend two and a half hours in preparation. You undoubtedly spend additional time, money and effort improving your speaking and writing skills. Many trainers take night courses in speech and communication, and every Toastmasters Club numbers teachers and trainers among its membership.

But how much time and effort do you spend developing your *listening* or *"receiving"* skills? Cathrina Bauby, author of *Understanding Each Other*, talks about person-to-person communication in terms of the "dialogue skills of listening, questioning and acknowledgment." Classroom communication is nothing if not an active, unpredictable process of dialogue. Were it otherwise, the role of instructor could and should be relegated to the boob tube.

## Listening requires practice, too

Most of us assume that listening is a natural ability we all possess. Certainly, hearing is inborn for most of us...but effective listening is not. Marshall McCluhan has quipped that, while we have no idea who discovered water, we can be pretty sure that it wasn't a fish. Listening and hearing are like that. You and I are so immersed in the daily stream of survival communication that we seldom realize that real listening goes beyond simple decoding of the literal meanings of the words we hear. Communications experts suggest that words and their dictionary meanings are only one-third of any speaker's message. Voice tone, body language, and even the tense and person of the words we choose convey that other, vital two-thirds of the message. To be effective in the classroom, we must be keenly aware of the three types of listening—selective listening, active listening, and "eye" listening.

## Selective listening: listening for facts

"What's he trying to say?" "Will she ever get to the point?" "Did I miss something, or did he forget to get where he was going with that?" Ever ask yourself those questions? If so, then you've experienced selective listening problems. If we listened only to trained public speakers all day, listening would be no problem. The "pro" invariably follows the sequence of introduction, thesis, body, and conclusion. The army used to call it the bull's-eye formula: Tell 'em what you're gonna tell 'em, tell 'em, tell 'em what you told 'em. Few of us speak in that organized fashion. Especially off-the-cuff. Especially trainees. Compounding the general disorganization of conversational or daily speech, the *rate of hearing* mitigates against effective fact comprehension. The average speaker delivers approximately 140 words per minute. Researchers have found that the average listener can comfortably comprehend messages delivered at 300 w.p.m. You

and I tend to fill the "dead space" by watching cars go by, inspecting the speaker's shoeshine, and talking to ourselves sub-audibly ("Will he *ever* get to the point?"). Small wonder that we are occasionally "out to lunch" when the trainee finally formulates the main point of his or her question, or that we sometimes fail to correctly sort and classify the speaker's facts and opinions.

According to Chris Hickey, product manager for Xerox Learning Systems' "Strategies for Effective Listening," we can double the effectiveness of our listening by developing the process skills of separating fact from opinion, distinguishing between main points and supporting arguments, and building mental outlines as we listen to people. A simple enough concept, but one that requires time and practice.

## Active listening: listening for feelings

If some messages are difficult to understand because the speaker is disorganized and has trouble making himself "perfectly clear," others are difficult because the message isn't contained in the speaker's words at all! According to Psychologist Thomas Gordon, author of *Parent Effectiveness Training* and *Teacher Effectiveness Training,* not all communication is self-evident and easily understood. The sentence "What time is it?" *may* be a request to know the time; but if the speaker is hungry and the dinner hour is at hand, "What time is it?" might actually mean "When do we eat?" The technique needed to decode these subtle messages is Active Listening.

According to Psychologist Carl Rogers, you and I could be superb at semantics—able to follow and untangle the most convoluted of scholarly arguments—and still be totally inept at understanding what people are "telling" us. Why? Because the symbols themselves—words—have nothing to do with the main message. Want proof? Simple. Say the following phrase aloud, emphasizing the underlined word, and you'll see how different a message the same words can convey:

*We're* not going to have a test today?
We're *not* going to have a test today?
We're not going to have a *test* today?

Active listening was created by Rogers for training therapists to work with patients. The method consists of "listening for feelings" and reflecting back your guess at the speaker's emotional state. With advance

Reprinted from TRAINING, July 1977

apologies to Rogers and Gordon, here's approximately how active listening works.

Charlie Trainee storms into your office, screaming at the top of his lungs: "I wouldn't work for this chicken outfit another 10 minutes if my life depended on it." You, a calm, cool trainer schooled in active listening, reply: "Charlie, it sounds like you're upset. And I know you wouldn't be upset without a good reason. Tell me about it."

"First they screwed up my housing allowance, and now my plane tickets are all wrong. They just don't care about us trainees."

"You don't think the company cares about your problems?"

"I've got to get home before seven on Friday night. It's our fifth anniversary, and my wife is planning a big party."

"You really want to leave here earlier than you're scheduled for now."

"And how!"

"Let's call travel and see what we can do."

Easy? No. Effective? Yes. Try it and see, the next time a communications problem presents itself. But, first, take a look at Gordon's work. To Rogers' active listening skill, he has added the skills of identifying problem ownership and "I"-message delivery to form a vocabulary for the developing technology of listening for feelings.

## Eye listening: the body speaks

The third part of listening isn't listening at all; it's looking. Watching what people do with their bodies, how they stand, move, and hold themselves, gesture, make eye contact and the like, in relation to other people—this is what is meant by non-verbal communication.

One aspect of non-verbal communi-cation concerns cultural norms. In *The Silent Language*, cultural anthropologist Edwart T. Hall suggests that you and I can communicate effectively only to the extent that we share three things he calls Key Cultural Isolates. These are time and its meaning, space and its use, and common experiences. While Hall was working for the State Department, he noticed that Americans overseas who failed to perceive and honor the ways different people use time and space accomplished little. Simple example. Americans tend to keep business associates literally at arms length; four to seven feet is the distance we normally maintain for talking to business-only acquaintances. But in the Middle East, business is often literally transacted nose to nose. American business people dealing with Middle Easteners often feel they are being attacked, and, conversely, the Middle Eastern business person is uncomfortable with Yankee stand-offishness.

A friend of ours, who spent four months in Iran for a computer man-ufacturer, began to fear he smelled offensive when he returned to the States. He couldn't figure out why people stood so far away from him. The problem? He had adapted so well to a different norm for using space that space use in his own culture actually felt uncomfortable.

Another example: eye contact. Blacks and whites in our culture have slightly different eye-contact rules. In general, whites avoid eye contact when speaking but watch the speaker closely when they are listening. Blacks tend to do the opposite. This leads to "He/She isn't paying attention to what I'm saying" interpretations of normal, subculturally sanctioned lis-tening behavior.

The second part of non-verbal com-munications is actual body language or Kinesics, as Psychologist Ray Birdwhistell dubbed this art/science in the 1940s. The listener or speaker who twists and turns in his or her chair while engaged in dialogue prob-ably finds the conversation unpleas-ant. Rubbing one's nose may simply be a response to an itch, but some body linguists contend that it might mean the speaker is nervous, disapproving, or even dishonest.

Here are some other gestures to watch for from your trainees:

• *Arms folded across chest*. This could mean the individual is implaca-ble, seemingly unbudgeable. His mind may be as tightly locked as his arms.

• *Sitting on the chair edge*. This is tricky because its precise meaning is ambivalent. It could be either that the individual has warmed to you and your ideas and is ready to cooperate *or* that he is turned off and is anxious to end the meeting.

• *Leaning back with hands behind head*. This suggests arrogance, ag-gressiveness, a propensity to domi-nate.

• *The poker face*. It successfully masks all feelings and reactions and confounds observers.

•*Excessive blinking*. It may indicate nervousness, apprehension about being backed into an uncomfortable corner. It may spell guilt.

• *Coughing and/or throat-clearing*. See blinking.

• *Steepling* (bringing the fingertips of both hands together to form a steeple): This generally indicates self-confidence, a sense of certainty that what one says is correct.

## If we have ears to hear

Our trainees want to communicate with us. They want us to listen and hear. But, as the CBers say, we can't hear if we don't have our "ears on."

Real listening requires three sets of ears, each specially trained—one set for hearing facts, one for hearing feelings, a third for seeing what you hear. **T**

Where someone is seated
can give you clues to
the interpersonal forces at work

# Watch where they sit in your class

by Kenneth Short

A few years ago, in an informal group of about a dozen people, a friend of mine sitting to my right about three places around the circle disagreed with me on a particular issue. The exchange between us became so intense (yet friendly) that my friend got up and moved to a seat directly opposite mine in the circle.

The issue under discussion has long since been forgotten. But my friend's movement started me observing something about the dynamics of groups that has proven both fascinating to me and amazingly consistent.

My observation is that in any group with a designated leader (DL), what might be called *dynamic leadership tension* tends to develop between the leader and the person sitting directly opposite him or her. It is as though the person sitting directly opposite becomes, even unwittingly, a counterweight. This person tends to respond in one of three ways: He or she either leads support for the leader, leads the opposition to the leader, or withdraws and leaves a curious leadership vacuum. In essence, this person becomes the Alter Leader (AL).

Whether in opposition or support, the alter leader is usually more aggressive than others in the group in challenging ideas or raising important questions that may further the inquiry. In fact, far from being an unrelievedly negative presence, this person may be quite helpful, thus creating a sort of leadership tandem with the designated leader. In groups with two leaders, the leaders often will position themselves directly opposite each other to accomplish this tandem effect, whether consciously or unconsciously.

Dynamic leadership tension creates a *charge of influence* on other members of the group which is directly related to an individual's proximity to the DL and AL, both to the right and the left. This is not, incidentally, inconsistent with research findings in regard to why persons tend to like or dislike each other. In his *Handbook of*

*Small Group Research* (Free Press, New York, 1962), Paul Hare indicates that persons who are near to each other in residence or on a job become friends more often than others.

Within the charge of influence that develops, persons closer to the DL tend to become more supportive of him or her, while those closer to the

AL more often than not lend their support in that direction. Further, those immediately to the right of the DL, and those most immediately to the right of the AL, tend to offer more unquestioned support to the corresponding leader to their left. Those to the left of either the DL or AL offer support, but with less intensity—in a more "left-handed" way. Charge of influence support, both to the right and the left, tends to wane about halfway between the principals in the dynamic leadership tension.

Recently, while leading several groups of nursing supervisors in training activities, I described this theory. In one group, innocently but predictably, the first person to respond was the person sitting directly opposite me.

"I don't agree with that," this nurse said at the first response point.

"You've just proved my point," I replied.

Her good-natured reaction evoked laughter, but the incident advanced both productive discussion and the theory. It was as if awareness to what had happened in that exchange created a sensitivity to the dynamic, and also insight as to how it might be used.

In another group, a charge nurse said she had been having trouble with the person who stood across from her in daily report. We talked about the possibility of the DL in a conflict situation moving to where the AL would

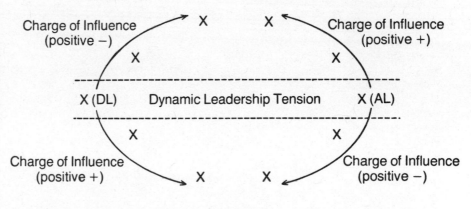

Charge of Influence (positive −) ... Charge of Influence (positive +)

X (DL) — Dynamic Leadership Tension — X (AL)

Charge of Influence (positive +) ... Charge of Influence (positive −)

**Figure 1**

be physically to her immediate right. This has the effect of making the AL the DL's potentially strongest supporter (but, of course, sets up a new AL across the group).

We also talked about the phrases we commonly use in our day-to-day dealings with others. For instance we say, "I'm not in a position to do anything about that now," or "those two really squared off against each other," or "he's my right-hand man," or "that certainly was a left-handed compliment."

The charge nurse decided to test the theory in report. For the next week, she moved to her adversary's left. The dynamic did indeed change. At first, she reported, it was almost more than the group could handle. Persons had taken the same positions for so long, and were so comfortable with what had come to be predictable tensions (albeit loaded with conflict), that even a small change was a threat. "All hell broke loose," she noted, "but it worked."

Leadership tension tends to develop across diameters. If, in a fairly mature group—one that has developed a comfortable level of trust and cohesion— the leadership shifts to a point other than the DL, the dynamic leadership tension also moves to cross between the newly assumed position of leadership and its alter leader. I have seen this dynamic operate in community committees, church groups, business meetings, classrooms, speaker-audience settings and counseling sessions. You probably have, too.

It is important to use the theory of dynamic leadership tension in positive ways. If you are a leader, for instance, this means you position yourself and your supportive strength to advantage, not to be manipulative or inconsiderate, but as a strategy toward productive results. If you know what to expect from different positions around the group, you can use the dynamic and avoid being trapped into agruments or other destructive activities. If your AL is not supportive, it is well to watch your eye contact in that direction. There is sometimes a tendency for a small group leader to look at that particular person in a way that suggests the leader's authority or approval must be won from that position. This can be defeating. The DL needs to consciously direct eye contact to all members of the group.

Should too much tension be generated in the group between the DL and AL positions, temporarily shifting the leadership role to a person on the DL's supportive right via a question or other device will change the direction of dynamic tension for at least a time and relieve the pressure. A creative leader will think of other ways to use or reduce tension so the group may function effectively rather than get bogged down in polarization and division.

If you have problems in your work group, check out this theory of dynamic leadership tension. If nothing else, get your group together, watch the positions people habitually take, then plan to use the dynamic in a creative way. Begin with your own supportive presence in the group and help build positive self-images among its members to develop a more harmonious working relationship.

Everyone is at one time or another a member of a group. If you can learn how dynamics tend to work within a group, know what to look for, and are aware of the potential forces you may create or contribute to, you can become a more effective and contributing group participant. ∎

These strategies and techniques are useful for those 'problem' trainees

# Handling the 'I'd rather be somewhere else' trainee

by Martin M. Broadwell

More often than not, there will be a certain number of students in every training classroom who simply do not want to be there. This does not necessarily reflect on the ability of the trainer or the subject matter being covered in the class. Many factors, some beyond the control of the instructor, can influence a student's "I'd rather be home" attitude.

Take for example the case of the trainee whose income is derived from commissions on sales. During the time he's in the classroom, he's making only his base salary, while someone else may be getting his sales. His customers might even be lost to a competitor. It's not enough to say that the organization ought to correct such inequities. As long as this situation does exist and the trainee is required to attend training sessions, there is going to be a problem.

There are other problems which relate to the student's perception of the course content. Some may see little or no relevancy in the material. This doesn't mean that the material is, in itself, bad or irrelevant, but it does indicate poor communication. The trainee's supervisor should be encouraged to take the time to discuss why the training is necessary, point out the advantages, and spell out deficiencies in the trainee's performance.

Some students may have feelings of inadequacy that can make them wish they were back on the job instead of sitting in a classroom where the material seems too complicated and confusing and the discussions beyond their reach. On the other hand, other students might consider the material too basic or trivial. This can make them feel uncomfortable about attending a class they consider beneath them because, obviously, *someone* thought they needed it.

Other factors are completely out of the instructor's control. A student may have personal, non job-related problems such as a sick spouse, a troubled child, or an important meeting to attend after hours.

Rather than argue the relative merits of sending such students back to their jobs, let's discuss the options for handling the problem at the training site. First, we can use the basic motivating tool we should use with every student to get them interested and keep them involved—try to show what's in it for them.

Typically, companies attempt to sell the importance of a training program on the basis of what it will do *for the organization*: "Our sales were off last year by 10 percent. This training course will help get them back up where they ought to be," instead of, "This course will help you increase your sales by 10 percent." Or a supervisor will say, "We can cut down on employee turnover if you'll learn more about human relations," instead of, "You won't have to spend so much time training new people with the skills you'll learn from this course." The solution is obvious: a training course should be presented to a student to appeal to *his* needs.

Another way of maintaining interest is to apply the recognition or status principle of motivating. If the employee/trainee has certain skills or special knowledge, the instructor can use these to enhance the course: "Anne has some good experiences to share with us, I'm sure. Would you tell us what you do when you find this happening in the real world, Anne?" In this way, the trainer gets good input from the students, uses their credentials to build credibility, and motivates the trainees at the same time. We shouldn't force this activity, of course, but neither should we worry about the results. If the employee is experienced and the experience doesn't relate to what we are teaching, then we'd better examine our curriculum!

Another useful technique is to ask the "problem" trainee to discover the relevancy of the training for himself—to determine just how the course can help him back on the job. Even if the employee is one of those who feels inadequate, looking for relevancy on the job will be a source of encouragement. It's a subtle way of helping him find the reasons for being in the class in the first place and discovering the weaknesses that explain the boss's reason for thinking the course could overcome this performance deficiency.

If more than one person feels they don't want to be in the course, this self-examination technique may be good for the whole class. Stop and let them brainstorm about the value of the course objectives. This will also get the committed students working, as the class as a whole tries to bring some reality and reason to the course. It may be that we can see some areas where we can change our direction and make the course more meaningful for everybody. This is a measure of the flexibility a good instructor must have to be successful.

We've not mentioned one of the most obvious things that can be done. Have a talk with the trainee in private and see if there's anything you need to know about the person that can make the course more valuable to him or her. A simple statement such as, "How's it going?" may be all it takes, if you follow the rules of good interviewing from that point on. If you don't get results at first, you may have to expand the questioning to be a little more specific, even to the point of saying, "I sort of get the feeling that I'm not making the course as meaningful to you as you would like," or, "Is there some way I can help you get more from the sessions? Your responses have indicated that the course isn't meeting your needs very well." You shouldn't try to put the trainee on the grill, nor make veiled threats. You want the employee to know you're sincerely concerned about maximum learning for every student.

It would be less than admirable if we didn't mention some ways to avoid the problem in the first place. Basically, the problem resulted because of poor communication. Somewhere along the way, the course objectives failed to be communicated to the trainee, his supervisor, or both. An instructor will do well to make a practice of asking himself, "Is there enough information about the course available to the bosses and potential trainees to let them know not only what we're going to cover but also what behavioral changes we're hoping to make? Essentially, what are the promises we're making? What will the employees be able to do when they get back to the job that they can't do now? What deficiencies are we aiming at?"

The important things to avoid are being so vague about course objectives that all employees will believe they need to attend and making so many promises that no one wants to be left out. We should give enough information so supervisors can sit down with their subordinates and decide—on an intelligent basis—who needs to attend and who doesn't.

These techniques cannot eliminate the problem entirely. Instructors will always have a few discontented students, but there's no excuse for building problems into the system by poor design and poor communication. Good trainers will remain alert and sensitive to symptoms, causes, and possible cures, and they *can* learn to deal with the "I'd rather be home" student constructively. **T**

# Ways to encourage your trainees to ask questions

"That winds it up for today. Are there any questions? No? OK, folks, see you Wednesday morning for our next session which will be on modulation principles."

The instructor puts his notes into his attache case, wipes the chalkboard clean of the 17 equations and three circuit diagrams he managed to squeeze up there during the last hour, and thinks smugly to himself, "Well, not one person asked a question so I guess they got it all! Not bad! I wasn't sure I'd be able to cover all those points, and I guess I did rush a little toward the end, but by golly, I covered them. And not one question!"

A far fetched story? Hardly. On the contrary, and unfortunately, that situation is often more the rule than it is the exception. "Look at some of the factors involved," says Milt Badt, training supervisor for Western Electric Co. "It is 11:56 AM when the instructor asks for questions. The presentation had been scheduled from 9:30 to 12:00. Five out of the 10 students in the audience of 30 who would have liked to ask questions do not, because they are hungry, tired, bored, and perhaps a bit snowed, and want to get the heck out of there. Two who wanted to ask questions simply do not, lest they incur the wrath of the others who want to leave. And three others are not about to ask under any circumstances, because each one thinks they must be the only one in the class who didn't understand the point, and they don't want to appear foolish."

Of course, much of what Badt was getting at is just as true of a nicely scheduled question period during the middle of a meeting. Just the simple question, 'Are there any questions?' can be said a great number of ways. And of that number of ways, there are some that will turn students off and make them reluctant to ask any questions at all.

How can an instructor encourage questions? Here are Badt's suggestions:

• Use phrases like: Don't be afraid to ask questions. Raise your hand, or just speak up. Please interrupt me. If you have a question, chances are others have the same concern, so you'll be helping more than just yourself by asking."

• Remember there is no such thing as a stupid question. Look for and mention the merit in every question whenever possible. This will make the asker feel important and encourage others to speak up.

• Repeat the question loudly and clearly so that everyone in the room can hear it as well as the answer.

• Don't say, "If there are no questions on that we'll get on to the next topic, since I'm running a little behind schedule." Allow time in your presentation planning for the asking of questions— at five- or 10-minute intervals if the going is rough. Don't lecture for more than 15 minutes without calling for questions.

• Allow some time for trainees to respond. Don't ask for questions and immediately resume your discussion.

• Pay attention to the back of the room, where it's easy to overlook a raised hand. And, don't ask for questions while your eyes are glued to your notes or while you are writing on the board.

• Don't ask for questions in such a way that your voice implies, "If anyone was really too dense to get that, speak up now and I'll see if I can get it through your skull." If you think that way about your audience, your tone of voice will betray you.

• Don't call for questions within two or three minutes of a scheduled coffee or lunch break.

• If you have a printed schedule, insert several 10 or 15 minute question and answer sessions right into the format. However, you must still encourage questions during this time by using the applicable do's and don'ts. **T**

I WISH HE HAD COVERED THE XYZ POINT WITH MORE DETAIL, BUT I'M PROBABLY THE ONLY ONE THAT DOESN'T UNDERSTAND IT!

I'D LIKE TO ASK WHAT THE XYZ POINT MEANS, BUT I'M PROBABLY THE ONLY STOOP HERE THAT DOESN'T KNOW!

MY HAND'S BEEN UP FOR TEN MINUTES, BUT HE IGNORES ME!

LAST TIME HE MADE ME FEEL LIKE AN IDIOT! DARNED IF I ASK ANOTHER QUESTION!

ASK A QUESTION AT THREE MINUTES TO TWELVE? NO WAY!

ANY QUESTIONS? NO? GOOD! NOW, BLAH... BLA...BLA.

by Marilyn Leak

Every trainer eventually runs into
an audience determined to resist

# Surviving—and managing—those hostile participants

by Carl E. Pickhardt

A trainer is always a target. Even when training within the organization to which you belong, your leadership position temporarily separates you from the group with which you are working. Every group makes a participant/leader distinction: the participants are *we* and the trainer or trainers are *they*. As an outside trainer this distinction is even more strongly felt: "You are a stranger; you are not one of us."

Participants do, however, assign you two roles as a trainer. You are an *authority* coming in to exert training control, and you are an *expert* coming in to enable the development of skills and understanding participants do not already possess, or possess in lesser degree than yourself. Having given you these two roles, participants have now identified you as a target, and some will feel impelled to move to destroy your effectiveness and legitimacy in each area.

Why? Because in all organizations there is always a certain amount of free-floating dissatisfaction, anxiety, frustration and anger which accrues from the daily pressures of organizational life— people feeling pushed, blocked and let down in their work relationships. There is a desire to express these negative feelings, but in a "safe" setting which will not jeopardize standing at work. The training situation can provide this outlet. The rules of social conduct which ordinarily govern work relationships are temporarily relaxed. The trainer becomes a safe authority target upon whom participants may displace frustrations with their superiors; someone they can with relative impunity challenge, criticize and punish. They may in addition compete with the trainer, elevating their own self-esteem by putting the "expert" down. Some may feel built-in resentment toward the trainer as well: "It's easy for you to talk about our problems since you don't have to live with them." That the trainer is free from the toils of the participants' problems can serve as an irritant itself.

Trainers are in a real sense paid to be scapegoats— to provide opportunity and target for this pressure release. We must accept this reality and learn (and this *does* take experience) not to take participant hostility personally. Any time you are going to work with a group which you know in advance is operating under undue pressure, you can expect basic attacks on your two roles. They will attack your *expertise* ("You don't know so much," "I knew all this before," "I know more than you"). And they will attack your *authority* ("You can't control me," "I'll do what I please," "I have more power than you").

## Hostility expressed

They will come at you in a variety of ways.

• There is *hostile withdrawal*— participants who refuse you both ver- bal and nonverbal response. "If you can't reach us you will fail to teach us," they seem to say.

• There is *hostile diversion*— participants who initiate their own social interaction independent of that which you are orchestrating for the larger group. "If we can secede from your control, we can encourage others to do likewise," they seem to say.

• There is *hostile attack*— participants who directly challenge your authority, oppose your directions or criticize your message. "If we refuse to go along with you, that rejection will undermine your confidence and destroy your poise as a leader," they seem to say.

Participants particularly resourceful with their hostility can use all of these in combination. For example, they first set up a *diversion* to invite your response. Then, as you move to recontrol that situation, they *attack* you from out of their support group. And finally, when you try to deal directly with their objection, they *withdraw* into stubborn silence and will not respond.

## What does it mean?

When participant anger is expressed in any of these three ways, it is always *a statement of protest*. The participant, beneath the overlay of hostility, is indirectly saying: "I don't like being placed under your leadership. I don't like being in this training situation. I don't like what you represent. I don't like what you are saying. I do not like what you are asking me to do."

Further, participants do not commit themselves to public protest unless they are trying to elicit a particular trainer response to their challenge. They may want to punish you, and indirectly those responsible for the training, until you defend or apologize for your presence. They may want to push you until you give up your agenda and give way to theirs. They may want to provoke you into a fight to allow them to vent frustrations hitherto suppressed and usually forbidden.

The choices of a trainer wishing to honor protest are to reflect back the concern you think that protest may be masking ("Would you like to talk about your dissatisfaction at being here today?"), to apologize, change the agenda or absorb the ventilation of grievances. The major problem in honoring participant hostility in these ways is that it does delay and divert you from fulfilling the training assignment. There is, however, one case where some diversion may have survival value for you as a trainer.

## When hostility triggers fear

In all relationships anger is the great intimidator. For this reason one cannot adequately talk about the management of anger without including some discussion about the management of fear. It is an unpleasant reality of the trainer's life that on some occasions the expression of participant hostility will trigger within you some fear. This is normal. And although beginning trainers are most vulnerable to this response due to inexperience, even the most seasoned trainers are not entirely immune to this anxiety.

When, in response to participant hostility, you experience sufficient fear to distract you from your training focus, your first priority must be to

> ## "Trainers are paid to be scapegoats— to provide opportunity and target for participants' pressure release."

accept that fear and move to reduce it as quickly as possible. Why? Because fear undercuts the three major self-supports upon which your leadership as a trainer depends: your confidence, concentration and momentum. You suddenly question if you can do the job, your mind wanders away from your training purpose into worry, and you lose the assertive and responsive momentum upon which the illusion of your training authority depends.

Like all teachers, trainers have three major needs when working with a group: to be liked, to be in control, to be effective. When these needs are frustrated the trainer can become afraid. The participant who attacks you can trigger your fear of rejection. ("They do not like me.") The participant who creates a diversion can trigger your fear of authority loss. ("I cannot control them.") The participant who withdraws beyond your reach can trigger your fear of failure. ("I am not being an effective trainer.") Training is risky. Potential anxieties are built in, and under pressure from

participant hostility they may become actualized.

## Coping with fear

The most efficient way to reduce trainer fear is to close the distance with the hostile participant. Although our instinct at these times is usually to move away (to flee) or to defensively attack (to fight), both of these responses only increase our own anxiety and communicate it to our attacker. Behaviorally, closing the distance means:

1) physically moving closer to the hostile participant;
2) making direct eye contact;
3) courteously soliciting information about the nature of their protest;
4) dialoguing in a positive and supportive way about their concerns.

Even if the participant will not respond to these last two overtures, going through these active motions can still serve an anxiety reducing function for you. The purpose of these four moves is to reduce your fear of the hostile participant by reasserting your initiative in the relationship, by gaining more information about them, by establishing through dialogue a working connection with them that you can manipulate. Having moved to regain self-control, you are then ready to consider your options for gaining control of participant hostility in a group.

## Responding to participant hostility

One way to conceptualize participant hostility is as a *resistance* to the training progression through which you are leading a group. In your choice of responses it is always well to consider that the harder you press against that participant resistance the more likelihood there is that the resistance will increase. This is an isometric principle. (Isometrics is the conditioning procedure where, by pushing hard against a fixed resistance, you increase the tension in the relationship.) This applies to managing interpersonal resistance. The harder you push against the resistant participant, the harder their resistance is likely to become, the more energy you are going to have to spend in maintaining that relationship, and the more fatiguing it will become to you over time. Trainers need to conserve their energies and should follow the path of least resistance whenever possible, particularly in response to participant hostility. The following five categories of trainer response

begin with the lowest and move to the highest amount of trainer resistance applied to manage the situation.

**Option 1: Avoidance.** There are three major strategies to be considered here. The first is to literally ignore the hostile action or remark and proceed with your program as though nothing untoward had occurred. Sometimes simply denying protesting participants the reinforcement of your response is sufficient to shut them down. A second set of strategies has to do with avoiding direct contact with the hostile participants while attending to their disruption. Here you solicit peer influence to shut them down. For example, you deliberately lapse into silence after the hostile outburst. If the majority of the participants want you to continue, they will move to quell their disruptive peer. A third set of strategies has to do with providing an indirect response to the participant. You appear to be avoiding the protest, but actually you are interpreting its intent and then responding to meet the underlying concern expressed. For example, a diversion builds in a group to your left, but you avoid looking at them. However, because you interpret their protest as a restless desire for an intermission, you go on a few minutes and then, apparently independent of the protest, announce a break. Notice that with none of these strategies do you actively engage the resistance.

**Option 2: Acceptance.** This strategy is a very direct one. When hostile participants push against you, move to find out the purpose of the protest and then give them their way— accept their resistance. Some people feel that a trainer sacrifices authority by "giving in" this way. However, allowing some latitude for participants to alter the content or conduct of the session to suit their needs can actually increase their sense of ownership involvement in the training. For example, a participant who is dissatisfied with a training agenda which puts his concern last may well be brought back into cooperation by altering the order of items to be addressed. Of course, acceptance of resistance is counterproductive when the participant's only intent is to disrupt the proceedings.

**Option 3: Adapt.** The strategy here is a manipulative one. What you want to do is to engage with the participants in such a way that you ultimately use the force of their resistance against them or for yourself. Thus when they protest and strongly disagree with what you are saying, you immediately switch sides and say, "You're right, that's a good point." Then you take their argument away from them; you begin arguing for them against the position you had previously taken. Having thus championed their argument you have defused their resistance. Sometimes this is sufficient for your purpose. At other times you may, now that you control the thrust of their argument, want to turn it back into the direction you were originally heading.

**Option 4: Stand fast.** This strategy is at once a very simple, but a very energy-expensive response to make. What you are doing is standing fast in your intent to do what the participant is protesting. You will not give way. You will not discuss. You will not negotiate. Perhaps the training was designed to include an evening session, and several participants are vociferously complaining. You simply stand there and let their resistance wash over you and wear itself out. Then you proceed with the program as contracted. Withstanding this onslaught of negative emotions can be abusive to the trainer, which is why providing a firm resistance against which the hostile participants can

level their protest is an energy-costly option.

**Option 5: Push back.** This is the most energy-costly response to participant protest. They push against you. You push back. When two resistances push against each other, of course, you have created the social formula for conflict. What you hope to gain by resisting is to overcome the participants' resistance, persuading them to back off. The problem with pushing back, however, is that if the participant doesn't back off you have just created a fight. In almost all cases, that is a no-win situation for the trainer. If you "win" the fight, participants tend to array against you out of sympathy for their defeated peer. If you "lose," then participants tend to have reduced respect for your training authority.

Pushing back is always a gamble. As a bluff it can pay off if the protest subsides and there is no conflict. Sometimes the stakes are even great enough where fighting back with a hostile participant can be worthwhile for the trainer. For example, you may have a participant so forcefully hostile that others are both intimidated from cooperating with you and afraid to stand up to and stop their peer. At

this point, if the program is to be salvaged, you are the only person there to beat this opposition down, restore order and reestablish the training framework. Obviously, pushing back is the option of last resort when dealing with a hostile participant.

**Surviving hostility**

When encountering participant protest, the most critical concern for a trainer is to maintain your "cool"— the capacity to calculate and choose wisely under pressure. Fear provokes impulsive responses not reasoned choice. The five management options just described are available to us *only* so long as we retain our power of reason. Thus the key to trainer control of a hostile situation is keeping fear down and all management alternatives open.

As trainers we need to accept the inevitability of participant hostility. We need to learn to deal with our fear when upon occasion it becomes aroused in a hostile situation. We need to keep our cool in order to preserve our power of management choice. We need to know and use the full repertoire of these choices. And we must not take participant hostility personally. It comes with the job. **T**

# Learn to read non-verbal trainee messages

by Charles R. McConnell

**Y**ou're about to begin a lengthy workshop with a group of relative strangers. A good start depends on early identification of some willing talkers for a participative activity. How do you find your participants?

You might begin, as I did for years, by asking for volunteers. You may even get some — eventually. Do you politely but firmly repeat the request until somebody breaks the ice? Perhaps, although this requires valuable time and risks generating resentment.

Although I still voice a friendly request for volunteers, I no longer repeat the query to the group as a whole. Instead, I'm guided by their reactions. The instant the request is made, most of the eyes in the room shift away from the speaker. Chances are, most of those who avoid eye contact don't want to volunteer; they may also be afraid of being selected against their will. Occasionally — but not often enough to depend on — somebody will volunteer and your worries are over. Usually, however, you're left with silence and perhaps a third of the people still looking your way.

Concentrating on the one-third, direct the request for participation toward them. Keep it good-natured, perhaps joking ("I really need the help, folks; I don't know enough to go it alone.") Try something like: "I haven't met any of you before, but most of you know each other. Maybe you know ot some willing talkers among you? People who like to argue?"

Watch the reactions. Smiles, a spurt of physical activity as people settle in more comfortably, and — most important — obvious glances toward a few particular individuals. You're also likely to hear comments about those with a reputation for garrulity.

A group of 30 people who know each other will usually yield two or three such central figures. With these few, you're on fairly safe ground for a direct, friendly request. You'll usually get your participants.

You may also accomplish some desirable extras with this process. In finding your central figures, you've probably also identified the group's informal leaders. And you may well have given your listeners the ice-breaking opportunity needed to create a loose, friendly atmosphere early in the session.

The process isn't infallible, but it works often enough to be worth trying. Although there's some verbal interchange involved, many of the key indicators are nonverbal: looks averted or returned; smiles; glances and physical reorientation toward certain people. As leader, you must "listen" to your group's wordless messages.

When we hear about the necessity for interaction, we tend to think of it mostly in terms of verbal exchange. Just as important is the kind of interchange that involves your response, whether verbal or otherwise, to your audience's silent signals.

A note of caution: There are few, if any, nonverbal signals that consistently have the same meaning, and none with precise meanings. A few scattered displays of any particular signal may or may not be significant.

The key lies not in the *what* of some nonverbal signals as much as in *how often* you see them. However, the occurrences needed to suggest a signal's significance vary according.

The classic folded-arms pose provides a good illustration. This position frequently indicates resistance, the listener protecting himself by forming a barrier against you and your ideas. But it can also indicate other things. Two or three sets of folded arms in a group of 30 people may mean, "At the moment I'm most comfortable this way," or "I feel slightly cold." But if a large number — say, 10 or so — fold their arms, you may be generating resistance in your audience. You might respond by changing the direction or tone of your presentation.

I recently had to present a controversial plan to a 13-member board of directors. About 10 minutes into the talk, I found myself looking at nine pairs of folded arms plus a few frowns. I frantically wondered what I was doing wrong and how to change it. Almost desperately, I condensed part of the material, skipped a few notes, and, with some impromptu transitional comments, went into another part of the presentation. Things improved. Most of the frowns disappeared and many of the arms unfolded. Only later did I realize I'd prepared a lopsided presentation, concentrating all the "bad news" in one part — and thus turning off the audience.

The frown, of course, is an obvious nonverbal message. The sudden appearance of a few scattered frowns while you're talking suggests disagreement and lack of understanding. Several responses are possible. You can back up and restate your last point. You can pause and ask for questions, perhaps mentioning that your last remark seemed to cause some concern. Or, if you feel you've established some rapport, you might zero in on a specific frowner and ask if you can clarify anything.

A number of simple signals can suggest boredom. The hand-over-mouth can mean a stifled yawn. Glances at watches, frequent recrossing of legs, fidgeting, and eyes wandering around the room can also mean a bored audience. These often increase alarmingly as the end of the allotted time period approaches — especially if the group feels the session is going to run overtime.

What do you do when signs of boredom appear? Something different. Move about if you can. Change your speed of delivery and vary your vocal tone. Don't depend on your material to put itself across. The best material can flop if the delivery is lifeless. But even dry material can find life through an animated presentation.

Watch also for people who habitually nod or shake their heads slightly as they agree or disagree with what's being said. A few of these give you some idea of how you're going over. You can also get helpful information from those whose eyes give them away. The "skyward glance" — eyes rolled upward under raised brows —may signal anything from "Heaven help us!" to "Now I've heard everything!" The other, likely to signal skepticism or disbelief, is the "conspiratorial cut"—the sharp corner-of-the-eye look that flashes between adjacent listeners.

Communication, including that which takes place between a lecturer and a group of listeners, is always a two-way street. Generally, new instructors and speakers require considerable time and exposure to become sensitized to their listeners' nonverbal messages. Most of us start by working on what we have to say and later learning to improve the way we say it. Eventually we consider the shifting needs and moods of the audience which are often communicated by wordless messages of posture, motion, and expression.

Learn to "hear" these silent communications. Some of the signals will be swift, subtle, and almost elusive. But some will leave little doubt as to their meanings. One of the latter made a lasting impression on me. Some years ago, my boss sat through one of my first classes, which was woefully dry and running overtime. My boss looked directly at me and yawned widely, then looked down and shook his watch as though it had stopped. I got the message. **T**

Reprinted from TRAINING, May 1978

Of dogs and elephants and burned-out managers: Here's how to restore an environment for training success

# Breaking the pattern of learned helplessness

by Mark J. Martinko

Every experienced trainer has had it happen. You spend hours of painstaking preparation designing a program to improve managerial effectiveness. Then, half-way into your presentation, someone sighs and says, "It won't work here We tried that before and it didn't work. That's okay for a manufacturing company, but we're different."

At that point you know you're in for a rough day. You may ask yourself why it had to happen to you. You may label the person a malcontent or write off the individual as another incompetent, burned-out manager. Or you may try to engage in direct confrontation (which you almost never win). But if you are a little more introspective, you may come to the conclusion that there are some very good reasons for that skepticism or frustration—or both.

*Learned helplessness* is the notion that experiences with prior, uncontrollable aversive circumstances interfere with later learning. The concept was first developed in experimental animal psychology, but studies also have confirmed helplessness behavior in humans, and the theory of learned helplessness now has been adopted as a possible explanation for depression. This same theory appears relevant to the helplessness behaviors exhibited by managers and employees in work organizations.

The early research was conducted with animals and is particularly instructive in the definition and understanding of learned helplessness. In the late 1960s, Martin Seligman and his associates immobilized dogs in a harness and repeatedly shocked the animals. At first, of course, the dogs reacted very aggressively to the shock—howling, whining, defecating and urinating profusely. After a series of trials, however, these behaviors diminished and the reaction became passive; they became resigned to their fate.

Later in the experiment the dogs were released from the harness. At this point they could escape the shock by crossing a small barrier. Instead, the majcrity of the animals remained passive, exhibiting few escape behaviors. Even when a conditioned dog was able to terminate the shock by crossing the barrier, it usually did not continue escape behaviors on subsequent trials. In sharp contrast a control group of naive dogs quickly learned to escape the shock on almost every trial. The conclusion of the experimenters, supported by subsequent studies, was that when organisms (including humans) are exposed to inescapable punishing conditions, they eventually learn that their behavior is ineffective and makes no difference. As a result, their behavior becomes passive and ineffective, even when circumstances and conditions change.

Since the early studies, a great deal of research has been done on the helplessness phenomenon. In general it has been found that helplessness can indeed be induced in human subjects, and many of the dynamics of this process are similar to those found in the animal literature. The effects of helplessness have been found to generalize across tasks, yet a complex discrimination process is also involved. (Human subjects, for example, may exhibit helplessness for one experimenter, but not another.)

Considerable research has also been devoted to the process of immunizing and alleviating helplessness conditions. Prior success experiences, for instance, usually result in human subjects resuming normal response patterns when the period of exposure to inescapable punishment ends. Helplessness has also been alleviated through attributional training, where individuals learn to attribute their failures to their own lack of effort rather than a lack of ability or

**Just as an elephant is conditioned** *to think it's the rope, not the tree, that restrains him, people learn to assume they can't change things. For your training to break through, you have to find where the resistance really is.*

circumstances beyond their control.

Research on the existence and effects of learned helplessness in work organizations has not yet been done, but the theoretical foundation developed in animal and experimental human psychology can help explain many of the passive and hopeless behaviors exhibited in organizations— behaviors often in evidence during the training of experienced managers. It may be that many of the managers who reject training as inapplicable or unrealistic are actually voicing their learned helplessness. How many efforts at innovation with techniques such as management by objectives (MBO) or organization development (OD) have withered and died due to lack of support— or even punishment— of managers? Small wonder that after repeated efforts are met with indifference, resistance or reprisals, many managers eventually conclude that their efforts make little difference; they believe they are helpless to improve their organizations.

## The elephant syndrome

In conducting OD interventions, there always seems to be a point in the process where the participants tell me they feel almost totally helpless to control or influence their situations. At that point I talk about "the dogs and the elephants." The dogs, of course, are those in the experiments of Seligman and his associates. The elephant story, on the other hand, I first heard from one of my students.

As the story goes, when the natives of Asia and Africa depended on the elephant as a major source of transportation and labor, they developed an intriguing technique for restraining the animals. When a mature elephant was first captured, it would be tethered to a huge baobab tree. After days of struggle, shaking and trying to pull the tree down, the elephant learned helplessness, becoming passive and ceasing its efforts to escape. From that time on, it could be restrained simply by driving a small peg into the ground. At the first sensation of tension on its tether, the elephant would stop and passively accept a condition it could easily have escaped.

What does this suggest for trainers? It suggests that many helplessness reactions can be recognized and at least partially alleviated by understanding the conditioning process that may have been involved and designing the training experience accordingly. There are several methods which can be employed for this.

**Success experiences.** A number of studies have demonstrated that prior success helps subjects return to normal response patterns even after experiencing helplessness conditions. This suggests that particular care be taken in orienting new managers so they experience success before they become involved in situations in which they are more likely to experience failure. Also, in introducing new concepts or techniques to experienced managers, role play and simulation exercises designed for success may effectively immunize these managers from experiencing helplessness when difficulties are encountered.

More recent evidence on the effects of success experiences in the alleviation of helplessness suggests that this approach needs to be used with some care. Some studies, for example, demonstrate that subjects who experience continued success may have problems later learning to respond appropriately to failure. On the other hand, subjects experiencing equal levels of success and failure may be more persistent in responding appropriately when failure occurs. This learned persistence is heavily dependent on an individual's own internal explanations for success or failure.

**Attribution training.** The concept behind attribution training is that behavior is a function of internal beliefs about the reasons for success or failure. Behaviors differ depending on whether success is perceived to be a function of chance, other people, personal ability or effort. Similarly people's perceptions of the probability that they will be successful also influence their performance. A number of studies have fairly conclusively demonstrated that feedback emphasizing the attribution of failure to lack of effort often improves performance.

Within a training environment, helplessness reactions might be modified by training subjects to attribute the results of their actions to factors other than luck or people and conditions beyond their control. Questioning and discussing attribution values may be particularly effective. Ask skeptics *why* they think a technique will not work, *who* will block their efforts, *why* they feel they cannot control outcomes. Confronting trainees with their attributions— and the assumptions on which they are based— may also be an effective strategy.

Watch for the feelings of helplessness participants consciously and unconsciously communicate. Many may be legitimate; be sure to recognize them as such. Many, however, may come from a failure to recognize that circumstances and conditions can change. Are your trainees tied to pegs instead of trees, or accepting shock passively when it can be avoided?

It should be recognized, however, that attributing failure to lack of effort may be unrealistic and even unhealthy in many circumstances. In some of the research on psychologically depressed people, for example, it has been found they sometimes attribute failure to themselves even when circumstances are not under their control. Care should be exercised to ensure that attributional training accurately reflects the real environment.

**Modeling.** Many people learn vicariously through observing the experiences of others. As such, a third strategy for alleviating feelings of helplessness during training is to provide trainees with a description of the success experiences of another manager they respect. Films and examples provided during training may accomplish this objective, or another manager within the organization might offer a short presentation of his or her personal experiences with the topic being discussed. If this manager operates in the same environment as the trainees, it will be very difficult for them to continue to maintain they are helpless because of *their* circumstances.

**Structuring/shaping.** Here the managerial technique is broken down into discreet steps, with success at each step being reinforced. By breaking down the procedure into successive stages, trainees can clearly see that they bear the responsibility for success almost completely within each particular phase.

The theory and research regarding learned helplessness appears to generalize very readily to organizational situations, particularly training environments, but the state of knowledge advanced by research in this area is still somewhat uncertain. There are, to be sure, many unanswered questions and theoretical controversies regarding helplessness phenomena. As such, care must be exercised in generalizing findings to situations outside controlled experimental settings. To the extent that theory combined with common sense can provide us with helpful suggestions and insight, however, recognizing the causes and ways of dealing with learned helplessness may facilitate our efforts to create healthy work environments. **T**

For the new trainer:

# How to survive the first class taught

by Martin M. Broadwell

No matter how much preparation you do, no matter how well you know your material, no matter how many times you practice, no matter how much instructor training you have...sooner or later you have to face the class for the first time. You've never taught before. You've been a good supervisor and you know the job well. As a reward for that, you've been chosen by your organization to teach a portion of the course that is designed to train employees in your area of expertise. The recognition of your job talents is flattering, but the motivation fails to veil the panic that soon prevails—and grows as the day of the first class session approaches. For all the *job* expertise, you doubt your expertise in front of the class.

"Don't worry. We'll give you instructor training." That made you feel better—until you had the training, and your worst fears were realized: You really don't have much native talent in this newly appointed skill! More panic. You develop your materials, practice with them, struggle with these fancy gadgets called AV equipment. The overheads keep moving to the left when you want to shift them to the right. The film comes out backwards with "The End" appearing upside down and reversed. At least you're consistent, since that's the way the slides project, too. The course is scheduled, participants' names arrive, then the fateful day is upon you. The students actually show up. Your prayers for a small catastrophe like an earthquake, hurricane, flood, or the end of the world failed to materialize, so you're really going to go through with it. And you wonder: "Could this have been avoided?"

## Why does it happen?

If you can identify with the above scene, then you may have wondered why the first days of instructing are so frightening and what could have been done to avoid it.

There are four main reasons why we get ourselves into this panic condition, and these are obviously intertwined. First, there are many things to be remembered, and all of them are unfamiliar to us—the schedule, the equipment, the topics, the breaks, the teaching skills, the handouts, the procedures for running the exercises, role plays, games. "Let's see, the slides come before the break, right after the first quiz..."

Second, there is that almost indefinable thing called "stage fright"—the fear of getting up in front of the group, the feeling that you can't talk, can't move, can't think. It strikes people of high estate and low, educated and not, the well informed and the unprepared.

Third, there is the matter of insecurity. No matter how well you prepare yourself, you still have those moments of wondering if the class knows more about the topic than you do. As you look at the simple subjects, you begin to tell yourself, "surely they know all about this!" Then you look at their credentials and realize they're coming right off the job, and you wonder, "What if they ask a question about...?"

Finally, the first teaching assignments are often frightening because you have no comfortable habits to fall back on. When you're on the job, you're almost always comfortable; and when you aren't, it's the exception rather than the rule. In the case of the teaching assignment, you're rarely doing anything that you do habitually on the job. Even when you're *talking* about the job, it's in front of the group, in unfamiliar surroundings, trying to remember all the things that the teaching part of the job requires. And when you finish one part of the assignment, the next part isn't going to be any different, so there's nothing to look forward to.

## What can you do about it?

Before we go further, let's insist—in the face of many witnesses—that it doesn't have to be that way, nor is it that way for everybody. If you're thinking about doing some teaching, this isn't intended to frighten you off. It's meant to show you that it can happen, it's normal, but there are some things that can be done to overcome much of the anxiety. There are also some things you can do wrong if you aren't careful.

First of all, let's discuss what can happen if you allow nature to take its course and just do what comes natural when these signs of fear and insecurity come upon you. Let's consider the matter of "so many things to remember," for instance. Usually one of two things happen. Either you try to put it all in your head, with no notes, or you write everything down and use a wheelbarrow to cart the notes around. Both extremes are self-defeating. In the first case, you get into an awkward situation of wandering around the classroom trying to look nonchalant while you kill time by fumbling with the equipment, hoping you will remember what to do next. Invariably you do forget something and have to decide whether it's better to go back and pick it up out of sequence, admit your error (or try to cover it up), or whether you should leave the gap in the teaching session, messing up the learning pattern as well as the time scheduled. If you have too many notes, you find yourself wedded to the speaker's stand, since you can't carry all those notes around. And you're constantly getting lost in the pages. What's the answer?

The answer isn't more or less notes, it's *better* notes. Not just notes, but well organized notes, showing activities of both the teacher and the student. Perhaps on the left page is the teaching action, on the right is the learning action. There can be a row or column for time, visuals, method, and key points. Looking at the whole page, the teacher can tell at a glance everything that should be going on. An open notebook offers tremendous space for guidelines for an hour or so of instruction. On the other hand, note cards are bothersome, limited in space, and tend to get out of order.

## What about stage fright?

Can you overcome the fear of getting up in front of an audience? What are you likely to do wrong if you just let your "natural" self come forth? Almost without exception, you'll overprepare, end up with hurried notes up the side of the paper, get in front of the class, and lose your way immediately. Usually this is done while leaning on (or should we say "choking") the speaker's stand. The more you fear the audience, the less you look at them; and the more notes you have, the less you look at the audience. Put them together and the students may never know what the teacher looks like.

What's the remedy? There's no substitute for preparation. Mostly, the solution is mental, but there should be some teaching skills thrown in for good measure. Regardless of what you

may think, there's little chance of the students eating up a perfectly good instructor, especially if the teacher is knowledgeable in areas where the students have shortcomings. Remember, they're there because they have a job performance deficiency of some kind, not because they're addicted to teacher meat. The teaching skill here is to build in a design that gets the students working, talking to each other, coming to the teacher for help, building a dependency on the teacher's ability to facilitate their learning. The other things you do, like lecturing, using quantities of visuals; solving their problems for them, build the wrong kind of dependency. They become dependent on the teacher for information, not facilitation.

## What about insecurity?

This, too, is mental. You worry that they might ask a question you won't have an answer for. Again, preparation is a key factor. If you know the job, the material, the policy, and the procedures, you aren't likely to get many questions you can't answer. If you do, then answer them the same way an experienced instructor does— "I don't know, but I'll find out."

Many instructors fall back on com-

fortable habits. The things you're likely to do include rambling, falling back on tales of the job like it used to be, giving background information in great detail, or, even worse, developing some incorrect habits. If you have "success" in overcoming stage fright by looking at the screen even when there's nothing there (screens don't bite), this "reward" may cause you to develop a habit of screen-looking all the time. If you find satisfaction in cutting down students (now they don't ask those silly questions), then you're likely to continue doing this. The solution: Intentionally develop some good habits. Say to yourself, "I'm going to try to redirect every question for the next hour, even if it's awkward," or, "I'm not going to draw a single conclusion during the period between break and lunch until after the students have had a chance." Watch yourself carefully and, when the period is over, see if you kept your promise. If you do this often enough—and you may have to write reminders all over the place—you'll end up with some good habits that will give you the right kind of rewards. The trick is to determine what habits you want and practice until "doing what comes natural" means habitually doing the correct kind of teaching. **T**

# Cooperative learning

A recent study indicates there are two good reasons to encourage your trainees to train each other: They'll probably learn more, and they may develop a spirit of cooperation, rather than competitiveness, essential to the success of your training program.

Students in a University of Washington social psychology course were grouped in pairs and told that their final grades would be determined not by individual achievement but by the average of both partners' grades. Each peer-monitoring group, as they were called, was expected to study together, and the partners were to motivate each other as much as possible. Although they weren't told this, students with low GPA's were roughly matched with students having high GPA's. Despite initial grumblings— that the arrangement wasn't voluntary, that each student's grade could be adversely affected by his or her partner's — the results were gratifying. The number of As and Bs in the peer-monitoring group (as opposed to the

control group, a separate class conducted in the traditional way) increased substantially. In fact, no student in the peer-monitoring class got a D or an F; 87% of the students performed above the 80% grading criterion established ahead of time (no curves allowed) for a B grade.

Contrary to early fears that score averaging would pressure students to spend more time preparing for this course while letting others slide, students in both the peer-monitoring and control groups spent about the same amount of time studying. As an added bonus, students in the peer-monitoring class were more interested in the subject matter and felt more motivated to learn the material; at the end of the quarter, they also rated the class more highly than did the control group.

No student in the peer-monitoring group got a lower grade as a result of the score averaging than he or she would have received had grades been based solely on individual performance. On the other hand, some students got higher grades than they would have under the old system. In

addition to performing better on tests and generally learning more, students made new acquaintances (unusual in large lecture classes), cooperated with each other, and became more aware of the need to work with and help each other while becoming more tolerant of others' values and approaches to life.

What do these results have to do with the trainer faced with a three-day seminar or a continuing in-house program? Since cooperative learning strategies such as this one seem to get better results than the "every man for himself" approach, it might be time to try the peer-monitoring system. And, since this system produces cooperative behavior in college classrooms, notoriously dog-eat-dog and overly competitive, it may also be good for the trainee whose final payoff depends on the performance of his or her group as a whole. In other words, the good old buddy system, which kept us from getting lost in the woods at summer camp or wandering off during field trips, may be just as useful today in your training program. — From *Journal of Educational Psychology*, 1977, Vol. 69, No. 2. **T**

When teaching is confused with learning, payoffs for effective training techniques are often overlooked

# Reminder: learning is a self-activity

by Martin M. Broadwell

If I were asked to give a novice instructor just one basic belief about teaching and learning, this would be it: Learning is a self-activity. The concept is, simply, that the learner is all important *to the learning process* because the learner controls the switch that lets learning happen. That may not be very scientific, but I suspect experienced teachers can relate to it pretty well.

When I used to teach mountain folks, I discovered that I usually learned more than they did. I first began to think about learning as a self-activity when I heard these folks say things like, "You can't larn them nuthin' " or "Somebody done a heap of larnin' on that boy." Obviously, they were substituting the word learning for teaching.

We more "sophisticated" types do that, too...but in reverse. We hear teachers say, "I taught them about statistics today" or "I taught a class how to complete the 2304-A form." We've even heard a class, unable to work a problem or recall data from a previous teaching-learning situation, chastised thusly: "Don't you remember? I taught you that yesterday!"

Learning is a personal thing. There is no such thing as a "group-learn" situation, though most of the formal training we do is in the group mode. We may teach in a classroom where there are a number of people, but whatever learning takes place does so on an *individual basis*. It is rare indeed when the whole class gets a simultaneous "ah-ha!" from something the teacher has done or said. Even those who have been involved in T-group or sensitivity activities don't claim that everybody in the group learned the same things at the same times.

This is no startling revelation, of course, but we tend to forget it in front of a group. Because the group all heard and/or saw something at the same time, we generally assume the students all "learned" that particular something just as, and when, we presented it. For the new instructor, this assumption can be a serious problem.

## Individual needs

What does it do for an instructor to believe that learning is a self-activity? It makes the job a lot harder, that's what. It means we must think of our students as individuals and recognize that they learn at different paces, have different needs, and bring to the class different amounts of desire to learn.

Acceptance of the premise should affect our design efforts, too. Acknowledging that our students are different, we'll begin to think more in terms of individualized efforts in teaching them. We'll become discouraged with certain existing group efforts, and find ourselves intrigued with things like programmed instruction, teaching machines, the open classroom and other individualized instructional concepts. We become advocates of anything and anybody that suggests the students should learn at their own paces, set their own goals, and direct their own learning.

*Then* comes the realization that there's no way the whole world of instruction can be converted overnight to this form of teaching-learning effort. Result? We become somewhat discouraged and plenty frustrated.

## Hopeless situation?

Next, we discover that others have been down this road of thinking before. Then we realize that these seasoned instructors are still engaged in what looks like plain old classroom teaching. Has their enthusiasm for individualized instruction dwindled? Or have they decided that, as a "cause," it is hopeless? We look at ourselves and our newfound convictions and eventually most of us decide we must continue to conduct business-as-usual.

Of course, different individuals react to these revelations in different ways. Many find themselves quite popular when they advocate the need for students to learn on their own. With their egos, stoked by this popularity, they devote more time to *talking* than *doing*. On the few occasions when they are involved in a teaching situation, they usually revert back to the old standby of lecturing, tossing in a sub-group exercise or two to keep it looking honest. Even in this incongruous situation—lecturing to a group—they often lecture on the need to cut down on lecturing.

Fortunately, change is at hand. Superior instructors are beginning to look at things differently in terms of the design and conduct of training programs. Those who are dissatisfied enough to desire lasting change are realizing that this change comes most easily and least painfully from within the system, rather than without. They begin by conducting programs that use *some* of the techniques that encourage self-pacing, self-choosing, and self-learning. They may even experiment with the open classroom or do some programming for self-study. Best of all, they become keenly aware of *individual students needs*.

This crucial awareness of individual student needs focuses all attention on the learner. It starts with the needs analysis—determining where the deficiencies are—and progress through

Reprinted from TRAINING, April 1977

the training process to the evaluation of the training results. When we examine the trainee's work world to decide what training, if any, is needed, we look at individuals, not groups. We may use individuals as samples of group needs, but we still insist on looking at individuals, not total populations. We see what a specific person is able and not able to do. We talk to specific supervisors about specific people, not groups of supervisors about nebulous groups of deficient employees. Once we've decided what training is needed to overcome the discovered deficiencies, we carry this same individuality over to our training design. We think about what the individual students will be doing at any one time. We think about pairing and grouping in sub-groups from the individual up, rather than from the large group down.

In other words, we take individuals and form groups or teams, rather than taking the whole group and breaking it down into some convenient arrangement of teams or sub-group, without regard to anything but numbers.

When the training is completed, we return to the work world to look at individuals and draw conclusions about the entire population based on what specific individuals have accomplished. This represents quite a departure from the days when we amassed quantities of data with total surveys and then made the applications to individuals within the group.

## Conclusion

Has this new-found bit of information about learning as a self-activity changed us so that it's blatantly obvious we're operating under another flag? Of course not. But because *we* know we're thinking differently and actually doing differently, we sleep a little easier, teach a little better, and sympathize a lot more with those who are struggling with the questions that once haunted us. Perhaps, since we've agonized along the same road, we'll even give them some encouragement. **T**

---

# A glossary of trainee types

Certain kinds of people turn up regularly in training courses, and as trainers we need a set of terms that we can use in describing them. At least that's the reasoned opinion of Don Ricks, president of IWCC Ltd., a Calgary, Alberta-based consulting firm specializing in writing training. Ricks, a frequent contributor to TRAINING, proposes the development of a glossary of Trainee Types that would provide trainers everywhere with easily remembered terms for categorizing people on the basis of their in-class attitudes and behavior. A word or phrase could be used to make the key identification, and a short motto could define the distinguishing characteristics.

*Someone Else.* "I don't need this course. I'm just here to find out if someone else should take it."

*Learned.* "Does your approach take into account Bruconowski's theory concerning the intermultiplicity of organizational relativities?"

*Reader.* "According to the last five books I read on this subject..."

*Over The Hill.* "I only wish I had taken this course while I was still young enough to learn something."

*Lookout.* "I'm on the lookout for Male Chauvinist Pigs."

*Me.* "If you and the others keep talking all the time, how are you going to listen to me?"

*Hide.* "Maybe if I look inconspicuous, you won't ask me any questions."

*Conditional.* "I'll learn if..."

*Vacation.* "It's good to get away from the office, even if it means sitting through a course."

*Bird Dog (Male).* "Charlie told me that a lot of horny chicks show up at these courses."

*Bird Dog (Female).* "Suzie told me that..."

*Wow.* "Lay another good one on me, teacher. I'm hanging on your every word."

*Critic.* "Unless I argue about everything, no one will know how smart I am."

*Smiley.* "You know I'm learning, because I smile and nod every time you look at me."

*Mask.* "You may be getting through to me, but I'll be damned if I'll let you know it."

*Signed Up.* "I didn't come here to do anything, I just signed up for a course."

*Blue Eyes.* "I'm trying to concentrate, but you're so distractingly sexy."

*Like Me.* "Learn? I'm too busy trying to make you like me."

*Sub.* "Don't look at me. I'm just sitting in for someone who couldn't make it."

*Belligerent.* "Nobody had better try to teach me anything."

*Live and Let Live.* "You just stand up there and do your talking, and I'll sit here and do my listening."

*We Always.* "But that's not the way we always do it."

*I Always.* "But I always thought that you were supposed to..."

*Last Time.* "But the last time our instructor said..."

*Never 1.* "That's great in theory, but it would never work in the real world."

*Never 2.* "That's a good idea, but my boss would never go for it." **T**

Reprinted from TRAINING, November 1977

Success or failure can
depend on group size
and seating arrangements

# Using small group activities in the classroom

by Patrick Suessmuth

**E**very instructor is familiar witl the advantages of dividing class into small groups for problem solving, case study, discussing or exploring a situation, answering a specific question, model building, developing ideas for further study, and even preparation of projects. Students learn best when they're actively involved in the learning process, and small groups tend to encourage this involvement in a number of ways:

● Non-talkers feel freer, less threatened by being wrong in front of large numbers of people if they do speak out.

● Each participant has a greater level of self-commitment to what has been said, hence a higher probability of following up the idea with action.

● Individuals are far less likely to be ignored in a small group.

● Individual tutorial type of learning, with its greater effectiveness, is more closely approached.

## How big should the group be?

My experience has shown that the following size groups will produce roughly the results indicated:

GROUP SIZE

2 only—Not really a group; suitable for one-to-one situations.

3—The barest minimum that forms a group, but limited in its capacity to generate ideas and develop thoughts. Not enough people to be effective in most situations.

4—Reasonably effective.

5 or 6—Best results are usually achieved from groups this size.

7—Reasonably effective, but starting to get a bit large.

8 or 9—Group structure starts to break down as subgroups form or splinter discussions occur. Satisfactory results can still be attained, but may take longer.

10 plus—Very unsatisfactory unless your purpose is to illustrate problems of groups. Any group of eight or more will create situations where participants get in each other's way and negatively affect group achievements.

## How should students be seated?

The most effective group seating arrangement is a tight circle, although it sometimes takes a bit of doing. Tell a class to form groups and they almost always will sit in a straight line. Even when told to form circles, they don't do it well; often all they do is form into a half-moon shape. The best formation is one in which all group members' knees are touching; this means the group members are facing each other and are close enough for easy communications and maximum group cohesiveness.

Tables can impede group effectiveness. The last thing we need is a table between group members. The table, though serving as a writing and working surface, also serves to 1) set

up sides and 2) add one more barrier to communications.

## What is your role in various types of groups?

There are six ways that groups are usually structured, and your function is different in each:

**1. Task group.** This type of group is established for a specific purpose such as building a list of points, doing a project, solving a case study, etc.

In this type of group structure the teacher's role is totally outside the group. He listens in unobtrusively and periodically to be sure the students understand the task and have the

**Task group-teacher relationship.**

resources needed. He also provides any feedback required.

**2. Discussion group.** This type of group gives the students a free and uninhibited opportunity to discuss a topic of importance; discussion groups usually occur at the end of group tasks when a free flow of feelings and reactions have been generated by the task performed.

The teacher should be careful not to impose his presence too obviously upon a discussion group; one of his main functions is judging when to cut off the discussion. The only guide to this judgment is the discussion itself. Usually lively at the start, when all participants are intensely involved, the discussion will gradually wind down as more and more people drop out. At this point, the instructor should step in and end it.

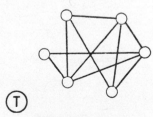

**Discussion group.**

**3. Brainstorming group.** This is usually a larger group (6 to 12 students) and rarely used by trainers. If you decide to hold brainstorming sessions, be sure to first train the students in brainstorming techniques. Consult

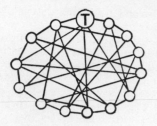

**Brainstorming group.**

Alex Osborn's books which are available in most libraries.

**4. Tutorial group.** There are two types of tutorial groups. In the first, the instructor presents material directly to all members of the group at once. Most of us probably react negatively to this approach as it resembles the lecture-type format we are trying to

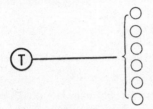

**Tutorial group—Type 1.**

avoid by using small groups. But it is undeniable that by using this form of tutorial group we can take a more personal approach and be sure our information gets across to all of the students.

The second type of tutorial group is not really a group situation as such. In this setting the group works on a task and the instructor assists the students individually. Normally one doesn't consider this as a separate way a

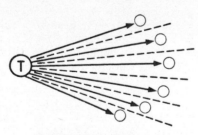

**Tutorial group—Type 2.**

teacher and group can interact, but it arises in any of three ways. First, a student may ask for help voluntarily. Second, the teacher may spot a person needing help or straying off the task. Third, the teacher may set up a task that specifically requires each student to work alone and need, at various points, help from the instructor.

**5. Explorer group.** This has the purpose of developing students' skills in asking questions leading to a suitable exploration of the subject at hand. In its basic form, the teacher is central. Students ask questions of the instructor as they progress through the material under investigation, usually in three stages.

Stage one consists of the students asking the instructor questions about the situation. In other words, the students are analyzing the situation to

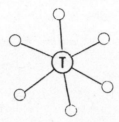

**Explorer group—teacher central.**

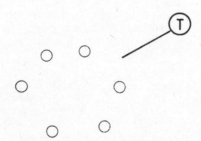

**Explorer group—teacher divorced.**

be sure they have an accurate idea of what they are trying to do. In stage two, students search for facts relevant to the situation at hand. In stage three, the students formulate and test various solutions to the situation.

Obviously the teacher is central in stages one and two, but he should take a passive stance in stage three. Ex-

plorer group activity can be used with verbal case studies, films, problem situations, or anytime students must search out further information in order to reach a valid solution.

Another format is to have the instructor divorced from the group though readily available to answer questions. The divorced arrangement usually leads to better questions being asked. Its disadvantage is that it restricts the flow of questions and often causes key points to be overlooked.

**6. Discovery group.** This type of group usually focuses on a problem which takes the form of "What can we do to...?" The instructor is part of the group and the group's findings repres-

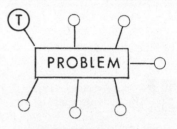

**Discovery group.**

ent discovery for him also. The instructor's role at the start is one of challenger. He responds to student comments with statements such as "Prove it!" "Why that?", "Are you sure" or "What do you mean?" In later stages, after the facts have been established, the instructor's role shifts to passive support in order to enable the group to reach its own solution and its own commitment to action.

Most instructors find the discovery group the hardest type of group activity to manage. This is because all solutions must come from the group and not from the instructor; the instructor must muzzle himself, even when he has a good solution he would greatly enjoy revealing to the group. The teacher can support various students, but only to assure that the whole group heard a particular point the student has made. The instructor supports listening—not student ideas or thoughts. ⊓

Group energy doesn't just happen. It takes careful planning and activities

# Five ways to get trainees to open up and get moving

by Judith H. Steele

*"I'm John Smith, manager of the up-town office," drones the gentleman in the first row.*

*"I'm Mary Jones, supervisor in the accounting department," recites the woman next to him in a flat voice. The trainees continue introducing themselves in singsong voices and sit back lethargically as the trainer mounts the podium to deliver a humdrum lecture.*

Of course, you'd never allow this tedious scene to unfold in *your* training classroom. You're aware that exposing trainees to one another's experiences sparks the exchange of vital job know-how. And, you also want your adult learners to generate their own problem-solving group energy. But group activity doesn't happen automatically. It takes more than noble intentions to get employees, from various branches or departments of the organization, to begin talking, sharing, and working together.

To make it happen, build group activities into your training agenda. Set an active tone early and reinforce it throughout. Ensure that your group "jells" near the beginning of training, and you can turn placid trainees into adults willing to take charge of their own learning.

Here's how you can translate your training ideals into workable classroom activities that harness group energy:

## Introduce people creatively

Remember those uninspiring trainees who could barely blurt out their names and job titles? Anxiously muttering their lines, they were stymied by lifelong exhortations to be modest— and by low training expectations. The grim results: a tense, "first day of school" feeling in the room, and little useful information for trainer or trainees.

Next time, try it another way. Channeling trainees toward their favorite topics— themselves— builds group energy fast. Make trainees abandon comfortable cliques and team up with new partners. Allow time for pairs to interview each other, venturing beyond the basics toward self-disclosure.

When your trainees introduce their partners to the class, watch your talented, multifaceted group come alive. No longer do stiffness and humility dull the atmosphere. Trainees publicly boost each other, announcing that Mary "has quite a bit of useful experience in sales," or that John "solved a stubborn office problem last month." They are also quick to point out common threads of experience that help bind the group: "Like John was saying before, Sue finds meeting the public the most challenging part of the job."

As an open-minded, open-eared trainer, encourage this process by making your own comments throughout the introductions. Your trainess will follow your cue and begin talking directly to each other. Here's the chance for you to pick up some subtle messages about your trainees. Have you spotted your classroom characters: Mr. Garrulous, Ms. Humorist, or Mr. Technicality? Seize this opportunity to review your plans, so you'll be able to gear your training to these newly revealed experience levels and personality traits.

For a more structured beginning, ask trainees to list facts and qualities which best describe them. Then, when they compare their lists with partners, the differences and similarities will spark lively discussions, and provide a vehicle for colorful introductions.

## Give trainees something to talk about

Do your trainees start the day as stonefaced, inert bodies? Break their passivity *before* they can fall back on their old, tight-lipped school behavior. Introduce the unexpected— a stimulating topic or an unusual format that your trainees can relate to course content.

A Polarity Worksheet exercise is one way to ensure that trainees don't doze through your class. These sheets contain an equal number of small boxes at the top and bottom. Each box on top has two captioned pictures illustrating polar opposites— a "noisy" lion and a "quiet" mouse, for example. Trainees select the pictures that best suit their self-definitions and draw them in the corresponding empty boxes below. If they balk at committing themselves to either pole, that's something to talk about, too, when they complete the sheets and introduce themselves to partners who have drawn different pictures.

Make sure your trainees are aware that there aren't any "right" or "wrong" answers—and no one is being judged for artistic talent. Avoid amateur psychological interpretation. Instead, relate the exercise to the rest of your training. Stress how a variety of personal styles can result in effective managers or salespeople and watch your trainees mirror your acceptance of human differences.

For your training session in Life/Work Planning, you might try Movie Screen Worksheets. These handouts contain outlines of three empty screens. Instruct trainees to "freeze the action" on the movies they're making about their own lives. On the first screen, they draw characteristic scenes of themselves at work. On the second screen, they zoom in on leisure time. The third screen might be X-rated— it's for a personal fantasy. Now everyone's active, involved, and focusing on the training objectives.

## Keep trainees moving

Add movement to your training activities by, for example, breaking up familiar seating patterns several times during the day. But your adult learners deserve more than an updated version of musical chairs. For example, when your trainees disagree on a topic, have them regroup according to shared views. When each group's recorder reports back to the entire class, new "converts" have the opportunity to change group affiliations.

To help trainees keep from gathering mental cobwebs, shift the size of the working groups during your training sessions. Alternate trainer input with trainee input, individual work with group work. But tailor the movement to your training content. Clusters of two or groups of 10 may suit your purposes at varying times.

Group shifting does more than just energize your training. It also caters to the diverse personal learning styles of your trainees, some of whom might, for example, clam up in large groups but participate freely in small ones.

### Ask, don't tell

If your trainees seem reticent and unresponsive, it could be *you've* been overworking. Next time, don't try to do all the work by yourself! Tap the resource buried in your trainee's rich body of experience. Resist the temptation to always "tell" your trainees with texts or lectures.

If you're about to hand out a list summarizing MacGregor's management theories, stop and reconsider. Change "telling everyone" to "asking everyone" with a thought-provoking questionnaire or survey. Ask trainees to rate their own degree of agreement or disagreement with the tenets of each management theory. Devise a method to graph individual and class results. Rather than a vague discussion on which theory is "correct," trainees can now decide which parts have meaning for their own jobs. Adrenalin is up—and so is active learning.

### Don't say it, do it

If you want to prove to trainees that participatory communication networks make for more effective management than hierarchial ones, you could cite numerous studies. But with a simulation, your trainees will feel the effects firsthand.

Seat the group in rows, each row being a team. Hand each team member a packet of pre-arranged playing cards. Together, each team holds an entire deck, except for one missing element—like clubs or nines. The game is to find out what's missing, and your goal is to show which manager-subordinate communication system does this best.

Play this in three rounds, with different card packets for each. In the first, no one— including the decision-making manager seated at the end of the row—can speak to anyone except the occupant of an adjacent chair. For the next round, vary the rules by allowing the manager, seated mid-row, to speak individually to anyone in the group. Subordinates, however, can talk only to the manager. Finally, play without any assigned manager and with no limits on communication.

Treat this simulation as more than a diversionary game. Have "managers" and "subordinates" discuss their reactions to the exercise. Ask them to compare the efficiency and effectiveness of each of the three rounds. Pay special attention to the emotions of the "subordinates." Find out which structure fostered the highest morale.

Rounding out your training agenda with group energy activities like these will make your sessions lively, controversial, and, most important, productive. With everyone in your group participating, you'll not only help adults take charge of their own learning, but win points as an effective trainer, too.  **T**

# How to handle the classroom sharpshooter

Every classroom trainer is, at some time in his or her career, confronted by the inevitable "sharpshooter"—the wiseacre who loves to put instructors on the spot by demanding an answer to what is usually a loaded question. In addition to being potentially embarrassing for the trainer, such questions can do considerable harm to a well-planned presentation, distracting the rest of the class from the important business at hand.

New instructors, especially, are vulnerable to this nemesis of the classroom. So how can you help your new trainers respond appropriately to sharpshooter questions? Milt Badt, an experienced instructor and senior engineer with Western Electric Co., believes preparation is the key. Badt offers the following list of defense mechanisms which, although basic, may serve to help the new instructor face his or her first sharpshooter with equanimity.

- Don't be afraid of the sharpshooter. If he were already an expert on your topic, he probably wouldn't, or shouldn't, be enrolled in your class.
- Don't bluff and don't be afraid to say "I don't know."
- Don't get drawn into a long dialogue or argument with the questioner because this will take time away from the material you are expected to cover.
- Smile. A pleasant smile is perhaps as disarming as anything else you may do or say.
- Let the sharpshooter off the hook easily (if he traps himself—and he probably will). You'll gain his respect and

that of the rest of the class.

- State loudly and clearly, "That question has merit!" Then attempt to find some merit, in your own mind, in the particular question asked and state what that merit is. Chances are, there is somewhere, buried within its treachery, some real value to the question. Find it and you may surprise as well as disarm the sharpshooter.

As with every technique of instruction, developing it takes practice. Undoubtedly, your new trainers would eventually find the best method for them, but it never hurts to be prepared.

Reprinted from TRAINING, April 1978

When it comes to motivating
trainees, trainers can learn
from good salespeople
and ad copywriters

# Help trainees believe they need to learn

by Martin M. Broadwell

**P**erhaps it's fair to say that people learn for the same reasons they buy toasters or don't buy mixers—because they have a need of some kind (or perceive themselves as having a need). One has only to read the newspaper ads or watch the sales efforts on the TV screen to see that much advertising is aimed at taking advantage of the "need" syndrome. The idea of getting more for less, better for the same price, avoiding the last minute rush and price increase, taking advantage of a one-time offer—all are designed to appeal to an individual's impulse to gain a reward or avoid punishment.

But good salespeople and ad writers don't just wait for the potential customer to figure out some need. They go out and create a need where it doesn't exist.

It's not often you have a salesperson come to the door of your office, lay a product on the desk or table and say, "Here it is. Wanna buy it?" But think how many times some trainers walk into the classroom, lay the books on the table and say to the students, "Here it is. Wanna learn it?"

Let's take it a step further. Imagine your reaction when the seller tells you, "You'd better buy it. You're gonna need it someday." If you're the naturally patient kind, you'll respond only by suggesting rapid departure. If you're less patient, you might aid that departure somewhat. When using this approach in the classroom, then, is it any surprise when the patient stu-

dents simply sink into a coma and the less patient ones begin a concentrated harassment program?

This may be an ideal time for each of us to look at every program and decide what there is in the course for the students. For those who have given up on real discernable objectives, what are you using to offer the students a reward or to help them avoid punishment? How are you creating the need? For those who still struggle with objectives, are you sharing them with the students? Are they perceived by the students as fulfilling their needs?

**Whose needs are you meeting?**

Here's an experiment you can try in your teacher training classes. Ask half of the group to list reasons why an organization spends money on training. Obviously, training costs money. There's the cost of the facilities, the trainers, the materials, the transportation, the trainees' salaries, etc. Money has to be approved, and the expenditures therefore must be justified. Have the subgroup list the justifiable reasons for getting approval for training dollars. While half the group works on that assignment, have the other group answer this question: "Why would a learner ever bother to learn anything?" It takes some effort, some mo' vation, some expenditure of time, and some commitment to learn most things. Why would a learner want to make the effort?

When the subgroups report, you'll probably have two completely different lists. On one side you'll see things like, "To improve efficiency, provide more services, increase profits, save

money, meet competition, keep up with changes, keep a backlog of promotable people, and reduce accidents." On the other side you'll find things like, "To keep my job, make more money, get ahead, make the job easier, fear of the boss, self-satisfaction, and curiosity."

There are reasons for the differences. Training programs are established for organizational reasons. People learn for self-oriented reasons. It doesn't have much appeal to tell employees they're being trained so they can produce more for the same wages, or that the organization wants them to be more efficient so it can get more goods or service without adding people or increasing costs. Remember, the employees are hoping to make their jobs *easier,* and more production or service sounds like *harder* work. We might kid ourselves and say that what's good for the organization is good for the trainee. That's often correct, but it seldom computes that quickly in the employee's mind.

What this suggests is that we don't use the information we have to motivate the students. We have the things that would turn the students on, motivate them, create within them a need for the learning to take place. We know (or should know) what's in it for the trainees. We know that we're training because there is a deficiency in job performance. We know what happens to employees who can't perform up to standard. We know what happens to employees who *do* perform up to standard. We know that safety has a direct bearing on the employee's pocketbook. We know that we're going to need a certain number of people with certain skills next year, or five years from now. Since we know these things, we ought to share them in such a way to get maximum motivation.

So can we motivate trainees? One way is to use a good sales approach. Create a need for the material—the learning. Create a desire for the objectives on the basis that there is something in it for the students.

Are you doing that now? Well, there are ways of telling. When was the last time you heard a trainee say, "That's okay, but we don't do it that way back at home"? Or, "That's interesting. I hope I get to use that someday." Or, "This is all well and good, but I can't use it until my boss has been here. When are you gonna send him?" And what is your reply? If it's "you'd better learn this or you'll be sorry," you'd better make a resolution to stay out of the selling business. You'll never make it by threatening the customers. As for making it in the training field, well...  ∎

# Learning from experience is a good learning experience

by Andre Nelson

**T**alk about your bright-eyed, bushy-tailed, wet-behind-the-ears trainers! You should have seen me 15 years ago. There I was, just out of college, an anointed training officer in a correctional agency in one of the largest states and burning with a zeal to prove myself.

But where to strike first? There were so many areas in need of my expert attention. Where could I look good and do good at the same time? Safety! Everyone is in favor of safety! Who wants to go to work alive and come home dead? Safety would be a perfect first triumph. I devised an elaborate program. My very own first training effort had films, statistics, lectures by safety experts and my own, very personal BS&T. The result of all this frantic activity? Apathy and resentment on the part of the trainees and a monthly accident rate which completely ignored my admonitions and kept right on inching up.

Of course, the presentations were boring. Safety is boring, isn't it? (It's like Latin. "Take Latin. It *must* be good for you, it's so awful.") A year of safety training, given once every two months, produced no changes in the accident rate. The solution? Cut back to safety training once a year. That'll show 'em. Besides, safety is such a nebulous subject that it wasn't my fault if the trainees were too obstinate to take advantage of my efforts in their behalf. That was the flimsy rationalization I used to salve my conscience.

Just recently, a chance comment made by one of our maintenance people jolted me out of my complacency about safety training. I think what I learned is of value to any trainer in any context. While my office was being remodeled to make room for some television equipment, one of the maintenance men, a welder, sat down wearily next to my desk. As he sank into the chair, he grimaced in pain, straightened out his leg, and grunted, "Man, it hurts all the way to my hips." Knowing he was an avid sportsman, I asked if he'd been hurt while hunting.

"No," he said, "I was on a ladder and fell. Landed on my left hip and side and strained and stretched muscles way down to my ankle. Boy, I sure hate to get up before that group again. This will be the second time in two months."

I was bewildered. Ed is a bull of a man, whom nothing seems to faze. To me, he always seemed about as sensitive as a Patton tank, and certainly the first to guffaw at any safety suggestion. His favorite phrase, when I was launching my safety program was, "Shove off, sonny. I've done this longer than you have years, and I'm still healthy."

I was more than mildly curious about what sort of meeting *he* would be reluctant to address. And *why*, I wanted to know, would he be talking to people about an accident.

It seems that a few months after I gave up my formal, stylized safety training approach, the chief of plant operations had, on his own, initiated a very different kind of safety program. He referred to it as a "tailgate" session, patterned after the informal safety sessions some public-utilities maintenance crews hold around the tailgate of a truck before the start of a work day.

The CPO had been holding informal safety-training sessions for half an hour once every month. During this meeting, every member of the maintenance crew who had an accident during the previous month would stand up in front of the group, describe his accident and suggest ways he could have avoided it. His peers were free to offer corrective suggestions, and, invariably, a discussion regarding that accident and similar ones would develop.

As Ed had confided to me, no crew member relished having to stand up and admit he had injured himself through his own carelessness. There was no breast beating or pleading for forgiveness, just a frank recital of an accident and what had caused it. And the causes the maintenance crew isolated were reasonable and avoidable —trying to take a short-cut to do a job, using improper equipment, or simply daydreaming on the job.

By any measure, this simple program initiated by the CPO has been an ongoing success. The men accept it as necessary, but once they appear before the group they don't wish to repeat the performance. The accident rate, which previously averaged three per month (one usually a disabling injury), has now dropped to less than one a month. And there has been only one disabling accident in a year!

As a novice training officer, I had failed—failed to realize that those for whom I set up safety programs had much more to contribute than I gave them credit for. The CPO, on the other hand, knew something I had forgotten. Safety isn't only rules, regulations and procedures. It's people working in certain ways. And who could have a greater vested interest in going to and returning from work alive and whole than the workers themselves? They are indeed the most valuable resource a safety program could hope for. **T**

Reprinted from TRAINING, July 1978

38    TRAINING/HRD

Socrates can provide
a powerful model for
classroom trainers

# The power of the questioning approach

by Paul J. Micali

There is nothing new, modern or revolutionary about the Socratic method. The man who perfected it, Socrates, was a Greek philosopher who lived around 450 B.C. His method consisted of asking a series of well-planned questions, through which the prospect's thinking was guided to the only correct conclusion possible— the ultimate truth. When Socrates did the selling, the prospect did most of the talking. As questioner, it was Socrates' role to evaluate his subject's reaction and determine the next question to fire out. He became so good at this that he rarely missed a sale.

Typically, trainers of our day spend a great deal of time and effort prompting salespeople, for example, to use the Socratic method. Why, then, is it so difficult for trainers to use it themselves? Trainers are far from college professors who can be content with lecturing, lecturing and lecturing some more. Adult learners have habits which have changed since their college days, if indeed they went to college. And the material is quite different, both in content and application. As Jay Beecroft, formerly of 3M, puts it, "Education is a simple process; training is not. Educators give people knowledge. Trainers help people put knowledge to use."

## The power of the question

In contrast to the lecture style of presentation, the Socratic method promises training that is impactful, that comes across with much more emphasis. And if it has positive results with adult learners, its use also serves to enhance the trainer's style and performance.

The Socratic method forces a trainer to prepare more fully. It is fundamental that you can't ask intelligent questions without first thinking them over carefully. It is also fundamental that you cannot jam too much material into too short a span of time and expect it to be absorbed. In both cases, the trainer is compelled to do a more thorough job— admittedly at some cost in time and effort.

In addition to enhanced planning of material and scheduling, there is the benefit of increased learner participation. By listening carefully, the trainer gets a feel for the intelligence level and overall preparedness of the audience, general morale and attitudes toward training, and attitudes toward superiors and the company. All of this makes it possible to adjust a presentation to not only fit the special needs of the group but also to correct any negative attitudes. And trainers may well learn as much from the answers they receive as they impart to their audience.

Participation also promotes tremendous rapport between trainer and trainees. For the latter, there is a myriad of benefits to be derived from the Socratic method. The best of trainers cannot keep an audience alert for hours on end single-handedly. The questioning approach avoids boredom since it is fueled by both trainer and learners. If trainees know that questions are the rule, they may arrive better prepared for learning, since there is an incentive to read over material very carefully in advance. In addition, the open forum promotes the feeling that personal views can be expressed and won't be criticized, which is always satisfying. The talkers get to talk. The quiet ones get drawn out. The experience is all the more productive for the enthusiastic participation encouraged in attendees.

## When wrong is right

Most trainers will concede the advantages of the Socratic method, but many will also offer a laundry list of disadvantages. The time schedule may not permit its use, they will argue, or the material may be new to attendees. Some trainees may be embarrassed by revealing themselves as novices or unprepared, and others will surely contribute the wrong ideas. And what to do with all those sophisticated visuals if time is to be spent in question and answer interplay?

In their simplest form, these arguments indicate a very real problem, though maybe not the predictable one. The Socratic method is ostensibly simple— conduct a training session by asking questions and handling the responses in such a way that the correct answer is ultimately arrived at. The tricky part is handling the answers properly, especially handling the wrong answers properly.

Those who oppose the Socratic method argue that it doesn't make much sense to entertain a bushel of wrong answers until the right one is finally arrived at, or— at last resort— is given by the trainer. It's a waste of time, they claim, since the wrong answers are of no value anyway. Not so. In learning, it is important to understand the wrong way of doing something along with the right way. In fact, when the wrong way is innocently voiced, it gives the trainer a golden opportunity to explain *why* it is wrong to the benefit of the entire group.

It's almost like handling objections. Done well, there is much to be gained; done poorly, much to be lost. And it really goes beyond that. The trainer must be able to answer *all* questions— right, wrong or irrelevant. Some answers aren't answers at all. They may represent an attitude, egotism, wise-cracking, or some other personal agenda. The trainer must remain in control, but in a positive manner, not by becoming pompous, irritating, insulting, abrasive or in any way terrifying. He or she must reflect the smoothest of salesmanship, appeal to reason where appropriate, and resort to tact and often humor in sidestepping delicate or difficult interchanges.

The acid test of a trainer's ability to set up and effectively maintain a Socratic dialogue is when a trainee offers a wrong idea. If wrong answers are handled properly, much is to be gained by all in attendance. In fact, wrong answers should never be discouraged, whether by ridiculing in any way the people who come up with them or isolating them from their peers as somehow less smart or less qualified to be a part of the group. This is intimidating as well as embarrassing to the individual, and ultimately counterproductive for the group.

The fact is that wrong answers are far from harmful to the cause. On the contrary, if trainees hear six wrong answers before the right one is finally nailed down, they (including those who offered incorrect responses) will understand the reasons behind the right one even better. It is naturally important to be judicious regarding how much time is spent on wrong answers. In any training, time is always a significant factor whose value is measured by the trainer.

What can be said regarding results obtained with the Socratic method? By many measures, trainees learn and retain more, though how much more is hard to quantify. In one case, however, the average test score of a group of 40 sales trainees after a two-day Socratic style seminar was 22% higher than the average score of a similar group of 85 who attended the exact same seminar in lecture format. **T**

# Why it pays to make a good first impression

**I**n their book, *Contact: The First Four Minutes,* Drs. Arthur and Natalie Zunnin claim that first impressions are lasting impressions. That is, the first four minutes we spend with someone we've just met can, and usually do, set the tone for an entire relationship. According to the Zunnins, we decide whom we will or won't buy from, hire or fall in love with in those first few critical moments of contact. Whether you're a salesperson, a job seeker or a cruising single, that can be a pretty startling realization. Obviously, it's important to know how to put your best foot forward in a first-contact situation.

Recent research by Drs. Brad and Velma Lashbrook, Wilson Learning Corporation, may shed some light on the dos and don'ts of that first-contact period. The Lashbrooks, working from the "counselor" model of buyer-seller relations, have been studying the factors that led prospective buyers to feel *comfortable* with salespeople.

Working with 605 salespeople, the Lashbrooks tested the idea that "a certain degree of social penetration (interpersonal comfort) is necessary for a buyer-seller relationship to develop to the degree that two parties can engage in a decision-making process." Their procedure was to have the salespeople in question distribute an interpersonal relations questionnaire, called the Interaction Feedback Profile, to their customers and prospects at the culmination of a sales call. The customer or prospect filled out the form and mailed it directly to the researchers.

At the end of the six-month data-gathering period, the researchers factor analyzed the data to tease out the elements that most affected customer comfort in the buyer-seller situation. Their findings indicate that variations in three perceptual factors — *competence, trust* and *propriety,* or "interactive integrity" — account for almost half (45%) the variation in level of customer comfort reported by the buyers in their study. That is, when a buyer perceived a seller to be *competent* (technically qualified to help solve a problem), *proper* (the right kind of person to be working with) and *trustworthy* ("win-win" motivated), then the buyer was most likely to report that he or she felt *comfortable with the salesperson.*

The Lashbrooks report that their data also suggest an order in which these three factors come into play. Apparently, the most impact on comfort occurs when the seller establishes the "normative" factors — competence and propriety — and then the "psychological" factor — trust. Establishing these client perceptions, they further suggest, may require more than one sales call.

Though their data analysis is a maze of complex factor analyzers, oblique rotations and regression modeling, the results are pretty clear. If you believe in and teach the "win-win" counselor or consultative approach to selling, your trainees should be aware of the critical impact of first impressions and should know how to make good ones.

According to the Lashbrooks' work, that good first impression requires the would-be seller to answer three questions for the buyer:

• Is this person enough like me to understand and deal with my problems? Do we have enough in common to work together (*propriety*)?

• Does this person have the knowledge and skill to help me solve my problem (*competence*)?

• What is this person's intent toward me? Does he/she really *want* to help me solve my problem (*trust*)?

When the buyer can answer all three questions positively, it means that the seller has established his or her *interpersonal integrity,* the buyer is comfortable with the seller and the problem-solving dance can begin. Be it buyer-seller, employer-employee, trainer-trainee or person-to-person, good relationships start with putting your best foot forward. A sincere effort to make the other person comfortable is clearly a step in the right direction. — R.Z. **T**

(Originally reported in "Applying the Concept of Interactive Integrity to the Sales Setting," an unpublished research report by William B. Lashbrook and Velma J. Lashbrook, Wilson Learning Corporation, Research Dept., Eden Prairie, MN.)

The world's great teachers have had the ability to illustrate their messages with simple but moving stories. You can, too

# Using the parable to make a point

by Lilith Ren

It earned Socrates the reputation of master teacher. It brought Abe Lincoln influence through persuasive power. And it's a crucial factor in a trainer's success. All of us can use it because it is a simple, trainable technology.

"It" is the ability to thoughtfully construct stories, or parables, that underwrite the training outcomes we want. For centuries, stories, anecdotes, jokes and other kinds of parables have been used to communicate important information, attitudes and skills. From Homer to Uncle Remus, storytellers trained while they entertained.

A parable is a bridge that can link my experiences and opinions to yours. Granted, my experiences and problems will never match yours, point for point. We see things differently, so what's true for me may feel off base to you. However, if in my communication with you, you recognize enough similarity between the situation I share through my parable and the situation you face, then you'll find ways to adapt my communication to your particular situation. This process, like all communication, is both conscious and subconscious. Consequently, the more subtle the suggestions I offer, the more likely it is you'll want to incorporate my ideas. Parables carry subtle messages. That's why they're particularly powerful.

Remember those "magic" speakers who've won your respect and atten-
tion with their right-on opening anecdote? It was more than just amusing. Holding clearly in mind their desired training outcomes, they could create and tell a story that danced right past your questions of credibility and began creating a mind-set for learning. The difference between using a story and letting it use you is aligning its underlying messages with your training goals.

Recently I was training a group of managers in effective communication. My partner and I were there because our needs assessment showed people were creating conflict by not sharing their opinions. I opened our first session with an adaptation of Dr. Jerry Harvey's "Abilene Paradox," an anecdote about family members who suffer the needless discomfort of a hot trek to Abilene because no one wants to speak up assertively. As I spoke, I watched my audience bob their heads in fascinated recognition. I had them. Or so I thought.

To our dismay, no one wanted to apply their new communications skills back on the job. "This stuff is great," we'd hear them say, "but my office is beyond all hope." Frustrated, I turned to my co-trainer and we discussed our work. What went wrong? Was it us? Was it them? It was neither. It was a poorly planned parable that sabotaged our previously effective design.

Learning from my mistakes, I opened the next course with a reworked parable. This time as the story ended, the family's new communication patterns led them to new
levels of teamwork and personal satisfaction. And this time we began to hear coffee-break tales of, "You know, this really works. Yesterday, I said to the boss...."

The parable has influence, whether we use it to warm up a group, motivate behavior change, deal with "yes buts," or point out an everyday application of theory. The parable also has power when we apply it outside our presentations. Imagine using this technique to help sell a proposal or next year's training budget. And you can see the possibilities of using informally delivered, but cleverly planned, parables to coach an individual toward more effective behaviors. Or, as the legendary sage will so often do, use a parable to get your point across while skirting an awkward question.

Well-planned parables sweeten advice with amusement and warm it with rapport, making it far easier to swallow. There's a very subtle— and very real— difference between giving advice and influencing via an effective parable. Part of this difference lies in the parable's ability to entertain. A parable will amuse your listeners while clearing a path through to their more creative, innovative subconscious. The better to hear you with...and problem solve.

The most crucial factor in the parable's power is your ability to construct it carefully, and with an eye to depth. Here's a seven-step process for effective parable engineering.

**1 Identify the problem.** We sabotage ourselves most often by telling jokes, stories and anecdotes before we think about the behavior we want to shape. To become more skilled at using parable power, first identify the problem clearly and define it in terms of behavior within the listeners' control. For example, increasing the division's budget may be out of their realm. Redefining department priorities isn't.

**2 Analyze the structural supports.** It's vital to clarify the structure of the situation. Looking at the perceived problem, what's the sequence of events to date? Specifically, when and where does this situation take place? Who are the characters involved? Most importantly, how do they relate to each other?

- **Hierarchy**     who reports to whom who supervises whom

- **Method**     who's a peer do they relate via writing face-to-face conversation non-verbally

- **Effect of their relating**  what happens physically to them
  what happens emotionally to others

**3 Find the balance point.** What's blocking the desired behavioral outcome? More importantly, *how* is that happening? Of course, be sure you identify a factor the recipients of your parable can effect. Throughout this clarifying, you'll discover "what" and "how" are more useful than "why."

**4 Script a parallel situation.** The analytic groundwork completed, you've a solid foundation on which to build a strong, effective parable. With a keen eye to this blueprint of the problem, change the names, costumes and settings to something more entertaining. A work team becomes a family with parents and children; in-laws or neighbors represent other departments or regulatory agencies. Or use animals in a forest, with the boss disguised as a fox or good-hearted but misunderstood troll. Keep your casting parallel to the data you collected in steps one through three.

To select relevant settings, cue in to common figures of speech your listeners already use. If they talk about "strategies" and "the big guns," create a war story. If it's "teamwork" and "first stringers," use sports as a backdrop. A note of caution: To make parables relevant, let listeners do their own detail work. "Those memories were strong whenever she saw him" will be more meaningful than "She felt furious about those memos whenever she saw him in the cafeteria." Listeners will provide the relevant details from their own experience.

**5 Provide a pragmatic alternative.** You've pinpointed the desired outcome. Now the question is what could the recipients of this parable be doing *instead* of what you see them doing now to reach the desired outcome? The alternatives you see can be changes in actions and/or attitudes. The essential thing is to encourage them to develop an alternative that *parallels and replaces* whatever ingredient it was you saw triggering their present problem.

Our clients aren't dumb. Sometimes the alternative to their problem is obvious to them. If the situation allows, check to see if they've already tried it. If so, what happened? Often, they'll recognize the way out of their quagmire, but feel they can't take that first step. That's why it's paramount you recognize *how* they stop themselves before giving advice wrapped in a parable.

**6 Point the way out.** The means to the end you've identified is the "connecting strategy." This is how you help them move from present situation to desired outcome. As you shape the parable, add something its characters either do, see or hear that helps them see the light and feel ready to act differently.

**7 Illustrate through a role model.** The connecting strategy dovetails into one or more of the following actions for the character who represents your listener(s):

- Character experiences old situation in a new way

  *"He began to see ways to use his angry feelings..."*

- Character engages in a new behavior and/or reacts with a new attitude
  *"...they became important signals that reminded him to share his views clearly so they could begin to negotiate..."*

- Character achieves desired outcome
  *"...listening thoughtfully and speaking assertively until their horse-trading ended in mutual satisfaction."*

Your finished parable will clearly show it's not the events, behaviors or emotions involved that are the problem. The problem is *how* characters are perceiving and using them.

Parables increase in power when built with skill and subtlety. David Gordon's *Therapeutic Metaphors* is a good book to look over as you develop more command.

There are two other tips useful in telling more powerful parables. First, build direct instructions into the parable. This is accomplished when you use active verbs rather than passive nouns and construct sentences that include direct suggestions. "Your *belief* in this system is something we need if it's going to be *workable*," translates to the more potent "We need to have you *believe* in this system if we're going to *make it work*."

When you use this kind of phrasing you can add more emphasis by using voice tone to underline phrases with instructions and desired outcomes, adding gestures for further emphasis and drawing listener attention to a phrase by inserting the word "you" or their name. ("If you like this idea, then, Terry, follow up on it.")

Second, most people pay attention to one kind of input. Some focus mostly on what they see. Some tune into sounds and speech. Some are generally in touch with what they feel and their sensory environment. By identifying those who are mostly seers, listeners or feelers, you gain a new key to establishing quick rapport. Listen to the verbs people use:

- Visual language: *focus on, picture, look for*
  "She scanned the situation for a new point of view."

- Auditory language: *tell, discuss, word of mouth*
  "Sounds like keeping your ears open for new ideas might work."

- Feeling language: *getting in touch, solid, joyful*

  "He was reaching for a new way to handle it."

Clearly, this can be a powerful tool in one-to-one communication. It can also be useful when training groups. For instance, to reach a larger number of listeners with your parable, choose words that guarantee you're understood by all three kinds of listeners.

If you discover an individual or work team paying attention to only one kind of input, teaching them to pay attention to another category can contribute to the connecting and empowering strategies you choose.

Like others who value their craft, as trainers it's rewarding to experiment with one more tool or technique that adds to our art. Honing the power of the parables you tell is just such a technique. With it, we make our entertaining more training and vice versa. **∎**

How well do your listeners 'see' what you mean? Boost the effectiveness of your training by understanding the link between what the senses say and the brain retains

# Using mental imagery to enhance learning

by Ron Zemke

**M**ental imagery, the ability we all have to "see" in the "mind's eye" an object, person or place not actually present, has been regarded as a powerful training tool since the time of Socrates. There is nothing especially spooky about it either. Dr. Joseph Shorr, director of the Institute of Psycho-Imagination Therapy in Los Angeles, maintains all of us use this ability to construct pictures in our heads all the time, sometimes consciously, sometimes not. He contends that regardless of the kind of wishing, thinking, reasoning or problem-solving we're involved in, we use some form of mental imagery to help us get the job done.

Skeptical? Try this: Picture yourself standing in your bedroom...now see yourself in your kitchen...now on an airplane endlessly circling O'Hare...now floating on an air mattress in the blue Caribbean...now reading...now on the telephone. In a flash you can be on a sandy beach, in a log cabin or at a special party. And you can slide effortlessly and at will from scene to scene. Similarly, you can *choose* to experience these scenes as vivid and real or in a more detached, distant manner; it's up to you. There are differences in the clarity and vividness of individuals' images, but if you simply relax and close your eyes you will most probably have mental pictures.

## A supple, subtle tool

This apparently intrinsic ability we all seem to have in some degree has a long history and many uses. The ancient Greeks taught a memory system based on the pairing of outlandish or unusual mental images with the object or idea to be remembered; a system popularized and refined this century by the likes of Dale Carnegie, Harry Lorraine and Robert Montgomery. Let's say you have to remember a list of three things to bring home from the market—a head of lettuce, a pound of ground round and a box of bagels. One memory system has a set of rhyming pegs for lists: one-gun, two-shoe, three-tree and so forth. To use these pegs you literally make a link between the items on the shopping list and the pegs. Coupling might go like this: "One-gun— I see a face on a head of lettuce and a bullet going through it. The face has little x's for eyes. Two-shoe— I see a football shoe kicking a meatloaf through the goal posts. Three-tree— I see a Christmas tree decorated with bagels." Believe it or not, making these connections verbally and then seeing these absurd scenes in your mind's eye, your imagination will put your shopping list neatly into short-term memory. And there's plenty of research that says it works.

But this "names-faces-dates-places" use of imagery may only scratch the surface of ways directed mental imagery can be used to enhance learning. Preliminary research suggests grade school students who are instructed to make a mental picture of the ideas in a story learn— and remember— new vocabulary more quickly and also tend to develop conceptual understanding of new words more quickly. *Brain Mind Bulletin* reports that a special imaging-based learning procedure developed by Synectics Education Systems, Cambridge, MA, has been shown to significantly affect reading and aural comprehension scores.

Other studies have shown that children who are told to make a mental picture of new spelling words perform better on recall tests; that university students learn lists of pairs of items faster and remember them longer when the word pairs form mental pictures; and that university students instructed to make mind pictures of what they read are able to answer more short essay questions than students who do not receive these instructions.

Overall, imagery as a direct aid to memory seems to work best for lists of numbers and names, and concrete objects. Overt activity with the objects increases the ability to form mental images and to recall the objects. As mentioned earlier, the Carnegie-Lorraine-Montgomery approach to remember names and faces has been researched and verified. A number of good studies have been conducted in England, and other researchers have found that the more bizarre the images used in the mental picture, the longer the name, face or idea stayed on the peg.

## Cold call daydreams

For all its uses in remembering words, ideas and concepts, imagery seems to be most powerful in the direct facilitation of behavior change. As far back as Freud, imagery— in the form of free association and dream recall techniques— has played a part in helping people change behavior. Fritz Pearl and other Gestalt therapists have used guided symbolic imagery instructions to help people get at what's bothering them and to help them seek out answers to problems. In one Gestalt technique, the Empty Chair, people having trouble confronting others are taught to construct an "image" of that person sitting across from them in a real empty chair. Their conversations with the empty chair have been known to become so real to them that more than a few have taken a poke at the imaginary adversary.

Reprinted from TRAINING, January 1981

Yale psychologist Jerome Singer says we all use spontaneous daydreaming to solve current problems, prepare for future events, ward off tension, relieve boredom, dispel fear and dissipate anger. He points out studies which show self-esteem and even bottom-line success can be affected by the way we image ourselves and the goals we are trying to achieve. Many sports figures, says Singer, report that they spur themselves on by imaging the act of winning. Philadelphia Eagles quarterback Ron Jaworski, for example, is known to spend time floating in a 20% saline solution isolation tank imaging the week's game plan.

Psychologist Frances Meritt Stern reports using imagery to help people slim down better and faster in her book *Mind Trips To Help You Lose Weight*. She also reports that executive stress can be managed by the use of short, pleasant mental imagery episodes, or what she calls "mini-vacations in your head." Likewise, salespeople who are having call reluctance or "phono-phobia" can reprogram themselves with carefully constructed success images.

What's the difference between the structured imagery that psychologists are pushing today and the 1950s sales motivator's cry of "What mind of man can conceive, man can achieve" and "Your success is only as limited as the dreams you dream of yourself"— or even Professor Harold Hill telling the children of River City they need only "think" the music to learn to play the instruments? For one thing, reality. For another, research.

For years the power of positive goal images was a popular platform topic. But people found that, just as with management by objectives, simply being able to picture a goal was not enough. There has to be a plan and a method—and a realistic chance—before attainment takes place.

One of the most frequently cited examples of the use of imagery in direct behavior change involves junior high students and free throw shooting. Three groups of boys were asked to take 10 shots from the foul line. Then one group was instructed to practice in the gym for 20 minutes every day. A second group was instructed to practice shooting free throws "in their heads" for the next week while a third group was given no instruction at all. A week later the practice group and the imagery group

both outperformed the control group. And, surprisingly, the imagery group outperformed the practice group.

But notice two things: First, the imagery practice group was working with a very specific discrete behavioral act: shooting free throws, something they had some prior experience with. Secondly, they were instructed to image those specific behaviors, not some wild fantasy such as playing in the NBA and making the free throw that won the game. In short, imagery seems to change behavior when the imagery used is concrete, behavioral and realistically attainable by the individual doing the imaging.

Fascinating literature is developing on the usefulness of this form of behavioral-specific, positive mental imagery. Among the more intriguing findings:

● Specific positive, pleasant mental images can be used as positive reinforcement for a variety of behaviors, from doing math problems to making cold canvass sales calls.

● New skills such as speaking before a group, acting assertively and eating with your mouth closed can be successfully practiced through mental imagery *if* a minimal amount of real practice is also interspersed.

● Directions to imagine a stressful event can actually trigger a physiological stress response. Conversely, instructions to picture a pleasant or peaceful event or place can reduce physiological stress responses.

● Debilitating fear of snakes, heights, open spaces and people named Big Al have been cured or eliminated by the use of mental imagery and a one-step-at-a-time procedure called systematic desensitization.

● Goal rehearsal of pass throwing, ground-ball catching, back hand hitting, slalom skiing and other athletic endeavors has proven successful in increasing performance for a variety of athletes, amateur and professional. (Researchers in this area generally conclude that if you are already good at some physical activity, the practice of goal rehearsal can make you better.)

● A number of medical problems— the so-called psychosomatic disorders— can be alleviated with imagery. Hypertension, dermatitis, ulcerative colitis, spastic colon and tension headaches have all reportedly been cured through the use of guided mental imagery. A few medical researchers are reporting that teaching patients specific "healing" mental

imagery seems to be useful in the treatment of cancer.

In addition, Dr. Albert Ellis, creator of rational-emotive therapy, has used imagery instructions to change the "self-talk" people use to assess, evaluate and guide their behavior. Research surgeon Wilder Penfield has found that electrical stimulation of the brain can cause an individual to see vivid images of things past and hear vivid echoes of sounds long ago faded. The late Dr. George Kelley suggested that the way people visualize the outcomes of anticipated events often shapes that outcome. Your imagery, adds Dr. Arnold Lazarus, can spawn an optimistic or a pessimistic life view. Thus, sadness and despondency can also be overcome using specific self-image, self-esteem enhancing imagery.

Lazarus believes we can even inoculate ourselves against future shock through imagery. His advocated technique is rehearsal through projected imagery. "To avoid future shock," he says, "it is important not only to think about events that are likely to occur in time, it is most important to picture them as clearly as possible, and to vividly imagine oneself dealing with these situations."

If you've just become a parent, you might want to inoculate yourself against the woes of parenting by imaging the good and bad things you are likely to encounter in years to come. For example, if it seems reasonable to you that there may be a shoplifting incident to deal with in the future, you will be better prepared to cope with it if you anticipate it now. That beats the heck out of the usual surprise, panic and blame that so many of *our* parents experienced when we failed to meet their expectations— images, if you will, of the perfect child.

We've only briefly touched on the many uses researchers are finding for the power of structured and unstructured mental imagery. Many of these uses have direct application to our work as trainers and human resources development specialists. Some techniques can be used to make the classroom experience faster and easier. Others can help incumbents handle the rocks and ruts of daily duties. Some can even help us make our lives and jobs more effective and fun. And *that* is an image worth imagining. **T**

No matter what your next class is about, a few choice ones from the likes of Mark Twain or Honest Abe make good training aids

# Why it pays to use quotes in your class

by Walt Robson

**M**any experienced trainers use the notable quote to support one or more of their principle premises and to give their audiences encapsulated summaries they can share with their colleagues. I often use this technique in my seminars in media communications, which I've been presenting for nearly 10 years.

Where do these nuggets of inspiration come from? Well, some from *Bartlett's Book of Quotations* and others from the speaker himself, inspired by circumstance to coin a phrase or two that has a ring of truth. "Inspiration," defined one sage, "is the instantaneous culmination of all previous experience." How true!

A case in point. I was giving a media communications seminar in Toronto to Canadian educators and was being intellectually challenged all morning by a courteous but persistent sharpshooter. He finally asked a question that would have required three graduate units of time and credits to answer: "Mr. Robson, how would you define the difference between teaching and learning?" Since I had never been asked that before, I had no prepared answer.

Fortunately, a thousand dusty synapses connected, my mouth opened, and, to my surprise, the definition he asked for came out: "Teaching takes place when the teacher is ready. Learning takes place when the learner is ready and, hardly ever, do the two coincide." "That," I concluded, "is the principle benefit of videotape." We are most motivated to learn at the moment when learning is critical. That's why we cram the night before final exams. It's also why the salesman really learns his new product just before he must make a critical presentation.

One of my favorite quotes comes from Mark Twain, and I use it when I'm asked how long a media presentation should be. For years, I've noticed that attention seems to wane after about 20 minutes and that shorter, single-concept modules seem to produce better immediate and long-term results. This pragmatic evidence was confirmed when we turned to Bartlett's and uncovered this terse observation from Twain: "No sinner is ever saved after the first 20 minutes of a sermon."

Suddenly the whole phenomenon makes sense. If the congregation is asleep, our chances for "saving" them is zero! Mr. Twain, in all his wisdom, gave us a simple guideline. If only we would listen! That quote has helped me—and, I trust, others—to win the battle against the long-winded 30- to 40-minute exposition.

## Massage the message, not the medium

Another battle we have to win is the rejection of personality-based instruction, especially where the "talking head" is a corporate giant or a well-known personality from the world of sports or entertainment. It is the *message*, after all, that is important, and no amount of "glamour" is going to make a poorly conceived message more effective. To that end, I coined the following: "If you have nothing important to say, have someone important say it."

Now and then, I'm struck by other people's off-the-wall logic which they have captured in a memorable phrase. A decision maker who didn't like to make decisions until the last moment (or after it) confronted us with this one: "Indecision is the key to flexibility." No one could defy logic as simplistic as that. If you don't make any decisions, you have left all your options open. From a communications design point of view, I offer this paraphrase of our friend's quote: "Indecision is the key to futility."

When I discuss the issue of credibility in communications, I often quote a newsman, who apparently had no love for the presidential press relations staff. According to him, a certain president's press secretary announced the sinking of the Titanic by saying, "The Titanic is pausing in mid-Atlantic to take on ice."

That story, of course, did not hold water, as it were. Neither did Watergate, and neither do some of the less credible corporate messages that have been released under the guise of corporate video newsreels. One firm we know of plans to interpret world news in its own way for its employees. Another organization found that when its video monitors played company propaganda, the employees turned the TV sets toward the wall.

## A lesson from Honest Abe

Honest Abe Lincoln is credited with apologizing to his friend for writing such a long letter, because he didn't have time to write a short one. Abe was right; it does take longer to write a clear, concise communique than it does to write a long, meandering missive. It takes time and stark objectivity, both of which often are in short supply.

A famous sports celebrity gave us a pearl of wisdom when he said, "Don't look back; something may be gaining on you." Who was that Socrates of sports? We will send a suitable award to the first five readers who identify this famous philosopher.

Onward, and upward dear reader. May your own quotes live on to serve as models to those who follow. William Onken, whose course, "Managing Management Time," is one of the best in the business, defined the "Golden Rule" in management as: "He who has the gold makes the rules." We always knew that. The boss is the boss and the client is the client, but the power of the quote makes the adjustment a little easier.  **T**

# End your programs with effective summaries

The summary is a crucial part of any platform presentation, from a one-hour briefing to a five-day workshop. Yet even the best speakers know the "MEGO (my eyes glaze over) effect" that overcomes an audience when the words "Let me summarize" are uttered.

David Monroe Miller, a New York-based training and human resource consultant and author, recognizes that most summaries suffer from dullness, lack of audience participation and time constraints. Miller says that while a summary should aid retention, most are ineffective because they require only passive listening on the part of the audience.

Graphically interesting visuals that show a sense of humor will help, according to Miller; but even they do not promote the two important purposes of a summary: retention and feedback. A handout listing key points is useful for later reference, but handouts often leave a feeling of anticlimax—if the program can be summarized on one piece of paper, why have we been here all this time? And asking for questions or comments at the end of a long day can undermine even the best of programs. The group will not feel like participating at the end of a long session, and such a loosely structured summary will cover only one or two points at best.

To combat the "MEGO effect," Miller has devised a summary and wrap-up method that involves the audience, promotes retention, clarifies key points, provides feedback and, importantly, does not run overtime.

Miller begins the summary of an all-day program a half-hour before the session is to end. He does not advertise it as a summary, only as another activity. He does, however, set his wristwatch alarm to "beep" mysteriously, a device guaranteed to pique audience interest.

Then participants are asked to jot down on a fresh piece of paper *one* point or idea that comes to mind from the workshop—not necessarily the most important point, just one idea covered. He allows no more than 30 seconds. Miller then asks for "samples" from the group, writing each contribution on the chalkboard. As Miller writes each point, he asks for a show of hands from all who had written down the same point, and calls on one of those participants to comment or amplify. This allows him to reinforce the points as they're mentioned. When all the group's points are listed on the chalkboard, he hands out his own list, clearly labeled "Summary." The group compares the two lists, looking for items that have been omitted or reworded in the chalkboard summary. To do this, the learner must review the entire program's discussion and perhaps ask questions—giving the instructor further opportunity to explain and clarify. Miller establishes that the list on the board is the master list, making sure that everyone copies it.

When the lists have been combined, Miller injects a little showmanship: "Now, I'll show you what to do with the printed handout." He crumples it and dramatically executes a "perfect two-point play" into the nearest wastebasket, reinforcing the participants' ownership of the summary.

With that preparation, Miller says, the speaker can launch into a "carefully rehearsed, uplifting, encouraging, 250-word-or-less rhetorical climax, complete with a built-in applause line." He does not take any questions, because the time for audience participation is over.

Miller considers the summary and the wrap-up two distinctly different parts of a program. The wrap-up is short and is done by the speaker alone. The summary has an important educational purpose and is longer, comprising between 5% and 10% of the total program time, and involves the audience.

A good summary cannot save a poor program, Miller says, but it can at least leave the participants with something approximating their money's worth. By the same token, a bad summary cannot kill a good program, but it can represent lost opportunity or even dilute the program's effectiveness. The "Miller Method," says its originator, can enhance learning, increase the probability that major points will be retained and understood, and give the group—and the instructor—a well-earned, positive feeling of accomplishment.—S.M. **T**

Reprinted from TRAINING, June 1980

These useful tips are
applicable for trainees
as well as trainers

# Teaching listening
# and questioning skills

Training in how to listen is fast becoming a key element in many supervisory training programs. That's not surprising, especially when you consider that without listening there can be no communication. And, of course, communicating is a major part of any manager's job.

Recent phone calls and inquiries from TRAINING's readers reflect increased interest in the area of listening. Many readers are asking us how trainers in other companies are teaching listening skills. We decided to ask Raymond A. Higgins, director of sales training and development at Armour-Dial, Inc., who has been teaching listening and questioning skills for 20 years. He calls these skills "the most needed (and often neglected) tools of any manager, supervisor, sales representative, parent, or training director."

Higgins bases his courses on the counseling tools developed by Carl Rogers. These techniques, often taught to professional counselors, are also part of the repertoire of most successful managers.

The problem, as Higgins sees it, is to put "handles" on the tools, to name them and present the techniques in such a way that trainees can grasp their significance and then practice using them. Asserts Higgins, "Sure, you can 'enlighten' managers on the tools available and they may even 'understand' them to the point where they can fill in the proper response on a written quiz or voice-back an 'example' in response to a staged tape recording. But we try to get them to 'learn-it-in-the-muscles' by practicing a la 'bedlam' with each participant-

manager trying to implement his solution to his real-life problem with a subordinate, peer, or boss."

In keeping with his "learn-it-in-the-muscles" principle, Higgins formulated his programs which progress through the following 10 steps.

**1. Use the participants' real-life problems, rather than hypothetical cases.** Each manager is required to submit one written case history of his or her most difficult problem in getting work done through people. This is their "price of admission" and the workshop revolves around these problems, which are numbered and reproduced in each participant's workbook. Before the class begins, the instructor chooses one-third of the problems for the first problem-solving session and divides the trainees on the seating chart into groups of three, each triad composed of one individual whose problem is being discussed.

**2. Provide a framework for good problem analysis.** "The best and simplest format I've found," says Higgins, "is an oldie (a generation before Kepner-Tregoe) by Dr. William J. Reilly, first published as *The Twelve Rules for Straight Thinking* (Harper Bros.). Reilly had defined how the mind works and how it ought to work, and believe me, they are not the same!"

Early in the workshop, Higgins gives a short, 15-minute lecture—that's right, a lecture—on the "straight-thought" process and progressively builds the steps with "slap-ons" on the hook and loop board. As he explains it, the process is comprised of four components: 1) factual and analytical observation, which

includes gathering facts like what, when, where, and who, and opinions; 2) definition of the *real* problem; 3) examination of possible solutions; and 4) conclusion(s).

Following the lecture, the class is split into the triad work groups and a case assigned to each. Since the participant who wrote the case is in the group analyzing it, there are no assumptions or suppositions necessary. After an hour of analysis, the class is reassembled and each group, in turn, reports on its assigned case, following a four-page form which lists: major contributing causes, their definition of the problem, at least three possible solutions, their conclusion, and why they chose it.

**3. Participants set up their own practice of implementing their solutions.** As each triad concludes its reported decision, the instructor asks what first step to implementation would involve a face-to-face confrontation with a person involved in the problem. A role-play situation form is then prepared by the triad and serves to help identify the personality and probable reaction of the subordinate.

**4. Conduct "bedlam" practice of the confrontations.** This is, in effect, a sort of "practice" session, intended to get a reading on how well the participants perform before they are introduced to the interviewing skills. The managers assume various roles and are videotaped while trying to solve the problems they've discussed.

"I used to give the input on 'Listening-Questioning' before any practice," comments Higgins, "but not any more! Our participant-managers—especially those district managers from supermarket chains—are grown, mature, successful managers. Each is directly responsible for eight to 14 stores and 40 to 60 million dollars in annual business volume. So I let them practice first. Then, during the videotape playback, I have always found several situations where the interviewer was doing most of the talking and/or was not getting true acceptance. Stop the tape!"

**5. Present the "Listening-Questioning" tools.** The instructor, using visuals and examples, explains each of Carl Rogers' tools. Higgins likes to start by hanging a face on the hook-board with the caption, "God gave us two ears and one mouth!"

**6. Pass out the billfold-size card which lists the six guidelines on how to listen and the six guidelines on how to ask questions.** If your class runs anything like Armour-Dial's, most managers have been taking copious notes. But don't bank on them retaining what you present without a "keeper." As the managers are tucking the cards away into their billfolds, Higgins dares them with "next Monday morning, just before walking into that first store, I challenge you to pull out the card and review both sides. See if you don't accomplish more!"

**7. Put the triads back to practice.** This time, they are supplied with two easel cards—one on listening and one on questioning. These are placed on the desk facing the interviewer. Back in bedlam practice, you'll probably notice a dramatic lessening of "telling" and complete involvement in two-way communication. Every once in a while, you may even notice an interviewer's eyes drop down to the easel cards, then back to eye contact with the "subordinate."

**8. Have one observer in each triad keep score.** The observer takes notes on how many of the listening-questioning tools are used and then conducts a private critique within the triad after the interview is concluded. Following the critique, the participants change roles and go back into practice until all three managers have been in all three roles.

**9. Replay randomly videotaped excerpts from the "after" practice.** During the replay, the instructor points out specific listening-questioning skills as they appear on the screen.

**10. Move on to more practice on handling difficult personalities.** You may want to use this step as the first exercise of the second day of your

---

### How To Listen

1. **Remain neutral.**
Do not give advice, agree or disagree, criticize or interrupt.

2. **Give your complete attention.**
Let him know you are listening. Nod your head — "uh huh, I see what you mean."

3. **Ask about his statements.**
Dig out information, invite him to tell everything. Say: "In addition to that is there anything else . . .?"

4. **Restate his main points.**
Let him hear his exact words restated by you. This prompts him to stick to the facts and to think intelligently.

5. **Put his feelings into words.**
State what his feelings seem to be. When he hears them voiced by you he evaluates and tempers them.

6. **Get agreement.**
Summarize what you have both said — encourage him to suggest the next step or course of action.

 ARMOUR·DIAL,INC

---

### How To Ask Questions

1. **No third degree.**
Use questions to help the other person think — never to degrade or to spy.

2. **Ask "W" questions.**
What, Why, When, Where, Who and How are the key words that will secure facts and information.

3. **Ask questions that make him go deeper.**
Ask for evidence, examples or explanations to discover reasons behind his thinking.

4. **Ask "suppose" questions.**
Introduce a new idea, break a deadlock or bring up an overlooked point with: "Suppose we . . . ?"

5. **Ask him.**
To encourage others to think or to avoid committing yourself, return the question or relay it to another qualified person.

6. **Ask questions that get agreement.**
Offer several solutions in the form of a question.

---

workshop, as Higgins does. The session opens with a discussion of close-mindedness and how to overcome it. Naturally, the listening-questioning tools come into play again as practice continues. Higgins also introduces some new techniques for dealing with such characters as "The Hot Shot," "The Old-Timer," "Mr. Excuses," "Mr. Belligerent," "Mr. Lazy," and "Mr.

Nervous."

Raymond Higgins and Armour-Dial have reported excellent results using this workshop format. You might try it on your next group of supervisory trainees and find that it works as well for you, too. And, remember, as Mr. Higgins cautions us all, "It isn't what you *tell* a man that counts—it's what he *accepts*." **T**

---

# Six tips on how to remember trainee names

**D**oesn't it feel good when someone remembers your name? Dale Carnegie said our names are the sweetest and most important sounds in any language. Most salespeople agree...just notice how many times a car salesperson or other "hard sale" representative calls you by name. Sometimes training is a "hard sell," too, and there's no sense making it harder by pointing to trainees or identifying them as "you with the blue shirt" or "the blond woman in the back row."

George Bell, Westborough, MA, memory expert, offers this advice for remembering names:

1. Pay attention to the name. Hear it the first time, or ask the person to repeat it.

2. Repeat the name yourself. Bell says this will improve recall by 30%.

3. Use the name in conversation. Repetition will engrave the name in your long-term memory.

4. Observe the face. Most of us can remember faces better than names, so really study the face and choose one outstanding detail.

5. Associate the name to the face. Form a mental picture, using an active image. Get the Bell to sway, the Byrd to fly, Waters to gush.

6. Use the name when saying good-bye. This final reinforcer also assures you that you know the name.

Of course, some names are easier to associate than others. Bell suggests symbolic phrases, such as an *ant* on a *honey*comb filled with *pellets* and *grain* for Anthony Pelligrino. And use symbols that immediately call up a name, such as a *walking slingshot* for David Walker.

Trainers have a special problem since they must often absorb 30 or 40 names at once when walking into a training session. Bell advises trainers to arrive early, so you can meet people as they enter by ones or twos. If possible, get a list of names in advance so you can devise replacement symbols more easily. During Bell's own memory classes, he has students fill out information cards. While the students complete a memory test, he picks up the cards at each desk and associates the name with the face.

To train others in how to remember names, Bell offers a three-part plan. First, explain the six points listed earlier. Second, provide worksheets so students can practice converting names to replacement words. Third, show slides of faces and gradually increase the number of faces students are asked to name. **T**

Reprinted from TRAINING, January 1979

Yes, you can help others to develop their brainpower. How? By treating 'thinking' as a teachable subject. Here's a model to help you do just that

# Teaching trainees how to think

by Karl Albrecht

Training trend spotters should note that mental fitness may well be to the '80s what physical fitness was to the '70s. The notion that you can increase your total brain power by comprehensively developing your entire range of practical thinking skills is taking hold. And it's the impetus behind a wave of interest in cognitive processes, thinking games and puzzles, and practical thinking skills and strategies.

For at least two generations, educators and trainers as a group have displayed a singular lack of interest in the skills of applied thinking as primary areas of teachable human capability. The focus has been almost exclusively on teaching *what* to think, rather than *how* to think. Considering what we now know about ways to teach the skills of thinking, and the many concepts, methods and techniques available, the thoughtful trainer might well ask why we have never considered Thinking as a subject in itself— as a legitimate topic of teaching and learning, just like history, English, mathematics, typing, music, carpentry, physical fitness or management.

This question invites some interesting speculations about the way we teach and the way we learn. How many of us have fallen prey to the same subtle messages transmitted to students by the structure of our academic curricula: the notion that each person comes into the world with a certain basic capability for thinking

and learning, and the only thing a teacher or school can do is help that person acquire a storehouse of information? How many of us unconsciously consider thinking ability more or less innately fixed and assume that, except for a bit of fine tuning, we can never significantly increase that ability? Years of preoccupation with IQ testing and other evaluative schemes for identifying "high-potential" people, and for indirectly slotting the rest of us as "low-potential" people, have probably contributed to this semiconscious belief. We have never seriously considered Thinking as a subject, and thus have never seriously approached the wide range of practical thinking skills as teachable and learnable.

## A new trend

Today, we see growing interest in total brainpower in a variety of areas. More and more periodicals are reporting new developments in research on brain functions and cognitive processes, and articles on memory research, attention, cognitive styles, neurolinguistic programming and the like are increasingly popular. Business seminars dealing with problem solving and decision making, creative idea production and innovation are burgeoning. Consider, too, the rapidly increasing sales of electronic thinking and learning games based on the revolutionary microprocessor chip, books of thinking puzzles and various other thinking games for children as well as adults. Finally, there's been a

slow but steady growth in the number of courses in primary and secondary schools and colleges that deal directly with the development of useful thinking skills.

These and other recent happenings suggest a significant increase in the priority given to thinking skills in some educational institutions, as well as in industrial training programs. We already have plenty of resources in this area and a large foundation of concepts and techniques. Now we must put them together into an overall structure of recognized value. In other words, we must make a subject out of Thinking.

### Define Thinking

What does it take for something to qualify as a subject? What common elements do we find among music, computer programming, welding, public administration, sales and physical therapy when we consider them as teachable subjects? From the standpoint of human resources development, we can call something a teachable subject if it meets the following criteria.

**It has a recognized body of knowledge.** In this case, we're dealing with knowledge about knowledge— more specifically, about how the brain takes it in, organizes it, stores it, manipulates it and acts upon it.

**It has a vocabulary.** This helps to describe the body of knowledge.

**It has a conceptual structure.** This enables us to study and apply the elements of knowledge.

**It includes a competence model.** This categorizes those greatest objectively identifiable skills we can learn and teach, and is perhaps of interest to the trainer.

**Training methods exist.** We must have techniques that one person can use to help another person master the elements of knowledge and acquire the basic skills. We already have a variety of these, and we need to organize them and systematically associate them with the various elements of competence.

**Resource materials exist.** The trainer and the learner need support materials they can use in their respective roles. Again, we have some of these, and we need to organize them and develop more of them.

Clearly, we can meet all six of these defining criteria for a subject called Thinking. But of what does Thinking consist? I consider 10 associated concepts fundamental to the subject. Each one serves as a kind of "bucket" in which we can capture some portion of what we know about Thinking. We can analyze each of these concepts,

Reprinted from TRAINING, March 1981

understand it and help others understand it.

**1** **Total brainpower**— the sum of a person's *acquired* thinking skills and so-called innate brain capability. This concept avoids the misplaced emphasis on IQ and focuses attention more appropriately on what a person can do to deploy available cognitive functions effectively.

**2** **Thinking about thinking**— becoming more aware of our thought processes, monitoring our mental procedures as we approach situations, and deliberately using mental strategies or techniques that help us deal with situations more effectively.

**3** **Using a vocabulary of key terms**— accepted terms like mental flexibility, problem solving, logical thinking, making inferences and deciding help to "capture" key concepts for study. Other less-known terms include option thinking, thinking on your feet, suspended judgment and such whimsical creations as decidophobia, opinionitis and mental arthritis. By teaching people to describe thinking processes with these useful terms, we can help them become conscious of those processes as they build specific skills.

**4** **Mental flexibility**—deals with the ability to adapt, suspend judgment, change your mind, tolerate ambiguity, think and speak nondogmatically, and remain open to new and potentially worthwhile experiences. We can contrast mental flexibility with mental rigidity in specific, behavioral terms— what a person says, how he or she uses words, how he or she forms and defends opinions.

**5** **Divergent and convergent thinking**— two highly contrasted and equally important modes of thought. In the divergent mode, one searches, explores, questions, examines multiple factors, identifies additional features and components of a situation, checks various points of view, generates more and more options and generally *expands* his or her field of attention. In the convergent mode, one zeroes in on a narrowly defined item or solution that meets rather specific criteria, casting out options, reducing the range of possibilities, evaluating, eliminating, choosing and generally *narrowing* the field of attention. By learning to recognize both divergent and convergent modes of thought, and to choose one or the other according to the situation, one can deploy stored knowledge effectively and deal with situations in versatile ways.

**6** **Option thinking**— refers to the skill of generating a variety of choices and reviewing them before making a decision. Many people will jump at one familiar or attractive course of action in a situation, or will consider at most only two. An effective option thinker makes a habit of alternatives.

**7** **The role of language in constructing thoughts**—eliminating dogmatic or absolute phraseology, minimizing either/or (black/white) descriptions, and describing concepts in flexible and adaptive terms can increase your mental flexibility. You also can maintain a positive frame of mind by changing negative language habits. For example, you can exclude from your speaking and thinking vocabulary those terms that have negative emotional connotations and use positive or neutral terms instead.

**8** **Brain lateralization**— a complex and subtle aspect of brain function. We can develop fluency in visual and spatial thinking, enhance intuitive processes and increase reliance on holistic pattern processing as adjuncts to our more familiar linear-sequential processes. We'll probably find that the *interplay* between the brain's right and left hemispheres has more influence on total thinking ability than the individual lateralized functions that have been getting an inordinate amount of media attention recently.

**9** **Problem solving and decision making**— by teaching people to pay attention to the *process* of solving a problem, rather than merely wrestling with the *elements* of the problem, trainers especially can help people significantly increase their mental effectiveness. A stepwise problem-solving model can play an important part in developing this "process awareness."

**10** **A new view of creativity**— abolish the word "creativity" as an abstract noun and replace it with an action-oriented description of what a person *does*. Current usage has apparently contributed to a common view of creativity as something you're born with, like your kidneys or your hair color. Psychological testing has, in my opinion, discouraged people from acknowledging and using the skill of idea production which re-sides in every normal human brain.

A competence model for Thinking lends structure to the subject and establishes some relatively objective target skills we can learn and teach. This aspect of the subject has lagged further behind than any other. Psychologists have given names to many micro-skills that play a part in a person's thinking processes but, to the best of my knowledge, no one has developed a categorical framework— a "Christmas tree" on which to hang the various mental functions and skills in relation to one another.

We can develop such a framework by classifying some fairly basic brain functions into larger-scale thinking skills. Out of the many overlapping terminological categories of brain functions that psychologists recognize, we can synthesize a useful working list of 10: concentration, observation, memory, logical reasoning, forming hypotheses, generating options, forming associations, recognizing patterns, making inferences and spatial/kinesthetic perceptions. These 10 categories can then be matched against six general areas of mental competence, or functional thinking skills, that amount to the effective deployment of basic brain processes.

While psychologists might prefer a more dignified and academic-sounding nomenclature, I've chosen some rather unorthodox vernacular names for the six categories I've identified. In designing your own training program in Thinking, I think you'll find these terms useful.

**Fact finding** includes all those thinking skills required to get useful information into your brain. It manifests the investigative attitude, a habit of perceiving and thinking that values evidence, new information, possibilities, relationships and points of view. Your skill at fact finding determines your basic storehouse of knowledge, which plays a fundamental part in the rest of your practical thinking capability. The more you know, generally speaking, the more effectively you can think.

**Crap detecting**, a charmingly blunt term attributed to Ernest Hemingway, refers to what psychologists euphemistically call "critical rationality." It means the skill of examining the structure and context of the message, as well as its content, and identifying ulterior messages, motives and logical fallacies. It involves an attitude of noncynical but nongullible examination. It also extends to the skills of questioning the status quo and constructively challenging basic beliefs and practices. A thinker who has his or her crap detector turned on and tuned in becomes very difficult to manipulate.

**Thinking on your feet** means effective adaptation in challenging situations. It involves psychological preparedness, having some useful "standard tactics," scanning the situation, identifying key factors, keeping your eye on the ball (that is, your real objective in the situation), communicating assertively, reviewing the options of a situation and avoiding getting drawn into unproductive digressions from your objective.

**Idea production** describes what you have left when you strip away the psychological mumbo-jumbo from what behavioral scientists vaguely label "creative thinking" (or the now-forbidden term creativity). Producing ideas simply means consciously combining two or more existing ideas to make a new and novel one. If the new idea turns out to be useful, so much the better. The skill of idea production rests on the attitude that *all* ideas may have potential value and the belief in idea-making as a far more valuable process than idea-killing.

**Problem solving and decision making** is a comprehensive skill which integrates many cognitive processes into an important personal capability. By developing a consciousness of the *process* of thinking through one's problems, one can anticipate problems, attack them more thoroughly and systematically, make more reliable decisions, and follow them through to results. In this way one becomes a more effective and productive problem solver, both in personal life and in business.

**Happying**, a term that admittedly involves a bit of grammatical license, means the active process of coping with your world in ways that enable you to maintain a highly positive frame of mind and to achieve those outcomes you value. Happying differs from "being happy" in that the former focuses attention on what one does. We can consider feeling happy a by-product of effective living and, therefore, a barometer of effective thinking, including the emotional dimension of our functioning. In this respect, happying means *doing* what-

# Try these tips and tricks for increasing classroom brainpower

Once we have a grip on Thinking as a potentially well-structured subject, many techniques for the trainer and the learner suggest themselves. Over several years of conducting seminars on various aspects of brainpower, I've collected and developed a variety of such techniques. If you review some of your own training resources with the subject of Thinking in mind, you'll probably find that many of them fill the bill quite well.

In working with groups, especially in management team building, I've had a great deal of success in using a structured problem-solving model. Getting everyone in a task group to adopt a common "process" model, to post it on the wall in the form of a large diagram, and to refer to it whenever they run into difficulties enables them to proceed more rapidly and achieve more effective decisions. It also eliminates the well-known "group-think" phenomenon, in which a few participants with strong personalities run away with the process, and uncommitted members get dragged into premature closure by a false impression of consensus.

Visual aids that demonstrate perceptual processes can help people understand how they take in information and organize their thoughts. The Uncritical Inference Test (published by the International Society for General Semantics in San Francisco), is a very useful little story-listening exercise that helps people identify their tendencies to jump to conclusions from insufficient evidence. You can also find plenty of thinking puzzles and games that challenge and develop various cognitive skills, such as sequential thought, logical inference-making, information organization, hypothesizing and idea production.

I frequently use a thinking challenge as a warm-up or ice-breaker. Once the participants have had a chance to solve it (I usually pick one most people can handle with a little effort), we review it together and become more aware of the kinds of thinking processes we employed to work it out. By collecting and analyzing these thinking games, you can identify the kinds of mental skills they challenge and develop, and catalog one or two for each of the kinds of skills you want to teach.

I've even used magic tricks to demonstrate thinking principles, such as the ways the brain forms and uses mental sets. The surprise effect of a magic trick comes from the sudden demolition of the mental set— an assumption the magician invited you to adopt, and which organizes your expectations and perceptions thereafter. The concept of a mental set plays an important part in understanding mental flexibility, and a few startling demonstrations make people aware of this normal feature of the brain.

In addition to problem-solving models, thinking games, magic tricks and practical illustrations, the trainer can also employ group discussion of specific thinking strategies and, of course, a certain amount of well-organized lecture. You can also use idea-production groups to give people experience with free-wheeling divergent thought. In this technique, participants in teams of four or five work against perhaps a five-minute deadline to produce the largest possible numbers of ideas that deal with some selected topic (for example, ways to improve the design of an ordinary piece of furniture). Following the skill-building experience, they can apply the idea-production technique to specific, practical problems of their choosing. The time limit, the element of competition and the emphasis on getting large numbers of options combine to get people out of their habitual convergent modes of thought and into productive divergent modes.

From the standpoint of specific resources designed for the learner, we can use games such as Master Mind, a two-person logical thinking challenge that makes skill-building enjoyable. The Creative Education Foundation, Buffalo, NY, offers a number of publications, and more and more consulting firms are producing training materials in this area. We also have a smattering of books on the subject, mostly on selected subtopics like logic, idea production and decision making. To the best of my knowledge, my recent book, *Brain Power*, is the first to attempt a comprehensive treatment of Thinking.—K.A. **T**

ever it takes to make you happy.

To extend this competence model, inventory the various micro-skills, such as sequential thinking, recognizing logical fallacies, asking divergent questions, identifying blocking assumptions, brainstorming, analyzing options and random association of ideas, and catalog them under their respective competence categories.

## Thinking in training

To design an effective training program on Thinking or to use a cognitive module as a part of some larger program aimed at an objective (such as positive customer contact), we first must explore the learning need. Suppose we find, for example, that our managers want to foster innovation among their employees but don't seem to know quite how to go about it. We might introduce them to the competence category of idea production and teach them skills under this category which they could then teach to their employees. We might focus especially on teaching the managers to use the cognitive skills of suspended judgment and divergent thinking as they listen to suggestions, concerns and new ideas from their employees. This will probably improve the communication process and encourage staff members to generate more new ideas as they see their efforts affirmed and rewarded.

Or suppose you've been asked to train a staff of counselors in the use of logical reasoning techniques that might help their clients deal with problems more effectively. In this case, you might focus on the area of problem solving and decision making, and teach them the skills of using a stepwise model as a communication aid in discussions with their clients. You could show them how to trace the process of personal problem solving— the basic dynamic of counseling— through the sequence of steps of a structured problem-solving model and help them develop thinking diagrams and other techniques for sharing the model with their clients.

These examples show that an overall competence model for Thinking, while not perfect or even all-inclusive, can provide us with a means for organizing our approaches and focusing our resources for learning and teaching. Many situations will call for multiple skills. In some cases, we'll need all six of the macro-skill categories. In others, we will need to combine thinking skills with skills from other subjects. The competence model will serve its purposes well if it enables us to isolate a useful skill and train others to acquire it.

## Learn what you teach

It's intriguing to speculate on the possibilities for approaching mental fitness just as explicitly as we approach physical fitness. Can you visualize, for example, a facility equipped as a mental gymnasium? How would you design one? What would it include? What can we do with the microprocessor? Will it finally make the long-awaited teaching machine a reality? Can it develop basic cognitive skills such as memory, concentration and logical reasoning?

As facilitators of learning, trainers generally can teach best what they have learned well themselves. To the extent that you have developed a high level of personal competence in Thinking, you can design effective training experiences for others. However, with an open-ended subject like Thinking, in which we find such a diversity of skills, learning never ends. You need not wait for some far-off day when you can confidently claim the status of "thinking expert" in order to begin to help others learn these important skills. Equipped with a workable competence model, a collection of training methods and resources, and an open-minded attitude that enables you to acknowledge which of your own skills you need to develop further, you can start now to train yourself and others to increase total brainpower. **T**

---

## FOR MORE INFO
Interested in more brain training theory and practice? You might find one or more of these texts a good guide.

**Books of brain stretching exercises**
Albrecht, Karl, *Brain Power;* 1980, Prentice Hall, $6.95.
Bry, Adelaide, *Directing the Movies of Your Mind;* 1978, Harper & Row, $18.95.
Buzan, Tony, *Using Both Sides of Your Brain;* 1976, E.P. Dutton, $5.95.
Edwards, Betty, *Drawing on the Right Side of the Brain;* 1979, J.P. Tarcher, $8.95.
McCarthy, Bernice, *The 4 Mat System: Teaching to Four Learning Styles Using Right and Left Mode Techniques;* 1981, EXCEL Publishing, $15.95.

**Books on brain theory**
Naranjo, Claudio, and Ornstein, Robert E., *On the Psychology of Meditation;* 1977, Viking Press, $2.50.
Restak, M.D., *The Brain: The Last Frontier;* 1979, Doubleday, $12.
Sagan, Carl, *The Dragons of Eden;* 1977, Random House, $8.95.
Smith, Adam, *Powers of Mind;* 1975, Random House, $10.

How the science of learning
affects the art of training

# Split-brain psychology

The idea that there are personal differences in the way individuals process information in the course of learning new concepts and principles is decidedly old hat. What is "new hat" is a relatively recent set of findings that locates these functional differences in the physical brain.

In the early '50s, neurosurgeon Wilder Penfield found that electrical stimulation of the physical brain caused old images, tastes, smells and thoughts to surface in the consciousness of the brains' owners. In the 1960s, another neurosurgeon, Joseph Bogen, was looking for ways to relieve severe epileptics of their seizures. Then-current brain function theories led him to experimentation with the surgical severing of the corpus callosum— the bundle of nerves which joins the two hemispheres, or right and left sides, of the brain— in some of his patients. Researchers subsequently found some interesting things about the functioning of these "split-brain" patients. While blindfolded, they could answer questions about objects held in their right hands but not in their left hands. Patients reported that they "knew" what the answers were but couldn't verbalize them. This jibed with the physiological theory that the neural pathways from each side of the body cross over and connect with the opposite side of the brain—information from a person's right hand is relayed to the language center in the left hemisphere of the brain and vice versa.

These experiments and a few more became the basis for claiming that the two halves or hemispheres of the brain, right and left, have distinct and separate functions. The ensuing hoopla was something to behold. In the popular press, the right hemisphere of the cerebral cortex became known as the "right brain" and was said to be the seat of everything artistic, emotional, aesthetic and, eventually, Eastern and "good." The poor old left hemi became the "left brain" and was tagged as logical, linear, controlled, analytical, ordered and, of course, Western and "bad." The true believers encouraged us to throw off our left brain thinking and being and ways of training and put the old right

brain in charge. Sprinting quite a bit in front of the actual research, these zealots claimed that split-brain psychology could explain virtually every heretofore unexplained sweet mystery of life. Among the notable quotes and claims:

- Marshall McLuhan proclaimed "bureaucracy is left hemisphere and the generation gap of the 1960s a conflict between right-brain kids and left-brain parents."
- Because so many artists are left-handed— right-brain dominant— many held that truth, beauty, justice and love must have their origins in the right brain.
- A prominent media research psychologist claimed that newspapers and magazines are left-brain media while television is a right-brain medium.
- The right brain was claimed to synthesize patterns from diverse-looking data, the left brain given the job of analyzing the nature and lawfulness of such patterns.
- Invention was said to be a right-brain act, while production was relegated to a simple, left-brain function.
- Managing was claimed as a right-brain dominated process, while planning was relegated to the left.

Balance came back into the picture when the researchers cleared their throats and asserted that the concept of hemispheric specialization wasn't intended as a social statement and that balance is a much more important concept. Among the modifying facts ignored by the faddists were these:

- Most of the early research on brain hemisphere specialization was purposely conducted on a unique group: right-handed males, right-eye dominant, with no left-handed relatives.
- The right side of the brain is *not* idle or out of gear when you're writing a letter or doing something linear. It simply is *less* active than the left side of the brain. Every mental operation requires many parts of the brain to be active.
- Japanese researchers found that patterns of hemispheric functional specialization in Japanese brains are quite different from those of

Western brains. This East/West difference holds for Japanese raised in the West and Westerners raised in Japan. These researchers are evolving a theory that suggests *language and culture* may play a role in assigning functions to specific brain locations.

- The brain has more than a right side and a left side. Because of its multitude of lobes and bundles and special function areas, the brain can just as easily be "split" from front to back or top to bottom.

Now that the zealots have moved on, those trainers and researchers who busied themselves panning for significance in the continuing stream of serious brain research are beginning to pluck up some useful nuggets. One of these hardtack hardies is Judith Springer, president of Bethesda, MD-based Athena Corporation. According to Springer, the study of the brain is just beginning to have learning and training payoffs.

Part of that payoff comes from the shedding of misconceptions. Take the great right brain/left brain dichotomy. According to Springer, "Physiologists have said all along that we in essence have *three* brains: the Reticular Activating System, sometimes referred to as the Dinosaur Brain; the Limbic Cortex, or Old Mammal Brain; and the Cerebral Cortex, or New Mammal Brain. It takes all three of these physical structures for us to be who we are, *not* just the cerebral cortex as some would have you believe."

The first system is the attention mechanism. When we focus on something in the environment, when we are simply conscious, we owe our thanks to the Reticular Activating System. We are part of that broad group of attentive organisms and not trees or shrubs because of it. The Limbic Cortex is the reason people and dogs and cats have emotions and aren't simply funny looking fish or paramecia. It is the home of the values that go with the facts and concepts we know. It may even be the seat of our feelings of internal and external locus of control. It's really an uncharted area that is just being learned about. And the Cerebral Cortex is where all the language and logic and associated "intelligence" functions seem to be.

Just knowing this set of facts, says Springer, gives us new insight into a couple of common training problems: "One of the things we've told each other, and researched a great deal, is this matter of a proper learning atmosphere. We've proven we need it, but the reasons have been nebulous. When the limbic system is aroused, when some other matter is affecting it, or when the learning environment is perceived as unsafe or the values implied in the training are counter to the values of similar material the person has learned, then forget it— no new learning will take place. We've all had our kids say, 'I don't like Mrs. Smith and I can't learn geography from her,' and understood it intuitively. Now there seems to be a reasonable, understandable basis for it. It's in the brain."

The new brain learnings explain why the darndest things can be so controversial. "Nothing we learn is free of values," says Springer. "All of the brain has to be functioning for an idea, fact or experience to sink in, and that means awake, attending, judging, and processing. Every fact, every thing in memory has to have some feel, some emotional loading, just to

be there. Remember the electrical stimulation experiments? Those patients remembered with their whole brain— sounds, colors, feelings, shapes, people, words, thoughts— all came rushing back as a set when the electrodes were activated." Small wonder some trainees are terrified by new learning experiences.

Springer sees the most immediate applicability of the developing new brain knowledge on the personal level. "Bernice McCarthy of EXCEL and Ned Herrmann of GE are both working on brain psychology-based style assessment instruments that can be used to help students on a one-to-one basis. But that is only helpful in a general way when you're working a classroom. It says for sure that during a speech you have to have attention-getting and keeping devices, and you have to present material in both linear-logical and pictorial ways. All those things about pacing and leading an audience make sense when you realize you are working with an organism that paces and tracks stimuli all the time."

Springer also has some tips for the management of one's own working/processing modes. Feeling melancholy or blue? "When people are sad, upset, unhappy, they slouch and look

down to the right," she says. To get them— or yourself— up, do what happy and excited people do: "Sit up straight or, better yet, stand up and look up, not down."

Need to be analytical and linear when you are really feeling creative and holistic? Have to stop dreaming and start writing? "If you are both in an emotional place and being very right-brain, try using some art to pull out and get linear. When you're feeling emotion, you have to go from limbic to right hemisphere and then across, so to speak. The connections between the limbic system and the right cerebral cortex are stronger, so it's hard to go directly to a left-cortex dominant activity from the limbic. Start with art. Look at some colorful abstract pieces; study them. Move on to more and more geometric sorts of shapes, paintings with less and less color and more regularity. Work your way toward an Escher painting. See if you can't figure out how he tricks your eyes with those impossible staircases or waterfalls or fish turning into geese. If you're really having trouble getting into a concept, try to flowchart it or diagram it visually. In just a matter of minutes you'll be perking along in a nice analytic, linear mode. Try it, you'll see."—R.Z.　**T**

Patterns of moving,
speaking and behavior are
indicators of wellness—all
of which can affect learning

# How to recognize and work with wellness—or lack of it

by Joanne Moses

As the "Wellness Movement" gains momentum in industry, trainers can take advantage of this interest in well-being to promote wellness within their organizations. At the moment, wellness advocates are emphasizing good nutrition, exercise and stress control. Each of these factors is important, and all of them are facets of a broader pattern of living that comprises wellness.

Wellness is a way of thinking, a way of eating, a way of exercising, a way of living. To change eating habits or exercise routines can be difficult if other aspects of life—social activities, for instance, beliefs, attitudes, even feelings about oneself— do not also change. Wellness isn't something you *do* for 15 minutes a day. It's something you *become*—a harmonious, integrated, "whole" person.

Here's where trainers can enter the picture. Our own professional background sensitizes us to interacting systems and how they affect individuals. The dictionary defines a "pattern" as a "complex of integrated parts functioning to make a whole." In this context, the "whole" is the person. All of an individual's patterns reflect the logic, the inner consistency, of who that person is. If the person is healthy, effective and spontaneous, then patterns of moving, speaking and dealing with people will reflect that vitality. If, on the other hand, the person has poor health or poor self-esteem, behavior patterns

will convey that message also.

Think for a moment of the times when you feel strong and sure of yourself. How do you stand, walk, talk, think? Recall, too, a time when you were physically or mentally not on top of things. What were your posture and speech like then?

Although patterns relating to wellness cover a range of factors those discussed here are most useful in a training situation. Breathing, posture, speaking, relationships and employment patterns can be easily observed. Thinking patterns can also emerge if the trainers have time to do some tracking with each participant. Underlying all these patterns is the basic one—self-concept.

## Recognizing patterns

Trainers can discover these patterns in participants as they go about their regular training activities. Looking at the person's behavior, observing how others in the group are responding to that individual, checking with the person on what is going on inside and getting the person's history of employment both in and out of the company will reveal consistent themes from four different vantage points.

To observe breathing patterns, watch the chest and diaphragm. A person who breathes fully expands his or her abdomen, rib cage and chest while inhaling; the chest falls and the abdomen contracts while exhaling. Few Westerners breathe that way,

though we ought to in order to enjoy full vitality. Full breathing carries a generous supply of oxygen throughout the body and invigorates all the cells. Many people are chest breathers only. They fill only a fraction of their lung capacity, so they have low energy levels. Others keep their chests locked to hold fear and other negative feelings in check. Still others fill their chests well, but don't allow breath into the diaphragm area. That way they maintain a sense of power without being vulnerable to feeling.

Posture patterns follow breathing closely. The shallow breathers will often be slightly round-shouldered. People who lock their chests may be erect but somewhat rigid. Heavy chest breathers throw out their chests and face the onslaughts of the world squarely.

Speech patterns will be consistent with breathing and posture. Shallow breathers are likely to seek approval and be apologetic in speaking; their sentences often end with "You know?" On the other hand, those with locked chests and stiff posture are likely to separate themselves from their feelings when they speak. They will take neither credit nor responsibility, and their speech reflects this equivocation: "Things are going very well" or "There were too many things to consider." Words like "it," "there" and "things" replace "I"; instead of saying "I'm disappointed" or "I'm excited," this person is more likely to say, "It's disappointing" or "That's exciting." The full-chest breathers will blame others instead of themselves: "You make me mad."

Relationships in the work setting will be consistent with body and speech patterns. The shallow breather is likely to be unassertive and dependent on others. The person with the stiff chest may need to be more assertive and less fearful. The full-chested breather may be aggressive and/or invite others to be dependent. These relationships can easily be observed in a training session.

Obviously, this discussion is highly oversimplified: people don't fit into such narrow categories. The intent, however, is to help trainers think in terms of patterns, both their uniqueness and their consistency. By so doing, they can help their clients integrate what they are learning into the broader fabric of their life pattern.

## Working with patterns in training seminars

1. First of all, know your own patterns and work toward modeling wellness yourself. Visualize your

Reprinted from TRAINING, November 1979

participants as healthy, effective people.

2. Help people recognize their own patterns. Videotape can be an excellent tool. If video equipment is not available, a tape recorder is good for speech patterns. People recognize habitual behaviors more quickly when they can see and hear themselves.

3. Help people evaluate their patterns. Do they work? Do you want them to be different? If so, in what way?

4. Help people realize the impact of changes they decide to make. If they change one thing, how will it affect the other patterns of their lives? For instance, if I become more assertive on the job, what will happen to my marriage when I take that behavior home?

5. Explore options. There aren't any rights and wrongs other than the person's satisfaction with life. If a person lives a limited, constrictive life but likes it, that's a matter of personal choice. However, a trainer can motivate people and help them find a wider range in their potential.

In brief, working as a change agent involves more than teaching people a system or technique. It means keeping in mind the life context and broader implications of new behavior. Helping people acquire skills from that perspective is likely to have a more lasting impact on participants than is stressing only one element, like diet or exercise. Wellness means "wholeness," from the inside out. **T**

---

# What's *your* facilitator style?

**C**onventional wisdom among T-group facilitators has it that the facilitator's job is to *build a culture or climate* for learning; establish mutual *trust*; *confront* inaction, disruptive norms and so on; and *influence* and *support* learning and change. Research has tended to support the conventional wisdom.

But an English researcher, Peter B. Smith, lecturer in social psychology, University of Sussex, Sussex, England, is challenging both conventional wisdom and the research supporting it. According to Smith, the facilitator's job is not nearly so simple and clear. In a major statistical study of 31 English T-groups, Smith found evidence that the most successful groups— those the groups' participants rated as "beneficial" to them and leading to "change for the better" five months after the training— were facilitated in a much more relativistic fashion.

Though agreeing that establishing trust and exerting influence appear to be necessary to effect a change and promote learning in a group, Smith cautions that, according to his data, building trust and influence is not sufficient to ensure effectiveness. Part of the alternative Smith suggests is that trainers need to behave in different ways with different types of groups to bring about a condition of effective functioning. This suggests that it is important for the trainer to analyze and understand the existing culture of the group before starting to intervene with its members.

Smith reports that, according to his data, there appear to be four group cultures, each differentiated by participant's ratings of one another on two scales— interpersonal trust and interpersonal tension. Each of the four cultures created by the 2 by 2 grid of these scores requires a different trainer intervention style.

**Type 1 Culture: High interpersonal trust/high interpersonal tension.** In the type-1 group or culture, the effective trainer is rated high on influence by the group. The pattern of Smith's correlations suggest that the effective trainer for type-1 groups is active in structuring events but not strongly involved with the group in a personal way.

**Type 2: High-trust/low-tension group.** In type-2 groups, the effective trainer is rated high on influence, trust and tension. Smith's data further suggest that effective trainers for type-2 groups are active and both confronting and supportive.

**Type 3: Low-trust/high-tension group.** In this group, the effective trainer is rated high on trust. The pattern here suggests a primary supportive style is critical.

**Type 4: Low-trust/low-tension group.** The effective trainer for type 4 appears to be confronting in style. Raising tension seems to be an important goal if this group type is to function effectively.

It appears that while all groups may require, or are at least not impeded by, high-influence, high-trust trainers, the degree to which the trainer generates tension is crucial. In high-tension groups (types 1 and 3), a high-tension-generating trainer is not required, while low-tension groups require such a trainer. In a sense, the required trainer role is reciprocal to the group culture.

Smith concludes his report this way: "Effective trainer behavior is seen as a pattern of responses to a group culture which trainers themselves cannot unilaterally create. The trainer's skill thus lies not in the fixed application of an 'effective' formula, but in diagnosis, in flexibility of intervention skill, and in timing....These findings strongly imply that the trainer is to be conceptualized not as a creator of group climate, but as someone whose interventions must be reactive to that climate. In this sense the trainer is more a prisoner of circumstance rather than an unfettered group facilitator."—R.Z. **T**

(Smith's research was reported in *The Journal of Applied Behavioral Science*, Vol. 16, No. 1, 1980, as "The T-Group Trainer: Group Facilitator or Prisoner of Circumstance?")

Reprinted from TRAINING, August 1980

# Classroom tips

by Marilyn Leak

## Don't flip your flip chart

The so-called Rip-Off—Stick Up method was brought to our attention recently by Milt Badt, a senior engineer with Western Electric Co., who has worked as an instructor and a trainer for several years while assigned to the Bell Telephone Laboratories and Western Electric field locations. Badt learned it from Mr. Alec Mackenzie, author of *The Time Trap*, and well-known lecturer on time management. Says Badt: "It's simple. Sketch or write as usual, using a felt-tipped marker, crayon, or other stylus. Speak clearly, stand back, use a pointer for emphasis, let the message sink in for a moment, look at your audience, and answer any questions. But then, before you proceed, pick up a strategically placed roll of masking tape, tear off two small strips of it, return to the flip chart, and *rip it off*.

"Then, instead of having folded the chart over the back of the easel, take the chart you've just ripped off, and with the two small pieces of masking tape *stick it* to a convenient surface where the audience can look at it if they want to.

"Think about it. 'Hiding it from view' is *exactly* what we do when we flip a chart over the back of the easel. And how frustrating it can be for the trainees who didn't quite get those extra 10 seconds to let it sink in, or to make notes, or who wish they could remember some detail from a previously flipped chart. **T**

Reprinted from TRAINING, May 1977

## Graffiti provides useful feedback

Emily Hitchens first observed the use of graffiti as an evaluation tool while working as a psychiatric nurse. The technique allows patients to ventilate their feelings and opinions in a public, yet anonymous, way. Hitchens adapted the use of graffiti to help her deal with a difficult group of students.

"One of my lecture classes was notoriously angry and difficult," she reports. "They'd been together through three years of college and were now second-quarter seniors in psychiatric nursing with a long history of lateness, talking in class and giggling during lectures." Hitchens tried most traditional methods of extinguishing this behavior, but found that none helped. "The class seemed to be at odds with itself," she explains, "and it seemed to me that they needed more than just a traditional course evaluation form by the end of the term."

During the last class period, Hitchens told the students that she would leave the room for ten minutes while they filled three large blackboard panels in graffiti style, under the headings of "course content," "methods of presentation" and "class participation." After discussion, all the panels would be erased.

The first two panels, she states, contained traditional comments expected in any course evaluation. But the third, "class participation," was entirely negative, peppered with words such as "rude," "inconsiderate," and other bad assessments of class morale and conduct.

This last panel provoked a long and revealing discussion among class members. Hitchens facilitated the conversation with questions such as "What can you do about this in the future, for next term?" "Though the discussion was brief," she concludes, "I believe it was a catalytic one. Afterwards, they all clapped and rushed up to erase the board. In the future, I will use the technique of graffiti evaluation even earlier in the term so the participants have more time to learn new behaviors."—J.S. **T**

Reprinted from TRAINING, August 1979

## Memory tips you can't forget

Most of us agree with the youngster who said, "Memory is what I forget with." We also know memory is particularly important in training. As the old hand told the new trainer who had just finished reading a presentation, "How do you expect us to remember your talk if you don't?" Yet no matter how poor we say our memory is, we have an inexplicable ability to remember certain items. For example, the executive who can't remember an appointment for the next day can recall the scoring inning by inning at last week's ball game.

# Chart productivity before class starts

Everyone has ebbs and flows in his or her daily productivity and alertness cycle which drastically affect performance. There are "day people," who love to tackle the tough jobs in the morning. And there are "night people," who are dynamos after dark but who have a hard time perking before noon.

You can schedule a lesson plan to best fit the alertness and productivity cycle of your class by using the following simple exercise developed by Kenneth Cooper of KCA Associates, St. Louis, MO.

Have each student divide a piece of paper into one-hour increments, from 7:00 AM to 5:00 PM. Instruct the students to rate their productivity and alertness for each hour of the day, using a scale of "10" for most, and "1" for least. Tell them at least one "1" and one "10" must appear on their rating. Next, divide the hourly totals by the number of students in the class. This gives a composite class productivity and alertness rating. It also shows how much less effective students feel they are in early and late overtime sessions.

This class in the example has a majority of "day people," whose best hours are from 9:00 to 11:00 AM. Before lunch, there is a drastic drop in performance which is never quite recovered. The rating picks up slightly after lunch, and then drops off sharply as fatigue sets in.

The trainer now has a clear picture of how best to schedule the day. Detailed lecture or lengthy material should be scheduled in the morning. As lunch nears, it would be advisable to allow for short breaks every 40 minutes or so, instead of longer ones every hour. If there is a large amount of workshop or interactive time in the course, it might be beneficial to break early for lunch and minimize the hunger plummet in class effectiveness.

After lunch, the trainer has approximately one hour of suitable lecture time available. Breaks should be more frequent as the afternoon wears on, and classroom activities should allow the students chances for increased participation and physical movement to help overcome fatigue. **T**

Reprinted from TRAINING, December 1977

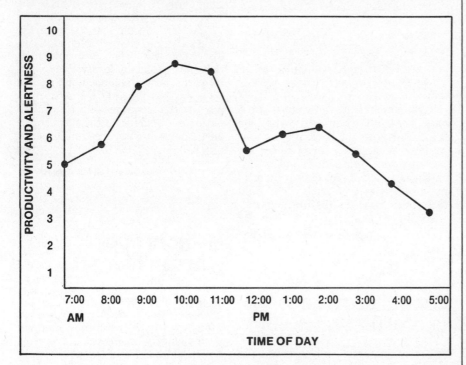

What information IS memorable? We most *remember* pleasant experiences, motor skills, and material that is worth remembering, talked about often, used frequently, given time to sink in, and stretched our learning capacities. We most *forget* names, dates, numbers, facts we don't believe, material not understood, "crammed" information, unpleasant experiences, our failures, times when we are sick, and times when we are mad.

We can turn those *most forgotten* items into *most remembered* items by using three simple procedures taught by Ken Cooper, a training consultant who teaches listening and memory techniques at the Civil Service Commission's regional training center in St. Louis.

**Pay attention to what is important.** We can't recall something never noticed in the first place. When meeting someone, we usually forget the most important thing—the person's name. While our body is shaking hands, our mind is elsewhere. The successful executive has learned what is important in his or her job. To find out what you are missing, carry a small notebook around for several weeks.

**Concentrate on the important facets of your job.** Most people talk about one-fifth as fast as you can think. This means that about 80 percent of the time they're talking your mind can be distracted by literally millions of bits of information presented to your brain every second. If you use your mental "idle time" to listen and observe reactively, you will think about what you are hearing and seeing. Evaluate it, analyze it, turn it over in your mind. Look for flaws, truths, similarities, or usefulness. Make certain you shift your attention and concentration to another subject only because you have exhausted the current one's value, and not because you have been lured away through distraction.

**Organize what is important.** A minister was shocked when a member of his congregation told him after a shortened sermon, "Where was your last point? You promised us four at the start of your sermon and I only counted three!" The member was trying to organize the sermon while listening. While most people believe that memory gets worse with age, memorization actually becomes easier the longer we've lived. The more we have experienced and learned, the more easily new information can be organized with respect to something we already know, or some similar fact or event. **T**

Reprinted from TRAINING, November 1977

## Better learning through laughter

Stories in the form of case studies, first person and apocryphal examples, and what-if illustrations are widely used in training and education. There has even been research done on the pedagogic power of children's stories from "Hansel and Gretel" through "Cat in the Hat." Child psychiatrist Bruno Bettelheim's book, "The Uses of Enchantment," is the touchstone for understanding the meaning and importance of fairy tales and myths in the educational process. While teachers may hotly debate the implications of teaching reading to rural and suburban school children using textbooks featuring tales of growing up in the big city, the use of the story per se goes unchallenged.

But another form of storytelling, the use of jokes, funny stuff and humorous tall tales, is far from accepted among trainers and adult educators. Just as PBS Sesame Street has been attacked as too much fun to be of educative value for children, the trainer who sounds too much like a Tonight Show guest host aspirant is often condemned as instructionally irrelevant.

Dr. Herb True, a psychologist turned "edutainer," believes humor is vital to a successful adult learning experience. True believes humor releases the tensions in a group and helps defuse any ill will trainees may have about their attendance in the program. "But," writes True in his book *Humor Power,* "applied as a communications system, humor does more than release tensions and evaporate hostility. It opens up channels to others, shows us how to communicate clearly, and reminds us when we aren't communicating."

Without evidence, the question of how humor affects learning is essentially a defensive debate between those who tell stories and those who don't. Fortunately, the controversy over Sesame Street has begun to stimulate research into the effects of humor on the learning of children and adults. Though many issues are unresolved, preliminary findings are interesting and instructive. Five examples:

1. Researchers at Tel Aviv University have demonstrated that students retain more information from lectures that have interspersed "humor breaks." Specifically, the researchers played routines from a recorded comedy album between segments of a lecture and found that these humor breaks somehow facilitated learning of the material in the lecture segments.

2. Researchers at a major U.S. university found that key learning points followed by a humorous story were better remembered than key learning points not followed by a humorous story. In addition, when the joke or humorous anecdote was in some way relevant to the key learning point, the greatest degree of retention was registered.

3. Media researchers at Indiana University have found that children learn and retain videotaped information when humorous, "entertaining" material is interspersed between "serious" content segments. In fact, when multiple segments of serious and humorous material are used in a long video sequence, learning of the serious content becomes progressively better. That is, the content of serious segment 2 is better learned than the content of serious segment 1, segment 3 better learned than segment 2 and so on, suggesting that the humorous segments have a cumulative effect on learning.

4. Brain researchers have found that humor creates remarkably intense attentional reactions. One researcher, Dalf Zillman of Indiana University, believes humor somehow stimulates the reticular formations in the brain, and that related diffuse projections to the cortex of the brain bring about a kind of vigilant behavior in the learner. The attention and vigilance stimulation seems to make the learner more receptive to information storage.

5. Humor has a positive effect on instructor as well as instructee. Trainers who regularly use humor in their training report they do so to help build rapport with trainees, to underline key learning points, and to relieve test anxiety among students. But these reasons may be secondary, since these same instructors report that the laughter of students decreases *trainer* stress and anxiety and gives feedback of student attention.

The research has yet to suggest the effects of telling one too many shaggy dog stories to a room full of highly motivated learners, ready for and *expecting* a straight, facts-only presentation. And until this and similar questions of parameter are resolved, we need to proceed carefully in the serious matter of making learning better through laughter.—R.Z.

Reprinted from TRAINING, May 1981

## Stand up, speak out, and look 'em in the eye

Speech teachers since the time of Aristotle, Cicero and Quintilian have been telling us that it's not so much what you say but how you say it that drives the message home. And according to Dr. Steven A. Beebe, University of Miami, numerous studies do indeed support the contention that certain speech-delivery techniques can both increase speaker credibility and enhance listener learning.

For some time, speech textbook authors, relying upon both research and personal experience, have instructed that *eye contact, varied vocal inflection* and *appropriate posture* are key to speech effectiveness. Likewise, audiences, when surveyed, almost always identify a *monotonous voice, stiff posture* and *lack of eye contact* as the three most distracting behaviors of public speakers. While each of these variables has been tested separately by speech and communication researchers, little is known about how they combine to affect an audience during the same presentation.

Dr. Beebe combined and manipulated these three influencers in the same speech and tested both the credibility they lent to or detracted from the speaker and the effect they had on speech content comprehension. Specifically, Beebe had a student give the same seven-minute speech—a talk about computer-generated music—to eight different groups of 16 students. Each time the speech was delivered, the speaker used a different combination of two *vocal inflections,* either varied or limited; two *body postures*—formal (upright body, face forward, feet together) or casual (body leaning, stance open); and two levels of *eye contact*—constant or none at all. Beebe tested this mix and match of effectiveness influencers on audience comprehension and speaker credibility.

Comprehension, or learning, was tested using a 20-item, multiple-guess test. *Speaker,* or *source,* credibility was measured using a set of nine, seven-point Semantic Differential scales that previously had reliably measured and defined source credibility as a combination of speaker *dynamism, believability* and *likability.*

Though somewhat complex and open to more than one interpretation, the results of Beebe's study were decidedly interesting and instructive to those of us who make a living "holding forth" to others. For starters, Beebe found that *eye contact* definitely is the most powerful influencer of both comprehension and credibility. Constant eye contact promoted significantly more learning among listeners than no eye contact, regardless of the other variables it was combined with. Beebe speculates that strong speaker eye contact helps focus the audience's attention on the speaker and signals message importance. Constant eye contact also seems to enhance the dynamism and believability factors of credibility scale.

Apparently, body posture has little influencing power compared with eye contact and vocal inflection. But a combination of constant eye contact, varied vocal inflection and casual body posture work together to decrease speaker believability slightly but simultaneously increase speaker likability.

Perhaps the most interesting result is the effect of contradictory delivery cues upon speaker credibility. For example, when the speaker combined constant eye contact with limited vocal inflection, she was perceived as incredulous; Beebe suggests this may have been because of an inconsistency between the verbal and nonverbal cues being sent. In short, whenever the speaker employed contradictory delivery cues, regardless of which cues they were, her believability was lower than when the cues were consistent.

A few years ago, maverick Canadian communication researcher Marshall McCluhan flatly proclaimed that the media *is* the message. Though he was referring primarily to television, his concept also applies to the classroom instructor and public speaker.

If you want them to hear what you're saying, believe it, comprehend it, and like you all in the bargain, then stand up and speak out and look 'em straight in the eye.—Dr. Beebe's research was originally reported to the 1978 Speech Communication Association in a paper titled "Effects of Eye Contact, Posture and Vocal Inflection Upon Credibility and Comprehension." (R.Z.)　∎

Reprinted from TRAINING, August 1979

This handy device can help you make media usage decisions faster and easier

# Try S.T.A.R.T.: the systematic training aid resource tool

by Bonnye L. Matthews
and Virginia Sweet Lincoln

**T**he designer of a new course often faces a difficult challenge when trying to select the instructional aid which best meets learner objectives. Sure, the trade journals are filled with complex charts, graphs, and diagrams for making such decisions. But, unfortunately, using these references involves a heavy time commitment for the trainer who must sort through this information before reaching a decision. Is there an easier way? Yes, it's called START—the Systematic Training Aid Resource Tool.

## Assembling the START wheel

At this point, it would be helpful to assemble the START wheel so you have your own instructional visual aid to use with this article. Cut out Figures 1 and 2, following the circular black lines. Using a razor knife, cut just inside each square on Figure 1 so that the black guideline remains on wheel. Then, place Figure 1 on top of Figure 2, and pierce a small hole at the center dot. Insert a paper fastener and secure so that Figure 1 will rotate on the surface of Figure 2.

As designers begin preparing their course, they must synthesize a lot of information. The face of the START wheel provides a recap of essential pre-course design considerations of domains, levels of cognition, principles and retention.

Once the learning need is established, it is critical to establish the learning domain(s) of the need as we have listed on the wheel. (We rely on Bloom's *Taxonomies for the Cognitive and Affective Domains*. At present, there is no single, widely accepted taxonomy for the third learning domain, the psychomotor.) We ask questions such as: Is the subject matter fact-oriented or attitude-oriented? Does it involve the use of motor skills?

Since effective course design is based on measurable objectives, the wheel includes the levels of cognition as a means of prioritizing tasks and ranking objectives regarding their relative levels of difficulty.

During the course-design process, evaluative skills involve testing the pre-test against the objectives, the instruction against the objectives, and the post-test against the objectives. Further evaluation skills determine whether the instruction can follow pre-test results for "beyond-entry-level" instruction, and whether the post-test is designed to measure the objectives of the course.

In designing a course, the designer must account for the principles of effective learning, and aim for a high level of learner retention of the material. The face of the START wheel helps the novice designer decide which training aid would effectively meet objectives, learning principles, and the retention goals.

## Using START to select aids

The START wheel works as a training-aid selector tool. Spin the wheel to overhead transparencies, and we'll run through this aid as an example. The first category on the wheel considers the relationship between the training aid and the domain of the objective. Overhead transparencies may be used to meet objectives in two domains—the Cognitive and the Affective.

The reusable category shows YES because transparencies require an overhead projector.

You'll observe that transparencies do not have special production demands; designers can make their own.

The next category identifies the audience for whom transparencies are suitable. They may be used effectively with both large- and small-group presentation.

The revisable category shows a NO answer because transparencies, once made, can't be altered; they must be redone. The second, need to show motion, also displays a NO answer because transparencies imply a one-dimensional, non-moving training aid. For example, they would not be the most effective method to teach the process of shifting gears from first to second.

The special-concerns box was left blank for you to list your own training constraints. These might include availability of equipment and classroom environment effects on the media.

Because no active participation is required of the learner when transparencies are used, the next category, active learner participation, also displays a NO. Regardless of the training aid used, one or more of the senses is involved in the learning process. For example, sight is the sense involved when overhead transparencies are used. Then, checking the retention listing, you can see that the retention rate for seeing is 30%.

The last two categories both show NO answers because neither learner control of pace nor color is essential to an effective use of transparencies. However, color may be used to highlight or detail information.

Transparencies, then, would be the training aid choice when all or most of the categories meet the need. But let's say the objective falls into the psychomotor domain, and the course designer wants to know if films might meet the need more effectively than transparencies. By rotating the wheel to the motion-picture category, you can see that films do meet needs in the psychomotor domain and are suitable for individuals as well as for groups.

On the other hand, let's say you had just considered transparencies and decided they were not best suited for use with individuals. By rotating the wheel to the right, and checking the suitable category, you can see that slides might be your next logical choice.

If this START wheel meets your training design needs, you can duplicate it on heavy paper. Using this wheel, you'll have both a head START on course design and a trainer's training aid. **T**

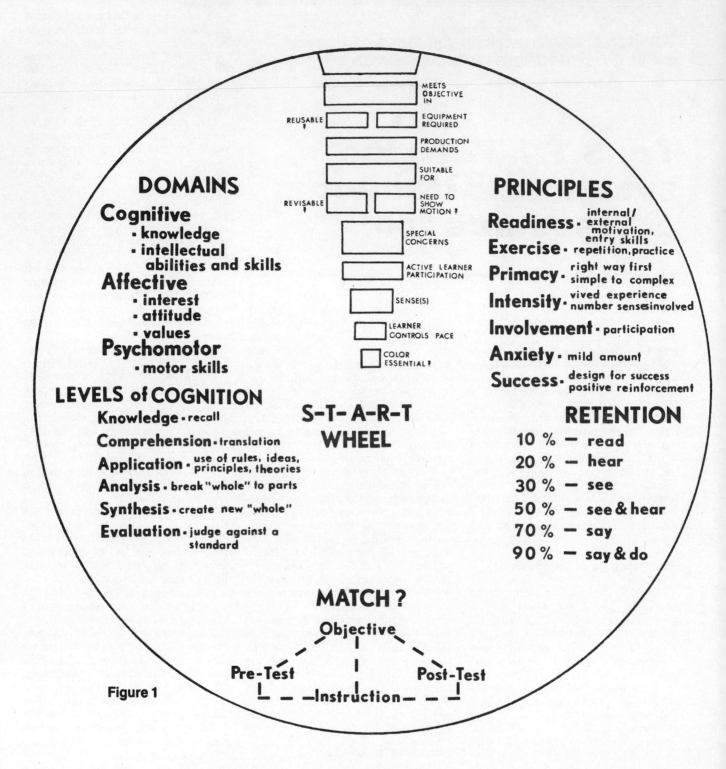

**DOMAINS**

**Cognitive**
- knowledge
- intellectual abilities and skills

**Affective**
- interest
- attitude
- values

**Psychomotor**
- motor skills

**LEVELS of COGNITION**

**Knowledge** - recall

**Comprehension** - translation

**Application** - use of rules, ideas, principles, theories

**Analysis** - break "whole" to parts

**Synthesis** - create new "whole"

**Evaluation** - judge against a standard

MEETS OBJECTIVE IN

REUSABLE ?    EQUIPMENT REQUIRED

PRODUCTION DEMANDS

SUITABLE FOR

REVISABLE ?    NEED TO SHOW MOTION ?

SPECIAL CONCERNS

ACTIVE LEARNER PARTICIPATION

SENSE(S)

LEARNER CONTROLS PACE

COLOR ESSENTIAL ?

**S-T- A-R-T WHEEL**

**PRINCIPLES**

**Readiness** - internal/external motivation, entry skills

**Exercise** - repetition, practice

**Primacy** - right way first simple to complex

**Intensity** - vived experience number senses involved

**Involvement** - participation

**Anxiety** - mild amount

**Success** - design for success positive reinforcement

**RETENTION**

10 % — read
20 % — hear
30 % — see
50 % — see & hear
70 % — say
90 % — say & do

**MATCH ?**

Objective

Pre-Test            Post-Test

Figure 1

Instruction

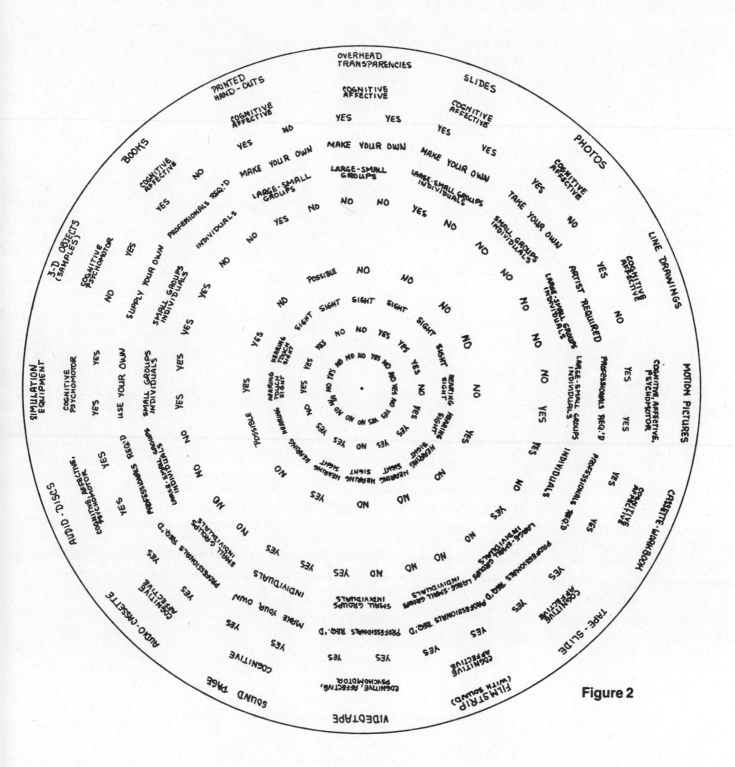

**Figure 2**

The learning by imitation concept is deceptively simple. But countless training programs still don't use

# Behavior modeling: The 'monkey see, monkey do' principle

by Ron Zemke

Monkey A sees Monkey B dig up a red root and eat it. Monkey B smacks his lips, jumps about excitedly, begins digging again. Monkey A "gets the picture," does some digging of his own, finds a red root, eats it, likes it, and digs for more. Simple as it may seem, this scenario captures the essentials of an emerging approach to the development of training. This new approach, based on the principles of social-learning theory, is known as behavior modeling.

## Behavior modeling and social-learning theory

Few trainers have more than a vague familiarity with behavior modeling and its parent, social-learning theory. Part of that unfamiliarity has to do with origins. Social-learning theory is a by-product of investigations by Albert Bandura, James Aronfreed, and others into the development of moral behavior in children. The specific question they investigated was: "If people tend to behave in ways that lead to satisfaction in any situation, why do they often appear to forego rewards in order to behave in ways that are socially acceptable, even in private?" The learning model they evolved to answer this question — social-learning theory —emphasizes two simple mechanisms: *conditioning* and the *observation of models.*

**Conditioning,** a la Bandura, is essentially Skinner's reinforcement-of-behavior concept but with a strong emphasis on interpersonal attention,

approval and affection as powerful reinforcers. As children, we learn to repeat behavior that gains parental approval, and we learn to avoid actions that bring withdrawal of affection and/or punishment and disapproval. The approval and disapproval of others remain powerful rewards and punishments throughout our lives.

The social-learning approach recognizes the importance of internal events, such as thoughts and memories, on the control of our behavior but insists that all behavior is at least indirectly controlled by external cues. As we become adults, we learn to reward and punish ourselves "internally" in imitation of previously encountered "external" reward and punishment. Once we've been burned by a hot stove, chances are slim that we'll touch one again, regardless of "social" pressures.

**Modeling** or observational learning is the way we learn from others' experiences. It takes place in two steps: acquisition and performance. In the first step, we see others act, and we *acquire* a mental picture of the act and its consequences. After the mental image is acquired, we *perform* or try out the act ourselves. This is, of course, where conditioning principles come into play. If we find the consequences of imitating the model rewarding, we're likely to act that way again.

Obviously, you and I don't imitate and try out every behavior we see others engaged in. In fact, adults seem to apply quite a few restrictions to whom and what they will parrot. We are most likely to try out a new behavior if we see someone prestigious, powerful and competent doing it. (How

many of us, for instance, dusted off our old tennis racket and ambled onto the court because a significant role model — some personal idol or strong influence — encouraged us through example?)

But our expectations and experiences with reward and punishment in similar situations also mediate the chances that we'll try the modeled behavior. A five-foot-five, 35-year-old male, watching Bill Walton play a magnificent game of basketball, may not be encouraged by the example to play a little one-on-one. But a five-foot-five, 15-year-old female might be.

A growing number of trainers are learning that the social-learning-theory approach leads to a radically different framework for designing training, one that is particularly useful to those who train others to do complex motor-skill tasks and those who train others in interpersonal communication tasks. The use of modeling in the technical-training context has long been recognized. Anyone who has tried to write or even read repair instructions for anything more complex than a rubber band appreciates modeling and learning by imitation. In technical training, the score has always been: talk about it = 0; see diagrams of it = 10; watch someone do it = 1,000.

The big news now is that interpersonal skills, such as those needed to sell or conduct effective performance reviews, can be effectively taught and learned using modeling and social reinforcement. Trainers at IBM, General Electric, AT&T, Levitz Furniture, and others are finding that supervisory, sales, and customer-relations skills are learned faster and more effectively when taught from a modeling base.

Bandura suggests that the social-learning theory is a successful training design tool because it mirrors critical features of the real world in the training experience. In fact, Dr. Bandura bluntly downgrades the efficiency of learning from textbooks and lectures, and from word descriptions of things learnable from direct example.

The marked discrepancy between textbook and social reality is largely attributable to the fact that certain critical conditions present in natural situations are rarely, if ever, reproduced in laboratory studies of learning. In laboratory investigations, experimenters arrange comparatively benign environments in which errors do not create fatal consequences for the organism. By contrast, natural environments are loaded with potentially lethal consequences for those unfortunate enough to perform hazardous errors. For this reason, it would be exceedingly injudicious to rely on differential reinforcement of trial-and-error performances in teaching children to swim, adolescents to drive automobiles, medical students to conduct surgical operations, or adults to develop complex occupational and social competencies.

There are several reasons why modeling influences are heavily favored in promoting everyday learning. Under circumstances in which mistakes are costly or dangerous, skillful performances can be established without needless errors by providing competent models who demonstrate the required activities. Some complex behaviors can be produced solely through the influence of models. If children had no opportunity to hear speech, it would be virtually impossible to teach them the linguistic skills that constitute a language. When desired forms of behavior can be conveyed only by social cues, modeling is an indispensable aspect of learning. Even in instances where it is possible to establish new response patterns through other means, the process of acquisition can be considerably shortened by providing appropriate models.*

Dr. William C. Byham, president of Development Dimensions International, a Pittsburgh, PA-based training company that uses behavior modeling in its program designs, suggests, "Modeling is the way we've all learned from day one. Our whole developmental history is one of modeling the behavior of others. Look, I talk to a lot of successful managers and quiz them about their success. To a person, they claim that the most important experience in their career was working for an exceptional manager at some time — usually early — in their career. They seem to be saying they had a manager who was a good model and mentor. Unfortunately, that's an experience most of us won't have. And that's why I'm so high on giving people good models to learn from instead of textbooks and lectures."

In short, then, social-learning theory and research strongly suggest that, when conditions are right, a trainee can learn rapidly and effectively from exposure to a model performing the desired behavior.

### Applying modeling and social learning to training

The first interpersonal-skills training using behavior-modeling techniques in industry was conducted in 1970 at General Electric by Mel Sorcher. The objective of this first course was to reduce the turnover of hard-core employees by helping them adapt to and cope with a job in industry. Both hard-core employees and

*Albert Bandura, *Psychological Modeling* (New York: Lieber-Atherton, Inc., 1971).

their first-line supervisors were trained in taking and giving constructive criticism, asking for and giving help, and establishing mutual trust and respect. The actual training was light on human-relations theory and attitude messages and long on visual examples — films of people *doing* good interpersonal relating — and role play. Basically, the training was exceptionally successful.

Six months after the original training, 72% of the 39 hard-core employees who had been trained and who worked for supervisors who had been trained remained on the job. Only 28% of the 25 hard-core employees who had not been trained and who worked for untrained supervisors did not leave. More important, Goldstein and Sorcher synthesized the important elements of the modeling-training approach, and it has been used widely in the development of interpersonal skills ever since.

Question: So what's the big deal? Don't we, more or less, use modeling in all our training? Most of us show movies — that sounds like modeling —and most of us give live demonstrations. That, too, sounds like modeling. And lots of us use practice and role playing, and that sounds like social reinforcement. So why all the hubbub?

For starters, simply exposing trainees to film and video images of people doing things isn't modeling. A recent stopwatch study of 15 commercial training films revealed that, out of 420 minutes of film, the largest block of time (235 minutes or 56%) was devoted to explaining the skills. Twenty-two percent or 92 minutes were titles and transitions, 13% or 55 minutes showed people doing the skill *incorrectly,* and only nine percent or 38 minutes showed people doing the skill correctly or modeling the behavior. That is an average of 2.6 minutes of correct-skill demonstration per film. Producers of training films would not be surprised at these numbers since they conceptualize their job as dramatizing and communicating an idea rather than providing a source of skill models.

The moral is that simply putting your message on film doesn't qualify the product as a source of behavior modeling experience. Even showing trainees a film or videotape composed solely of examples of people doing the behavior or demonstrating the skill correctly isn't a learning shoe-in. By analogy, you and I can go to a tennis tournament, watch Connors and Evert play perfect tennis and not learn anything new about the game. *Unless* we attend with the conscious intent of "going to school" on Conner's footwork

or Evert's backhand, we won't come away with any new backhand or footwork models.

In training based on modeling and social learning, care is given to facilitating three processes in the trainees:

● Attention — making sure the trainees attend to the pertinent aspects of the behavior being modeled;

● Retention — helping the trainees remember the original observation points in the form;

● Reinforcement and motivation —using practice and positive reinforcement to translate observational learning into skilled performance.

Development Dimensions' Byham suggests that these three processes are promoted by adhering to a specific sequence of events in the training:

1. *Overview.* The instructor discusses the objective and importance of the skill module.

2. *Critical steps.* The instructor describes the specific behavior or critical steps of the activity to be learned.

3. *Positive model.* A film or videotape shows an individual effectively utilizing the skill.

4. *Critique of the film.* The instructor and participants discuss the things done correctly in the film, with particular emphasis on how the model utilized the critical steps.

5. *Skill practice.* Trainees practice the skills in pairs, with one trainee acting the supervisor, salesperson or whatever and the second acting the employee, buyer and so forth. At least one other trainee observes the practice, using a prepared guide.

6. *Skill practice feedback.* After the practice session, the trainee receives feedback from observers and the instructor that emphasizes things done correctly. Where the behavior could have been more effective, alternative positive behaviors are suggested.

7. *Transfer.* Participants write out, practice, and receive feedback on situations they will face back on the job.

Byham also passes along the following tips and tricks for those who contemplate building a program around modeling concepts.

● Do a good needs analysis. Solving the wrong problem is *still* the trainer's number-one pitfall.

● Determine the specific situations where the new behavior is expected to manifest itself.

● Determine the minimum critical steps of the activity or skill to be mastered; don't complicate matters by listing too many critical steps.

● Spend up to 50% of the training time on the trainees on-job problems. (Development Dimensions courses typically devote 10 minutes to viewing the filmed model in a three-hour training sequence.)

• Keep the feedback sessions positive. The goal is to create a series of success experiences for the trainees.

• Develop the training group into a mutual support group.

• Don't expect a one-shot training program to yield a big behavior change. Work on one skill at a time over a period of weeks. Give trainees time and space to try out the new behaviors and come back for consultation with the rest of the group and the instructor.

Research on the effectiveness of behavior modeling in clinical and school settings is persuasive. Most assertiveness training is done through modeling, and has an impressive composite track record. But how effective is the approach in our world, the normal adult learning context? There is an equally impressive accumulation of studies that say the approach is effective in business and industry.

We have already mentioned Sorcher's work and the book based on his and Goldstein's successes. Robert F. Burnaska, also of GE, reports that a course developed to improve the interpersonal skills of the managers of professional employees was equally successful. A one-month follow-up comparison of 62 trained and 62 un-trained middle managers showed that trained managers were better at *performance problem discussion, work assignment discussion,* and *giving recognition to an average employee* than were the untrained managers. In addition, a five-month follow-up found trained managers even better than they were at the one-month follow-up.

At AT&T, Joseph L. Moses and Richard J. Ritchie developed a behavior - modeling - oriented supervisory-relationships training program following the Goldstein and Sorcher model and evaluated the results, using an assessment-center approach. A team of specially trained individuals observed and evaluated 90 trained and 93 untrained first-level supervisors performing a variety of simulation exercises. Two months after the program, both groups were given cases of excessive absence, an alleged discrimination complaint, and a case of suspected theft. In all simulated situations, the trained group utilized "appropriate skills" and handled the situations significantly better than did the untrained group.

Preston E. Smith of IBM office products division reports that modeling training of *meeting effectiveness skills, discussing opinions survey results,* and *customer complaint handling* has paid off handsomely for his organization.

Trained managers were rated higher on employee opinion surveys after training than before. In addition, customer-satisfaction ratings and sales-quota results were higher for branches managed by trained managers.

Lest we seem about to leap too quickly onto the behavior-modeling bandwagon, let's review three *facts* about the technique. First, the behavior-modeling approach comes from a learning model — social-learning theory — that has an impressive set of credentials. Second, a number of trainers are finding that the application of modeling principles is further reducing their dependence on the "spray and pray" approach to training. Third, good, solid evaluations are verifying the effectiveness.

But, as the folks at "Ma Bell" remind us, "The system is the solution." And no new training program or technique can overcome bad products, poor market positioning, or a management team that fights change. With this in mind, we should avoid setting expectations for behavior modeling that it can't fulfill. But we also should be glad we have an innovation, a new tool, that helps us perform better professionally. Who knows what will happen if we begin to model the professionalism we profess. **T**

# What your trainees can learn by simply watching others

**B**ehavior modeling or imitation learning was a virtually unre-searched and unknown topic prior to the 1941 publication of *Social Learning and Imitation* by Miller and Dollard. Their studies lead them to view imitation learning as a special form of the behavioral conditioning process. Essentially, the trainer must provide a sample of the behavior, the learner must respond in a way that matches the sample, and the imitation must be positively reinforced. In Dollard's and Miller's view, the "model" simply informs the learner where to go or how to behave for reinforcement. The learner does not acquire new, previously unexhibited behavior from the model. Though much of Miller's and Dollard's interpretation of results and theorizing has been questioned recently, they deserve credit for priming the pump, for beginning to research the question, "How and what do people learn simply by watching others?"

Groundbreaking and impressive modeling research has been conducted by Dr. Albert Bandura of Stanford University. In a typical experiment, Bandura, Ross and Ross showed nursery-school children a motion picture of an adult displaying "aggressive behavior" toward a large, inflatable rubber clown — the kind that bounces back for more because of a bottom full of sand. Boys and girls who watched the film behaved aggressively toward the clown themselves, closely mimicking the adult in the film. They lifted and threw, kicked and hit, and beat the clown with a hammer exactly as the adult had. Bandura has repeatedly found that most children will, with little or no prodding, thus imitate the novel behavior of a model.

In addition to establishing that modeling does occur, Bandura has investigated the ways in which it can be increased or decreased. He has found, for example, that children are more likely to imitate the behavior of a model they see rewarded than one they see punished. In one experiment, three groups of children watched films of a model who yelled at and punched a Bobo doll. In the film one group saw, the model was punished by an author-ity for punching the doll; in the film a second group saw, the model was praised for his aggressive behavior; in the film the third group saw, the model received neither praise nor punishment. When put into a situation similar to that of the model, the children who had seen him praised were much more likely to imitate him than those who had seen him punished. Bandura hypothesized that the children identified with the model and experienced reward or punishment vicariously as they watched the film. Therefore, when given a chance to act as the model had, they tended to behave as if they themselves (instead of the model) had earlier been praised or punished for hitting the doll.

Bandura's approach to understanding the modeling phenomenon is more complex and cognitively oriented than Dollard's and Miller's. To Bandura, models influence learning in an information-transmitting fashion. The observer acquires a symbolic representation of the modeled activities rather than a group of stimulus-response associations. Because there are cognitive or mental, as well as behavioral, components to modeling, Bandura suggests that there are four processes governing the modeling phenomenon: *attention, retention, reproduction,* and *reinforcement/motivation.*

## The attention process

The principle here is that a person cannot learn much by observation if he or she does not attend to, or recognize, the essential features of the model's behavior. The learner must be sensitized to look for the things we want them to learn or they will learn something else — or nothing at all. Research suggests there are the following natural factors which shape the attention patterns of learners:

● *Similarity of model and learner.* The people with whom one regularly associates influence the types of behavior one will repeatedly observe and learn thoroughly. Opportunities for learning aggressive behavior are most prevalent for children of the urban poor than for offspring of the rural Quaker.

● *Functional value.* Behavior which has an intuitive value for the learner in the learner's environment is more likely to be attended to. Subway-map reading doesn't have a high functional value to a Los Angelino.

● *Interpersonal attraction.* Models who possess interesting and winsome qualities are sought out, whereas those without such characteristics tend to be ignored or rejected, even though they may excel in other ways.

● *Media attractiveness.* Models presented in televised form are so effective in capturing attention that viewers learn the depicted behavior regardless of the presence or absence of incentives for learning.

## Retention processes

If one is to reproduce a model's behavior when the latter is no longer present to serve as a guide, the response patterns must be represented in memory in symbolic form.

● *Mental images.* There is an almost automatic mental imaging function, but for practical use these "mind pictures" should be associated with common symbols, such as words. As Plato suggested, a bowl may be only a poor example of the concept bowl, but the concept name bowl invariably pulls forth an image of a specific bowl one has had experience with.

● *Verbal coding.* Observers who code modeled behavior into words, concise labels, or vivid imagery learn and retain the behavior better than those who simply observe or are mentally preoccupied with other matters while watching the performance of others. Consciously counting Mark Spitz's strokes per lap will help a swimmer retain and retrieve a mental image of Spitz's swimming style.

● *Rehearsal.* People who mentally rehearse or actually perform modeled patterns of behavior are less likely to forget them. For example, mumbling your "opening lines" over and over to yourself makes them automatic.

## Motoric reproduction processes

To actually *do* the behavior, the learner must put together a given set of responses according to the modeled patterns. The amount of the model which can be exhibited depends on acquisition of component skills.

● *Parts must equal whole.* A learner could have all the parts but not succeed with the whole. A young child might watch and be able to exhibit all the components of driving a car but still run the family Hupmobile through the garage wall.

● *Skill level.* Even if all components are learned, can be identified and talked about, performance of the whole will be poor until all the components are practiced and fitted together in a whole. A would-be tennis player can learn a lot by watching others play, talking about it and banging balls against the house. *But,* until one goes on the court and hits with another person, honing and fine tuning to the level of the model can't take place.

## Reinforcement/motivation

A person can acquire, retain and possess the capabilities for skillful execution of modeled behavior, but the learning rarely will be activated if negatively sanctioned.

● *Positive incentive.* When positive incentives are provided, observational learning, which has been previously unexpressed, is promptly translated into action. Reinforcement influences not only the demonstration of already learned behavior, but it can affect the level of observational learning by influencing attending, coding and rehearsal phases.

● *Anticipation of reinforcement.* If the learner sees the model reinforced positively or avoiding punishment, learning is enhanced.

● *Familiarity with subskills.* If the learner has all the subskills and also has names or a coding system for them, seemingly complex skills can be modeled verbally — a factor most technical-manual writers rely upon heavily.

● *Multiple models.* The more models the learner is exposed to, the less likely he or she is to learn only one way of behaving. Learners exposed to three or four models exhibit behavior that is an innovative mix of all of the models seen. This would seem especially im-portant for learning interpersonal skills that are personality dependent, such as selling or interviewing.

● *Outcome for the model.* How the model is treated influences both the probability of the learner learning the behavior and the learner's attitude toward the model and the behavior the model exhibited. This concept has been especially useful in helping people de-learn phobias.

During the last decade, there has been copious research on modeling applications. And at least some should interest the training and development professional.

● Problem-solving strategies— both linear and creative — seem to be enhanced by a combination of process rules and extensive modeling of the processes.

● Rule following and positive attitude toward procedures and rules seem to be enhanced through discussion and viewing of filmed vignettes of people successfully following rules and procedures.

● Interviewing skills can be quickly and effectively learned by watching a videotape of a model conducting an effective interview.

● When watching a model of supervisory skills, trainees also tend to learn and assimilate the leadership *style* of the model.

● Self-disclosure in a closed group increases when the facilitator models self-disclosure and makes a high number of self-disclosing statements.

● Assertive behavior can be effectively learned watching a videotape of a low-assertive person becoming assertive with the help of an assertiveness trainer.

● Complex motor skills can be learned by watching a film of a correctly performing model *or* a film of someone learning to perform the motor skill.

● Tolerance to pain can be learned from watching a model endure what the viewer perceives to be a painful experience. (Especially useful for those who must conduct or endure long meetings or seminars.)

● And, finally, one researcher has determined that we are what we watch. Specifically, he found that those who watch "All in the Family" most frequently are most tolerant of and in sympathy with Archie Bunker's attitudes and views. The researcher does not suggest a causal relationship but if some Sunday morning you notice the "Gilligan's Island" rerun you're watching is one you've seen three times before — and you're still enjoying it — it might be time to consider the effect behavior modeling is having on you. **T**

Trainers everywhere can adopt this step-by-step approach, which works so successfully

# How to set up, run and evaluate programs based on behavior modeling principles

by Terence O'Connor

**A**t St. Luke's Hospital Center, 108 supervisors have improved their skills, thanks to behavior modeling. The program is so successful that some of us have spent our vacations offering the technique at other organizations. Employees of an international insurance company, a multinational shipping firm and more than 20 health care institutions have benefited from our classes alone, and dozens of large and small consulting firms now offer supervisory training that utilizes behavior modeling techniques.

You've probably read other recent testimonials to the concept of learning by imitating the behavior of models. Numerous publications ranging from TRAINING (June 1978) and *Business Week* (May 8, 1978) to the *Journal of Nursing Administration* (April 1978) have explained how and why the process works. But these and other articles generally have steered clear of the nitty gritty details of how you go about setting up, running and evaluating a training program that revolves around behavior modeling. I would like to do just that.

First, I suggest that you read *Changing Supervisor Behavior*, by Arnold P. Goldstein and Melvin Sorcher; this is the theoretical framework for the technique. Next, read one of the many good books that stress improving communications through increased empathy, respect and warmth. One particularly good

one is *Human Relations Development—A Manual for Health Sciences*, by George Gazda, Richard Walters and Williams Childers.

A further review of the literature shows the variety of situations that respond to behavior modeling. At St. Luke's, we use seven frequently:

- greeting the new employee
- introducing a new policy or procedure
- improving poor work habits
- improving poor performance
- the discipline interview
- performance appraisal
- reducing conflict between two subordinates

Your organization's records and needs analysis may indicate other situations that require the employee to make a positive individual commitment to alter his or her behavior. Analyze how your best supervisors handle these situations. Compare them with your worst supervisors. From these extremes of behavior, you can identify key points (usually five to seven) in the best supervisors' communications process for each situation.

Generally, these key points include:

- greeting the employee warmly and appropriately
- identifying the situation being discussed
- soliciting the employee's suggestions for improvement
- writing down those suggestions

the employee chooses as most likely to be effective
- setting a follow-up date to review the situation
- expressing confidence in the employee's ability to handle the situation properly

For each problem situation, adapt the key steps to reflect the language of that interaction.

Develop a script for a model interview between supervisor and employee, for each situation. The script should model the supervisor's behavior, not the policy or procedure—hence the term "behavior modeling." Because the model stresses the process of the interview, not the content, it requires a certain brevity and pace that are not necessarily realistic. The model will be attacked in class if it contains too many references to organizational policies and documentable facts.

In the script, the supervisor should cover each key step in sequence. He should not move onto the next step until the prior one has been completed. The listener should hear the supervisor control the interviewer's pace. The subordinate should do most of the talking, but the supervisor stays in command.

Now, videotape your model interviews. (Using videotape recording and playback equipment is, of course, optional but it makes the next step much more effective.)

Don't worry if your players don't follow your scripts. What's important is that the model follows the key steps for each interaction. If it does, then encourage your actors to use their own words and mannerisms.

At St. Luke's, we began with supervisors from one department. We have since done groups from many departments and, on occasion, from more than one institution. We also mix experience with inexperience. Members of the group, however, must have difficulty with the same interactions.

At this point, our needs analysis is not complicated. Of our prospective participants, we ask, "What do you want to do better?" In a separate meeting, we ask their managers, "What do you want them to do better?" Each group will use words like "morale" and "motivation"; get them to speak in terms of specific interactions, and you will find a remarkable degree of agreement between the two groups. You may have to bridge some minor gulfs, but the two will tell you quickly which of your models you will use—and if you will have to make more.

I prefer to do this needs analysis orally, rather than by questionnaire.

This lets me probe below the generality and also lets me explain what I'll be doing. But you can use printed surveys before the meetings, if you wish.

Groups size in our classes has varied from four to twenty. The bigger the class, the longer each session lasts. We find 10 is the best size. Classes are at least two hours long and meet once a week. The participant receives a notice of time, place and topic for each class but no preliminary reading.

The first class is devoted to explaining in detail the program's specifics. The camera is turned on, and the group is seen on the monitor, but nothing is recorded. When the group is comfortable with the TV, we turn off the equipment. The remainder of the class is spent reviewing the duties of a supervisor, the importance of communication skills and the techniques of effective listening. Because the class is to learn behavior, not theory, the latter is never mentioned.

Each week thereafter, we cover another interaction. The format of each class is similar:

- Distribute the key steps, read them aloud, answer questions about them (10 minutes).
- Show the model tape for that interaction (10 minutes).
- Talk about the model (5 minutes).
- Have the class in pairs, rehearse the model behavior; after 10 minutes, reverse the pairs, so each person is the supervisor (20 minutes).
- Turn on the television and record a pair rehearsing. At the end of the rehearsal, ask the "supervisor" for his review; then solicit remarks from the "employee." Play back the tape. Allow comments from anyone in the room (30 minutes).

Who goes on the tape? Everyone plays the supervisor at least once. Who goes first? Ask for volunteers. No volunteers? I pick the least aggressive person in the room to star as the supervisor first.

What order for the interactions? Start with the least threatening, and end with the most threatening. Do at least five; the key points are basically repetitive, and five weeks are needed for the rehearsals to be learned effectively.

What is the pass-out material? Only the key steps for each week. Participants should refer to these as they rehearse and be encouraged to have them handy on the job. We also have these key steps in a check-off form and may distribute this to encourage the class to follow the televised rehearsals.

At one time, participants also received brief outlines of situations to use as they rehearse. But we discarded these because few were used. Or, if they were, the actors got involved in our written words and not their oral ones. It's best to let them use their own styles of communication to cover key points effectively.

Who acts in the model tapes? Anyone who is believable. At one time, we used actors from each department as we trained in it, but this had little effect and wasn't worth the effort.

What about tests? The final class is a test, both written and behavioral. Participants arrive alone, complete the written test (on communication skills, not theory) and choose one of three situations. After a few moments to prepare, a tape is made; the instructor usually plays the employee. Total time is about 30 minutes.

Who works the TV equipment? No one. In reality, the trainer turns it on to play the model and then puts on the tape that records the rehearsals. Operating time takes no more than two or three minutes.

Evaluations can take the form of written tests, rehearsal tapes and/or the final test tapes. At St. Luke's, we rely most heavily on the final test tapes. Participants are graded on: control of the interaction, ability to move the employee to a positive response to the problem and ability to follow the key steps.

Outside the classroom, statistical follow-up reveals that problems do respond to the program. For example, new employee turnover decreases when participants study orientation of new employees.

Validation? In December 1977, we requested nine randomly chosen graduates (10% of our total), trained from January 1975 to June 1977, to visit our training department. Arriving singly, each was given a typed description of a problem: One of their employees had a pattern of recent Monday lateness. After a few moments preparation, each indicated a willingness for the interview to begin. A trainer played the employee.

Some "testees" were stern and disciplinary, and some were paternalistic and helping. Each revealed his own personality and used his own communications style in the interview. Each graded high in interactive control, employee contribution and following key steps. Even those who had participated three years earlier and who had received no overt reinforcement from training scored well.

For before-and-after comparisons, these interviews were compared with the first taped rehearsal interview of each "testee." Nontraining administrators scored each pair of interviews. In each case, "after" scored higher. Retention of skills, even after 35 months, was significant.

At St. Luke's, where the technique is called "behavior rehearsal," we stress rehearsal rather than the model. It is rehearsal time that allows the participant to make mistakes in the classroom, not the work room. Rehearsal lets each person explore how best to play the role illustrated by the models. **T**

The technique is attractive, and the uses seem almost limitless, but it is not guaranteed cost-effective or appropriate

# Questions to ask before using behavior modeling

by James C. Robinson
and Dana L. Gaines

Since behavior modeling began as an experiment with a few supervisors at General Electric in 1970, it has grown into a learning technology that will be utilized in the training of more than 500,000 supervisors, managers and employees this year. Certainly, the numbers are impressive. But the pragmatist should ask, "How do we know that behavior modeling is the most effective learning experience for every one of those 500,000 learners?" The answer is, "We don't know and probably never will know."

Nevertheless, we must ask that question each time a decision is made to use behavior-modeling programs in our organizations. We all have a responsibility to our organizations to use behavior modeling (or any other learning technology) *only* when it is the most effective and cost-beneficial approach to a given problem. Only through careful deliberation can we determine when and under what circumstances behavior modeling should be used.

After several years of experimenting, we have developed a seven-step decision-making process (see table 1) that will enable organizations to examine any training situation to determine whether behavior modeling is appropriate. To illustrate how each step leads toward the ultimate decision, we will use a hypothetical organization, the Homespun Insurance Company. Homespun has 3,400 em-

ployees, with the majority located in a major city. There are 200 first-level supervisors in the organization.

## Given: Possible training need exists

The decision-making process starts when a possible training need is identified. This training need can pertain to employees, supervisors, managers, top management or any segment of the organization. It usually refers to a current performance deficiency (for example, not achieving a current job expectation) or some future problem (for example, learning to market a new product).

In the Homespun Insurance Company, the possible training need involved the ability of first-line supervisors to put an employee on probation without causing the employee to leave the organization. In the previous year, supervisors justifiably had put employees on probation 48 times; 20 of these employees eventually left the organization. Because rehiring and retraining for the 20 open positions had een costly to Homespun, the company hoped that a training program might reduce the expense.

## Decision #1: Could he/she do it if his/her life depended on it?

The decision is to determine whether the performance deficiency is a result of a lack of skill and knowledge or due to other factors. When the performance deficiency is a result of something other than skill or knowl-

edge, management should seek non-training solutions— which often involve changing the conditions in which the person is expected to perform— rather than training that person to do something he or she already knows how to do. According to Mager and Pipe, if a person has a genuine skill or knowledge deficiency, then the primary remedy must be either to change the skill level (teach the individual how to do it) or to change the job responsibilities. If, on the other hand, the person is able to perform the job, the solution lies in something other than enhancing skills and knowledge. "Teaching" someone to do what he or she already knows how to do isn't going to change that person's skill level. Instead, the remedy is to change the conditions in which the person is expected to perform.

Supervisors at Homespun obviously were struggling to conduct effective probationary conversations with employees. In almost every instance, it was in the company's best interest to have a poorly performing employee correct performance deficiencies. Supervisors, however, felt so pressured by these disciplinary conversations that their primary objective was to "get it over with." Consequently, the supervisors did not clearly delineate the performance standards expected of the employee. In addition, the discussions often provoked defensive reactions from the employees. To further complicate the matter, the supervisors were not consistently following corporate policies when placing employees on probation. But the crux of the problem was that many supervisors lacked the skill to conduct such conversations effectively.

## Decision #2: Is it a skill deficiency?

The second step in the decision-making process is to determine whether the deficiency is one of skill or one of knowledge. Behavior modeling is a feasible method of teaching skills; some other process, however, would be more appropriate for cognitivelearning. Since the performance deficiency often involves a combination of skill and knowledge, behavior modeling frequently is used in conjunction with another type of learning experience.

For example, if we were to design a program to teach student pilots to fly aircraft, we would confront a situation in which the students would have to learn several things. First, they must learn the theory of flying so they would know why an aircraft leaves the ground at given speeds. They also

Reprinted from TRAINING, December 1980

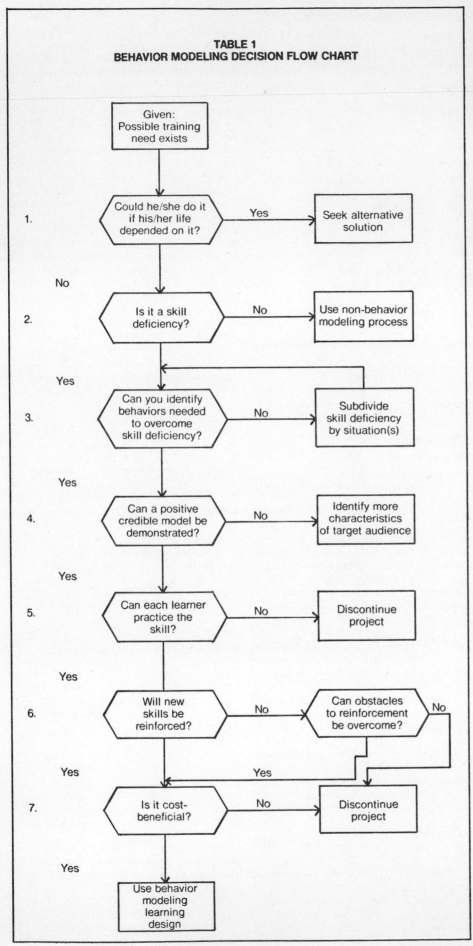

**TABLE 1**
**BEHAVIOR MODELING DECISION FLOW CHART**

Given:
Possible training
need exists

1. Could he/she do it
if his/her life
depended on it? → Yes → Seek alternative solution

No

2. Is it a skill
deficiency? → No → Use non-behavior modeling process

Yes

3. Can you identify
behaviors needed
to overcome
skill deficiency? → No → Subdivide skill deficiency by situation(s)

Yes

4. Can a positive
credible model be
demonstrated? → No → Identify more characteristics of target audience

Yes

5. Can each learner
practice the
skill? → No → Discontinue project

Yes

6. Will new
skills be
reinforced? → No → Can obstacles to reinforcement be overcome? → No

Yes                              Yes

7. Is it cost-
beneficial? → No → Discontinue project

Yes

Use behavior
modeling
learning
design

would have to develop the skills of applying power during takeoff; of controlling the aircraft's rudders, ailerons and elevators; and of reading the instruments during takeoff. We would utilize a non-behavior modeling process for the theory of flight, while we might consider behavior modeling to teach the new pilots how to control the aircraft.

At Homespun, the training need did require skill *and* knowledge training. Supervisors needed knowledge about corporate policies and documentation requirements regarding probation. They needed skill training in *how* to conduct an interview that would maintain employee self-esteem and minimize defensive reactions. Supervisors also needed help in learning how to participate with employees as they attempted to solve performance problems jointly. These are skills that could be acquired in a classroom.

### Decision #3: Can you identify behaviors needed to overcome the skills deficiency?

Although we might assume that we can readily identify the behaviors to be learned in *all* skill deficiency situations, many times one set of behaviors is not enough because the skill must be used in a number of significantly different types of situations. For example, in attempting to train salespeople to build rapport with clients or potential clients, we may find that one set of behaviors is not sufficient because there are many different types of potential clients. Potential clients may, for example, be categorized as: a) reluctant, b) openly hostile, c) needing help in solving a problem, d) friendly, but uncertain of specific needs; each of these requires a different set of behaviors.

The first general rule for determining if behaviors can be identified is that behaviors that are very similar in several different situations need *not* be subdivided by situation. Secondly, if a specific behavior is a make-or-break behavior (as is the case of building rapport with an openly hostile potential client) and if it doesn't occur in other situations, you must describe separately the behaviors needed to handle this situation.

A review of the training need at Homespun indicated that it would be advantageous to train supervisors to do the following:

1. Provide the employee with specific, descriptive behavioral feedback (for example, "You've been absent

from work five times in the past two months.").

2. Solicit the employee's reasons for the problem and a commitment to solving it.

3. Outline, in specific detail, the terms of the probation.

4. Set a date for a follow-up discussion.

5. Express confidence in the employee's ability to overcome this performance problem.

## Decision #4: Can a positive, credible model be demonstrated?

If you're going to use behavior modeling, you must demonstrate a model of the specific *positive* behavior to be learned. For example, in developing a model to teach a person how to operate an automobile, we wouldn't model an accident, which would be negative behavior. Instead, we would show the model taking action to avoid an accident; defensive driving would be positive behavior. Also, the learners must view the model as credible. They must feel that the model "could have happened in real life." If the learners don't perceive the model as positive and credible, we must identify more characteristics of the target audience. Knowing these will enable us to develop a model with behaviors that would be positive and effective in that environment, while remaining credible to those learners.

A positive model for the Homespun supervisors was provided in a film in which two office workers were shown discussing the employee's probation. The supervisor followed the appropriate skill behaviors, while the employee expressed some hostility and defensiveness in order to demonstrate a credible situation. The trainees focused on how the supervisor worked through the defensiveness to a problem-solving orientation.

## Decision #5: Can each learner practice the skill?

In a behavior modeling program, each learner must have an opportunity to practice the new skill. In most cases, it is possible to provide practice opportunities. In certain situations, however, it might not be cost-beneficial to do so. Imagine, for example, that someone advocated that all airline passengers boarding transoceanic flights practice using flotation equipment in water before flying. The purpose would be to ensure that everyone could float with the flotation device when fully

clothed. Those who couldn't do this would be provided with feedback and coaching on how to use the flotation equipment.

Obviously, this would be a costly skill practice. Although it's possible to provide every passenger with an opportunity to skill practice in this manner, it's not probable that it would be done. After all, passengers would have to arrive at the airport early, and flotation equipment and water tanks would have to be available, with lifeguards present. Some provision would have to be made for drying the passengers' clothes or providing them with an extra set. The decision to be made here is whether the benefits outweigh the costs.

For the Homespun supervisors, the opportunity to skill practice could be provided in a classroom situation, where groups of six to eight trainees could try out their new skills in realistic situations based on their office environment. Even better, they could be asked to describe a situation they had to deal with on the job. While two supervisors skill practiced, the remainder of the group could observe and take notes. Following skill practice, they could provide feedback on supervisors' proficiency in handling the situation.

## Decision #6: Will the new skills be reinforced?

The learner should be reinforced for using the new skills, both in and out of the classroom. Classroom reinforcement is quite easy to achieve; properly trained instructors can manage the group dynamics so that there is social reinforcement. But on-the-job reinforcement is often more difficult. First, you must do an analysis to determine whether sufficient reinforcement exists to assure sustained use of the new skills on the job. Because sufficient reinforcement is not present in most cases, you must discover the barriers to reinforcement. Only then can you decide whether these barriers can be overcome.

There are several possible barriers to reinforcement:

● **Peers**— If the peers of a newly trained supervisor are not using the skills, that supervisor is unlikely to continue to use them. Conversely, if a supervisor sees many of his or her peers using the skills, the tendency will be to give them a try. The best way to provide peer reinforcement is to train all peer supervisors in the same skills.

● **Workers**— If workers don't respond favorably to the supervisor's

use of the new skills, the supervisor will quickly stop using those skills. To ensure favorable worker response and, therefore, work reinforcement, supervisors must be trained to handle various types of employee reactions.

● **Managers**— The manager of the supervisor frequently does not reinforce the supervisor. Actually, managers can reinforce supervisors' use of the newly learned skills in three ways. As a coach, the manager can offer supervisors suggestions on how to handle specific on-the-job situations. As a reinforcer, the manager can recognize and praise the supervisor when the latter uses the newly learned skills on the job. As a positive model, the manager can show the supervisor that the skills are worth using on the job.

● **The Organization**— Many times, the organization doesn't reinforce the use of the skills. In that case, you must examine the rewards and punishments within the organization. Unfortunately, some organizations not only don't reward the use of newly learned skills, they actually punish those who practice them. For example, it may be punishing for a salesperson to handle a customer complaint effectively, because the time lost could be used to make other sales leading to commissions.

In Homespun, it was felt that the newly learned supervisory skill of effectively conducting a probationary interview could be reinforced in several ways:

1. All supervisors were to participate in the training.

2. During the actual discussion with the employee, the supervisors probably would find employees much less defensive than previously. While not guaranteed, it seemed probable that having supervisors approach probationary conversations in such a manner would produce positive problem-solving results.

3. All managers were shown how to reinforce the newly learned skill and how to coach the supervisor whenever a situation warranted probationary action.

4. Finally, the personnel department would reinforce the skill. Since all documentation of probations passed through this department, employment personnel would be coached to give positive feedback to supervisors as the quality of this documentation improved.

## Decision #7: Is it cost beneficial?

The real issue is whether there will be a positive return-on-investment from the proposed training. In this determination:

$$\frac{\text{Value of the training}}{\text{Cost of training}} = \text{Return-on-investment}$$

The value of the training is determined by computing the value of correcting a skill deficiency, preventing a problem from occurring or maximizing an opportunity. The cost of the training typically includes front-end analysis, development or purchase of the training materials, the salaries of the learners while they are in the classroom, the salaries of the instructors and the cost of overcoming the barriers to reinforcement. Return-on-investment is computed by dividing the value of the training by the cost of the training. If the return-on-investment is positive and within the organization's guidelines, behavior modeling should be used as a learning experience for the specific training situation.

For Homespun, it was determined that a complex analysis was not required for this training need. Rather, a break-even analysis was conducted on the cost to Homespun of employees leaving the organization. In the previous 12 months, 48 employees had been placed on probation—mostly for lateness and absence. Of these, 18 employees were finally terminated, and two voluntarily resigned at the time of probation. The average annual salary of these individuals was $9,200. Therefore, the cost to Homespun for these employment terminations could be computed:

| | |
|---|---:|
| Loss in productivity during the 90-day probationary period | $1,300 |
| Recruiting/hiring costs for replacement | 135 |
| Training costs and lower productivity during a four-month training period | 1,530 |
| Total cost per termination and replacement | $2,965 |

Also analyzed were the specific costs of training: for example, materials and classroom time, for learners and instructors. The training materials could be purchased from a supplier. In fact, the materials for this training need were part of a multi-modular program Homespun purchased to meet other supervisory training needs. The program cost included student materials for 200 supervisors ($700) and one modeling film ($400). In addition, one instructor had to be trained, at a pro-rated cost of $100. Therefore, total expenses were fixed at $1,200.

The average annual salary of supervisors to be trained was $14,000. The proposed training program required three hours away from the job. The cost of salaries was computed to be $20 per supervisor, or $4,000 to train all 200 supervisors.

The instructor in this example earned $20,000 per year. Therefore, hourly costs of $10 had to be applied against both the three-hour class time and the one-hour preparation time required. A total of 33 classes would be required to train all 200 supervisors. Instructor costs totalled $1,320.

Forty managers at Homespun needed training in a one-hour program so that they would know how to reinforce the newly learned supervisory skills. The proposed program was to be conducted five separate times, with eight managers in each class. Their average annual salary was $22,000 or $10.50/hour. These costs were computed to be $420 for the managers to attend and $50 for the instructor to teach.

Total training costs were:

| | | |
|---|---|---:|
| Training materials | = | $1,200 |
| Salaries of learners | = | 4,000 |
| Salary of instructor | = | 1,320 |
| Reinforcement training | = | 470 |
| | | $6,990 |

The financial benefit to the organization for each employee who was retained was $2,965. Since it was impossible to project what percentage of the 20 employees who had left the organization could have been retained, a break-even analysis was done which showed:

$$\frac{\text{Cost of training}}{\text{Value of retention per employee}} = \frac{\$6,990}{\$2,965} = 2.4$$

According to this break-even analysis, if three or more employees were retained because of the training received by their supervisors, the program would pay for itself. Because of this, Homespun decided to implement the training.

## Summary

Behavior modeling may soon begin to be used with senior managers, in matrix organizations, with service employees and in patient care, to name just a few. In addition, it will be used to teach more sophisticated skills, such as goal negotiation, opportunity identification, fact finding, planning, conflict resolution and team building.

Despite its attractiveness and almost unlimited possible uses, we in the training profession are still responsible for making sure that behavior modeling is used *only* when it will be effective and cost-beneficial. By judiciously using the seven-step decision-making process described here, you'll be able to make the correct decision about behavior modeling for each training situation. If you decide behavior modeling would be ineffective in a given situation, then move on to another technology. If you decide behavior modeling shouldn't be used because it is not cost-beneficial, you also should select another approach.

If, however, the decision is, "Yes, behavior modeling is effective and cost beneficial," then the real fun starts as you begin to design an effective behavior modeling program. **T**

If the right game is matched to the situation, both trainees and trainers can be winners

# Using games to help meet your objectives

## Why use a game?

by Linda Standke

The training session has started and the instructor has announced that part of the program involves playing a game. There is a box of Tinker Toys placed in front of you. According to the directions, you are a supervisor who has been asked to build a four-sided object with "something hanging in the middle." You've only a few minutes to get your subordinate (the person sitting next to you) to accomplish the task. Do you get involved in the doing rather than the directing? How does your subordinate feel about your assignment methods and leadership style?

The outcome would reveal not only a lot about you and your leadership style, but also set the stage for a discussion about appropriate supervisory behavior and the effects of non-specific directions on the final work product. And, if the setting was one where the emphasis was on interactive learning in a positive atmosphere, with good guidance from the trainer, then you probably would have enjoyed the experience and remembered the point of it back on the job.

It's for reasons like these that more and more trainers are using games to achieve their training and development objectives.

## What makes a game a game?

Before we review how and why to consider using games in your training, it's important to define our terms. What we're talking about when we say games runs the gamut from board games ("Fair Play," a distant relative of Monopoly, but with affirmative action EEO as the subject) and card games to computer simulations and even some types of role plays and in-basket exercises.

Complicating things further are the various game classifications. For example, the management development branch of the International Labor Office classified games by subject covered, type of competition required (between participants, between the actual self, or between the players and the environment), and how results are processed and fed back to the participants. Others classify games by nature of model (abstract or based on fact) and by purpose (for training or for research).

For the trainer's purposes, perhaps the most useful way of classifying games is whether or not they attempt to simulate reality. For understandable reasons, simulation games, ones where game rules and roles are drawn from real-life, tend not to have predictable outcomes. Non-simulation games, by contrast, involve temporary suspension of real-life rules and roles and the substitution of game rules and roles.

So what's the difference between a role play and a simulation? In a simulation, trainees generally respond to a situation by assuming a role using their own values, attitudes, beliefs and behavior patterns. For example, a trainee might be assigned the title of manager in a simulation where his or her subordinates are nonproductive. Although the label of manager would be assigned, the trainee would be given a part to act out as a manager. This type of role play is generally less effective than simulation in encouraging growth, because, unlike simulation, it doesn't promote abstract thinking and encourage players to react

with their *own* feelings. Pat Eady, principal in Experiential Learning Methods, Inc., Detroit, and developer of numerous games, points out that people don't learn from their experiences but rather by thinking about them. By their very nature, simulations induce reflection on seldom-analyzed situations.

*Experience is the teacher.* One of the advantages of simulation games, as opposed to several other interactive instructional design formats, is the extent to which they encourage trainees to explore their attitudes and values. It's very difficult, for example, to escape the feelings and emotions that accompany the tension between players of Value Options, a card game designed by New York City-based Mobley, Luciani and Associates. This game questions and explores values in light of their applicability to the choices day-to-day events force us to make. Played over a two- to four-hour period, Value Options has three critical stages. The first requires participants to upgrade the value cards they randomly receive. This is accomplished either by trading cards with other players or by trading and picking up cards from a large table. At the conclusion of this "upgrading" phase, each player holds at least two cards that reflect his or her values.

The second stage, called community building, requires individuals to form themselves into groups based on shared values. These groups then report on what commonality pulled them together.

The last and final stage, depolarization, requires each participant to pair up with someone holding a value that is in opposition to his or her own. These two individuals then work toward establishing a new value statement both parties can agree with. These stages crystallize the processes involved in making a value choice, recognizing its implications, and finding either common interests or compromise with participants holding different values.

*Games can help trainees grasp total course content.* An advantage of using a game at the beginning of a workshop is that it can give trainees a chance to experience the whole before discussing the parts. For example, starting a cross-cultural training session with a simulation game such as Bafa' Bafa', is a great way to prepare people, being transferred abroad, for the frustrations, joys and insights that come from contact with a foreign culture. Participants usually spend an hour playing

# Make sure your next training game meets these criteria

**W**hether you plan to buy a game or design one for your next training program, here are some desirable game characteristics you need to consider. These tips are excerpted from *Instructional Simulation Games* by Sivasailam Thiagarajan and Harold Stolovitch, Volume 12 of *The Instructional Design Library*, ©1978, Educational Technology Publications, Englewood Cliffs, NJ 07632. Although they are discussing simulation games, this list is a good guide to follow regardless of the kind of game you're looking for.

**Conflict.** Successful simulation games incorporate a fairly high degree of conflict. However, this conflict need not be in terms of cut-throat competition. Simulation games can effectively reflect the challenge inherent in using limited resources to achieve strategic outcomes.

**Constraints.** An ideal simulation game has the least number of constraints imposed on the player's behavior. Complicated and lengthy rules are seldom appreciated by players. The designer should attempt to simplify the rules of the game as much as possible and eliminate any superfluous constraints. If a game becomes too complex, it may be divided into two or more simpler ones. Or, a simplified version of the simulation game may be designed to introduce the basic play; more complex variants may be attempted later.

**Type of closure.** Effective simulation games end with a bang. Nothing is more anticlimactic than a simulation game that goes downhill and the players then quit. It should be possible for all players to "win." To be interesting and instructionally effective, a good simulation game has multiple criteria for measuring success.

**Contrivance and correspondence to reality.** The game should be realistic enough to involve the players. There should be sufficient correspondence between the game and the real-life it simulates so that it is obvious to the most naive player. But at the same time, there should be sufficient safeguards within the game to prevent permanent damage to a player's emotional health. To a large extent, the simulation game's success depends upon how easily the players get into and snap out of their roles.

**Replayability.** An effective simulation game should be replayable any number of times. This permits the players to try out alternative strategies and learn from the resulting differences in the game. Ideally, the game should lend itself to a number of minor variations to keep the players guessing.

**Time requirement.** A fast-paced simulation game can be very exciting. A slow-moving simulation which drags on forever can be deadly dull. The majority of players prefer simulation games of about 45 minutes duration.

**Equipment and materials.** The rate of adoption of a simulation game is inversely related to the quantity, complexity, and rigidity of equipment and materials. While commercial producers may profit in the short term by requiring players to buy specialized equipment or consumable materials, they lose in the long run through consumer rejection. There is a current trend to package simulation games as books that have perforated forms and tokens to be torn out because this increases trainer acceptance and reduces the price of the materials.

**Number of players.** Simulation games which involve small groups of three to five players are more flexible than the large (20-30) group versions. A small-group simulation game can be played by parallel groups in a large classroom, but a large-group game cannot be easily adapted for fewer players. Parallel play by a number of small groups has an additional instructional advantage: The groups can compare their experiences during debriefing.

**Purpose.** Successful simulation games lend themselves to a variety of purposes. An ideal simulation game should involve aspects of motivation, instruction, evaluation, and experimentation in a proper balance. The designer should keep these different purposes in mind and attempt to accommodate as many of them as possible. An ideal game also achieves a perfect balance among the elements of instruction, simulation, and gaming. If any of these elements is emphasized out of proportion, the result is likely to end up as a dull, confusing, and meaningless activity. **T**

the game and then up to five hours discussing how stereotypes are formed and perpetuated. Further discussion examines these stereotypes in a nonthreatening and constructive manner.

*Games can help "test" performance,* either before or after the learning experience. Playing a game at the beginning of a course allows the trainer to identify those skills which already exist and those which need to be strengthened. Playing the game at the end of the course enables the trainer to assess the instructional experience— how well the trainee can transfer training knowledge to on-the-job skills. Incidentally, game experts tend to agree that the closer a game's structure simulates reality the more likely and extensive the transfer of training.

What's the correlation between game success and work success? "The closer the situation is to real-life, the more valid an observation you can make," says Francine Foster, vice president of Creative Learning Systems, San Diego, and one of several game producers interviewed by TRAINING for this article. "A good simulation is a compressed reality. Typical behaviors can be highlighted because of the highly structured situation. This, then, becomes a powerful diagnostic tool when assessed by a qualified outside observer." The trick, though, is in making sure the trainees realize the objective. Lynn O'Mura, a product manager at Detroit-based Creative Universal, marketer of the well-known Performulations workshop that includes the use of Tinker Toys, believes the trainer or facilitator must not only monitor the rules, but also be aware of what the transfer relationship is between the game objective and the job skills— and help the trainees see that relationship, too. "People can't walk out after the game feeling the same way or doing the same thing they did when they walked in," she says. "If they do, it has only been an enjoyable experience for the trainees and a dog and pony show for the trainers."

## Starting and ending the game

Without the right beginning, even the best of training games is bound to end badly. For one thing, some people just don't like games and may not be willing to go all the way through one before learning the moral. Others find it hard to believe that playing with, let's say, Tinker Toys, can have anything useful to teach them about being better managers. The way you introduce and begin the game therefore, is crucially important.

Erica Keeps, Detroit-based consultant 'and long-time game user, offers some pointers, based on her experiences as corporate training manager for Hudson's, the Detroit-based retail chain. She utilized Performulations as part of a workshop on improving subordinates' performance. This simulation involves Tinker Toys and blindfolds— not typical management tools.

"What we found is that if the Tinker Toys are out on the table as people are coming into the classroom, someone will start playing with them. It's usually been so long since they've had an opportunity to play, that they really get into it. By the time the class starts, elaborate models have been built, usually with the help of the person sitting next to them. Then we announce the session by welcoming trainees to Tinker Toys-101. This breaks the ice."

Sometimes getting into a game involves carefully planned rounds or phases that not only allow role switching and the practice of different solutions to the problem, but also set some psychic distance between players. This is particularly important when the game is being used in a team-building effort and the group is feeling some tension or hostility just by being together in the same room.

Generally, effective games end logically—for example, when the time is up, the goal is achieved, the task is completed, or the competition is eliminated. Or do they? Many game users believe that the most important learning doesn't even start until the playing ends and the debriefing begins. Talking about what has just happened is crucially important, explains Foster, not only to bring the learning into consciousness, but also to take advantage of peer pressure toward positive change. Join, the name of one of Creative Learning Systems' games designed to boost effective teamwork, uses a two-step debriefing model. Debriefing guide cards are used to help each team debrief themselves and then the leader debriefs the class enmasse.

## What makes a game good?

Most people find games enjoyable because they provide relief from real-life pressures and usually contain an element of chance, the latter because of the game's structure and/or the unpredictability of other people's responses. Then, too, games users TRAINING contacted agree that the most enjoyable and effective games they've used tend 1) to be sophisticated enough to hold player interest and 2) not to be so detailed as to thwart natural response. (The structural elements of a successful game are covered in the accompanying boxed article.)

Frequently, good games have at least two agendas, the first being the rules, roles and goals that are announced to the participants. The other agenda, usually not mentioned to the trainees until the end of the debriefing, is the moral lesson the trainees are supposed to learn. Take, for example, a game called Desert Survival used at Hudsons. Players are told that their plane has crashed in the desert, that the only item on their agenda is to survive and that only certain items are available to help them. In the first part of the game, players must decide how to survive individually. Then the game is replayed with groups. In both cases, answers are compared with those of a group of experts. Pat Eady, developer of the game, has found that invariably teams "survive" better than do individuals.

The announced mission is, of course, simply to survive. The "hidden agenda"— the lesson participants invariably learn only at the end—is that teamwork pays off and boosts their chances of survival.

## When is a game not a game?

Like any other training medium, games are not a panacea. Used with the wrong group at the wrong time, a game may do more harm than good. Used appropriately, they can be an enjoyable and effective teaching technique. As Erica Keeps reminds us, though, it's important to remember not to expect a game to do much more than make participants aware of the consequences of their actions. A game, she points out, does not set up strategies for change. **T**

# The name of the game is Frame

by Hank Hutson and
Diane Dormant

As a trainer, you take pride in your resourcefulness. You adapt, borrow and create successful training activities to fit the needs of the moment. You customize training designs to meet shifting priorities and tight schedules. And where do you get these activities and designs? Often from your own past experiences. Every trainer has a personal kitbag of training tools developed over the years. A Framegame is just such a tool. And, since it is a highly effective, efficient, and versatile tool, we hope you'll add it to your kitbag.

Framegames are interactive training techniques that can be pressed into service without fuss or fanfare. Framegames provide structure which is open for your own content. You can use them in various ways — icebreaking, team-building, idea-generating, problem-solving — and you can easily load or insert content that is relevant to your training topic.

The concept of a Framegame is apparent in its two root words. A frame is an open structure made for enclosing something. In a Framegame, the open structure is a game. And, as in other games, there are rules, play-like rather than real-world events, and contested outcomes. But the "something" to be enclosed — i.e., the content of the Framegame — is left to you. Framegames are content-free until you put them to work. Bumper Clumper is an example.

You can readily see why Bumper Clumper is a Framegame. It has rules and it is a simulated rather than a real-world exercise. (Obviously, no one is going to derive a set of training directives from such a procedure alone.) Furthermore, Bumper Clumper is a contest, although not a very serious one. Individuals vie for "best" cards, and groups vie for the most amusing or profound slogan.

As for Bumper Clumper's "content-free" quality, note that the kicker statement "Training should..." could be written to suit any topic about which the participants have knowledge or opinions: "Affirmative action should...," "Management should...,"
"Our department should...," "Our competition should...." Participants should be reminded that negative statements are acceptable, too: "Affirmative action should *not*..." and so forth. The possibilities are as rich as your imagination and, in our experience as trainers, the outcomes are always lively.

Bumper Clumper, like most Framegames, is simple to load with content, easy to lead and highly flexible. It can be used at the beginning of a seminar to get things off to a roaring start, after lunch as a "wake-em-up," or at the end of a session for evaluation. Again, the frame and the game are there — all you need to do is plug in the content.

Let's look at another Framegame. R.S.V.P. is content-free, and it can serve many purposes. For example, it has been used to generate alternative solutions to world food problems, to management problems, to sales problems. It can be used to anticipate possible results of proposed courses of action. Because of its anonymous procedures, people can "green light" or "bad mouth" in relative safety.

---

## Bumper Clumper

**Possible Uses:** Icebreaker; initial focus on training topic; perception check of attitudes and opinions; evaluation exercise

**Participants:** Desired minimum of 15 (could be as few as 5, as many as 200)

**Time:** 20-40 minutes (depends on number of participants)

**Materials:** Index cards (about 5 per participant), flip chart paper, markers, masking tape

**Rules:**
1. Pass out 3 cards to each person.
2. Instruct participants to write one opinion on each card to complete a statement. (Example: "Training should...") These can be opinions held by the participants themselves or by others.
3. Take up cards and mix with handwritten "sweeteners." (To make the procedure failsafe as well as to enrich it, prepare extra cards ahead of time, twice as many as there are participants.)
4. Redistribute 3 cards to each person. Instruct them to prioritize cards in order of their perceived importance. Meanwhile, the trainer should arrange all leftover cards, right side up, on a large table.
5. Instruct them to improve their hands to better represent their own thinking by exchanging cards with those on the table. They must always have a total of 3 cards.
6. Instruct them to improve their hands by exchanging cards with each other. (Optional rule: participants must hold hands to make exchanges, and once they take a hand they have to make an exchange.) Participants should try to see as many cards as they can.
7. Instruct them to form coalitions. Say, "Now you know something about what others value with regard to the topic. Let's see if you can find kindred souls who will agree as a group on a total of 3 cards, discarding all others."
8. Ask each coalition to make a "bumper sticker" (using markers and chart paper) based upon the 3 chosen cards which communicate the group's position.
9. Ask them to join in a large group show-and-tell. Each coalition should select a representative to read the 3 cards and to present the bumper sticker to be displayed on the wall. Discussion or reactions may follow.

---

Reprinted from TRAINING, April 1981

Another value of R.S.V.P. is to provide a mechanism for people to solicit responses to a question or problem of specific concern to them. An alternative strategy is for the group or the trainer to select a set of general problems (perhaps five) ahead of time and to write these on the envelopes for each table. All tables then are working on the same set of questions, and fruitful large group discussion can follow.

Framegames are easy to use and they can result in motivating, effective sessions. Framegames are not, nor are they meant to be, heavyweight techniques to be taken very seriously. But they are once-over-lightly exercises that can serve several purposes, not the least of which is to have fun. (What's wrong with that?) Perhaps the best use of a Framegame is to set the stage for another training technique that is designed to carry a more substantial instructional or decision-making load.

Remember to keep Framegames in proper perspective. As the facilitator, be ready to change a rule or invent a procedure on the spot. Be flexible about time. Don't let things bog down.

The Great Debate, like other Framegames, has been used in many settings with a wide range of topics and dimensions. At TRAINING '79, we used it as a concluding activity for our Framegame workshop. The topic was TRAINING '79 itself and we used four dimensions: facilities, ideas/content, people and New York. You can imagine the foolishness sparked by that fourth dimension, but the other three dimensions provided a forum for some useful evaluation of the conference.

If you try them, you'll like them—and want more. A good source for additional Framegames is Harold D. Stolovitch and Sivasailam Thiagarajan's book, *Framegames*, published by Educational Technology, Englewood Cliffs, NJ. Also, once you have the notion of a content-free frame, you begin to look at all structured activities a bit differently. For example, John E. Jones and J. William Pfeiffer's two series— the *Annual Handbook for Group Facilitators* and *A Handbook of Structured Experiences for Human Relations Training*, published by University Associates, La Jolla, CA— are rich in activities which can be simplified and adapted to new content. **T**

## R.S.V.P.

**Possible Uses:** Way to elicit problems or solutions in a group with common concerns or expertise.

**Participants:** Any number of small groups formed into circles (5 persons in each group is a workable number)

**Time:** 20-40 minutes

**Materials:** Index cards (5 per participant), letter envelopes (1 each)

**Rules:**
1. Pass out blank envelope and 5 index cards to each person.
2. Ask each person to make a personal mark on the back of the envelope (e.g., a letter or squiggle) for later identification.
3. Say, "On the front of the envelope, write a question or pose a problem for which you want an answer or solution." (Of course, the question or problem should lie within the training topic selected— the content of this Framegame.)
4. Instruct them to pass the envelopes to the right.
5. Say, "Read the envelope, write an answer or solution on an index card, and insert the card in the envelope."
6. Instruct them to pass envelopes to the right again and, without looking at the card in the envelope, repeat step 5.
7. Continue the process (Steps 5 and 6) for several turns.
8. Instruct them to place the envelopes face down in the center of the table and retrieve their own.
9. Ask them to read and prioritize the cards.
10. Ask them to take turns sharing favorite responses, adding new thoughts, posing additional questions.

## The Great Debate

**Possible Uses:** Final evaluative event in a lengthy training session; a safe way to elicit negative as well as positive comments.

**Participants:** At least 18 preferred (as few as 12 or as many as 75 possible)

**Time:** 20-30 minutes

**Materials:** As many index cards as persons. Sets of 6 cards are marked with plus or minus in 3 different colors. (Example: One card marked with a red plus, one card with a red minus, one card with a blue plus, etc.)

**Rules:**
1. Pass out one card to each person.
2. Explain procedure: "You are going to debate such-and-such along three dimensions. Those of you who have a red plus on your card will go to one corner of the room and list the positive aspects of the topic along the dimension indicated for red. Those who have a red minus will go to a different corner and list the negative aspects of the same dimension. (The same for the blue dimension, etc.)"
3. Write dimensions and related colors on a flip chart or blackboard.
4. Allow 10 minutes for preparation, then ask each of the groups to choose a spokesperson.
5. After all have returned to their seats (or seated themselves with their debate group), call for the debate. Ask for the negative side of a dimension first, the positive second. Each spokesperson makes a one-minute presentation. End with the safest and/or most fun dimension.

# Prompt cards end those transparency fumbles

by Pat Lynch

**M**ost trainers will agree that it's awkward to try and follow an instructor's guide while manipulating a set of transparencies. Yet it may seem necessary for an instructor who is unfamiliar with the lesson content. It can be equally frustrating for the student who is counting on a stimulating class session but who must wait while the instructor refers to a guide for directions on what to do or say next. While the instructor is determining a path of action, the captive student must decide whether to sit patiently and concentrate on the subject matter just covered or dream about an upcoming vacation.

Sure, it's easy to criticize. But what can I offer as a substitute? How do I plan to keep the class running smoothly without a guide? Actually, I *do* have an alternative to that cumbersome guide. They're called prompt cards. Combined with overhead transparencies, they will help you be a more effective trainer by giving you quick access to a linear path through your materials.

The cards themselves are inserted between the overhead transparencies, thus eliminating the need for an instructor's guide. Prompt cards are prepared on .010 or 10-point card stock and are cut to the same outside dimensions as your overhead transparency frames, about 11¾ by 10¾ inches. The exact dimensions may vary, depending upon the size of your particular frames.

The cards carry directions for the instructor and the student for all items to be covered in the class other than the comments to be made about the overhead transparencies themselves. Any comments that you, as an instructor, wish to make about the transparencies can be noted on the frames (see Figure 1).

Figure 1 shows that the instructor plans to cover advantages and disadvantages; therefore, a prompt card is unnecessary. Likewise, if the instructor is covering only information about a *number of transparencies* and not other materials (handouts, quizzes, etc.), there would be no need to use prompt cards at all.

When preparing the cards, it's helpful to divide them into two sections. The left side of the card carries the directions that apply to the instructor; the right side of the card carries the directions that apply to the student (see Figure 2).

Placement of the directions on the card is critical. You'll notice, in fact, that the directions are placed in a staggered arrangement (see Figure 2). This makes it easy to follow a step-by-step process when presenting the materials.

The number of directions or instructions shown on each card depends on the complexity of the material that must be covered. In cases where there is a great deal of detail, you may need to staple several cards together. Then, again, there may be times when only a few instructions are necessary.

To keep the cards in the proper order, cross-reference the card with the preceding transparency (see Figure 3). You'll notice that the prompt card carries a numeral (1) plus the letter (A); the overhead transparency carries its numeral (1) plus the (1A) to designate that a prompt card follows.

By cross-referencing, you'll quickly be able to tell if a prompt card is missing. If the overhead transparency carries a numeral plus a numeral and letter, you'll know that a prompt card should follow.

In essence, your final presentation might be numbered, in part, like the sample set in Figure 4.

One final tip: If you use prompt cards for different programs, place the initials or the acronym for the program in the lower right-hand corner of the card (see Figure 5). If revisions must be made on the card, you'll know immediately where to reinsert the card after revision.

You may, of course, design your own format for the cards. And you may find other applications for the cards, too. For example, you may wish to use them in your meetings or for a public speaking engagement or anywhere you plan to use overhead transparencies. In any event, I think you'll find that prompt cards and overhead transparencies are a winning combination and one that frees you from that cumbersome instructor's guide. **T**

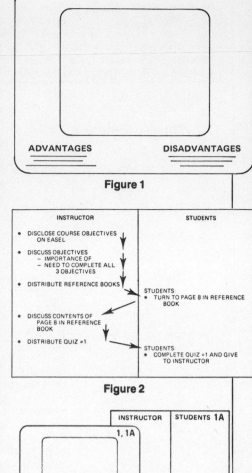

**Figure 1**

**Figure 2**

**Figure 3**

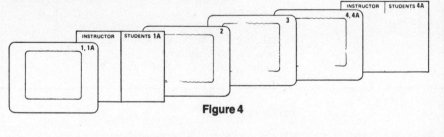

**Figure 4**

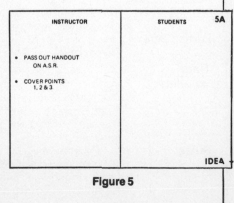

**Figure 5**

Reprinted from TRAINING, June 1979

Developed from the scientific research on learning behavior in older adults, the Discovery method is probably the most carefully studied innovation in learning technology since programmed instruction

# The discovery method

by R.M. Belbin

The Discovery method refers to a style of teaching that allows the pupil to learn by finding out principles and relationships for himself. It stands in contrast with the traditional style in which the pupil memorizes what he has read in his books or what the teacher has taught him.

The trouble with general phrases like "finding out for oneself" is that they can be quite misleading. The Discovery method is not at all like "sitting-by-Nellie," for example.

## Discovery is planned method

First of all, the Discovery method is a planned method. Its success depends on how well the training designer thinks out the progression of problems which the trainee is required to solve, relates this progression to the capacity of the trainee, and ensures that learning is based on intrinsic rather than extrinsic factors.

By intrinsic one means that the keys to progression in learning are provided within the immediate situation. The trainee does not need to rely on previous knowledge and experience, nor does he depend on outside assistance (i.e., extrinsic factors). The teacher may help the trainee, but only if he requests help. It is better that he should use the intrinsic information rather than that he should be shown or told.

With the trainee finding out through a planned progression of steps and no longer relying on the teacher, it might be said that the Discovery method bears a closer comparison with programed learning than with "sitting-by-Nellie." But programed learning is a very broad term. It usually refers to a way of presenting information bit by bit to trainees and then testing them regularly to help them to consolidate what they have learned. This has nothing in common with the Discovery method. A systematic presentation of instructions and information does not accord with the idea of Discovery learning.

But while programed learning is sometimes operated along lines that are diametrically opposed to Discovery learning, it can also be designed to incorporate the basic concept of a Discovery learning approach. The essential differences lie in the type of sequences chosen and in the type of problems posed.

In applying the Discovery method, the initial stage is demanding. One requires a good deal more than a listing and analysis of all that has to be learned. First the training designer has to identify the crucial concepts and remove all the nonessentials so that the training material can be appreciated in its most simple form.

But the second stage is the most difficult: the training designer has to get inside the learning situation and decide what are the principal obstacles to understanding. It is very hard to envisage these obstacles in advance with any accuracy. The more the expert knows, the more out of touch he is liable to be with the learning problems of those who are starting from scratch. The training designer must observe the problems of trainees and understand the reasons behind them.

Step three is the stage at which our training designs are fashioned. There are innumerable alternatives. The selection of our method will depend on the information we have gathered about trainee problems and on our knowledge of learning generally.

Stage four is the testing of the program with real trainees in pilot trials. It is more than a formality. I can hardly remember a case in our training program where this has not led to some modifications or additional finishing touches.

Let's take a look at a concrete illustration of the Discovery method. To find out the potential of the Discovery method for retraining older workers in industry, the Organisation for Economic Cooperation and Development, which is based in Paris, sponsored an industrial experiment in four countries. British Railways provided the project in the United Kingdom. Other projects were carried out in Sweden, Austria and the United States.

The demonstration project in the United Kingdom involved the training of 83 steam locomotive drivers (aged between 29 and 62) in electrical theory in preparation for their transfer to driving diesel-electric trains. Forty-nine of the drivers were "older" learners aged 40 and over, of whom 31 were trained by Discovery methods and 18 by traditional methods; then we had a group of 34 under-40s, with 16 trained by Discovery methods and 18 trained by traditional methods.

The idea was to give the trainees controlled experience so as

Reprinted from TRAINING, November 1973

to allow them to discover principles of electricity for themselves. Trainees worked in pairs. I will confine the illustration to one of the test boards they used, Board Three. This carried a battery, an ammeter, a switch, three pairs of motors connected as three series pairs in parallel, isolating links for each pair of motors and the accessory circuitry to simulate the elements of the power circuit of a diesel-electric locomotive. The ammeter was calibrated to simulate current consumption in an actual locomotive. In brief, we had motors, which we could isolate, linked in a circuit with an ammeter to give us current readings.

The trainees were directed by the instructor to make various changes to the apparatus and to make observations of the consequent meter-readings and of the behavior of the apparatus. From time to time conclusions had to be drawn and some simple statement completed. The instructor was available to help out with difficulties, but he gave no information. His response to questions was usually to ask a further question, to rephrase his directions and so on.

From this set-up, the trainees could "discover" a number of things:

- Closing the switch caused all the motors to rotate.
- Isolating one pair of motors caused a current fall of one-third.
- Isolating two pairs caused a current fall of two-thirds.
- Shorting out one motor of a pair caused a spectacular overload.
- Isolating the pair, including the failed motor, ensured a return to safe working at reduced power.
- Attaching the magnetically operated contacts of the adjacent Board Two to appropriate points in the power circuit of Board Three enabled the motors to be stopped or started by an independent control system.

This helped the trainees to understand the principles which were derived from experience of the events. When you conduct one of these sessions, you can see that learning is something qualitatively different from what we normally find in the classroom. The trainees working in pairs on the tasks tended to engage in excited discussion. They confirmed each other's readings, checked and re-checked the behavior of the equipment, argued and pointed out discoveries, some quite simple ones.

Many of their comments were illuminating in that they revealed a complete lack of electrical knowledge, like: "I never realized the current had to go all the way round," and, "I now see why you have two wires in a piece of cord." Not exactly a great discovery, perhaps, but pretty important by their standards.

Although we did not conduct any formal interviewing to determine whether the trainees felt they were learning more under this method, we did hear a lot of appreciative remarks, like, "If kids do things this way at school, they ought to learn fast." An older man said, "Less of a strain than watching the blackboard; you take your own time." This was an interesting remark, because a common complaint was that "the time went like lightning." I think the method created an infectious enthusiasm about learning. It even spread to two instructors who were not invited but who came in to observe the new methods. They said, "A pity all the learning couldn't be done this way."

As to results, briefly, the Discovery group trainees learned more, and did so in half the time. The part of the electrical program which was relevant to our examination was covered in sessions lasting 90 minutes on the traditional program and 45 minutes with our new experimental Discovery program.

### 'Learning' judged by tests

We judged "learning" by giving trainees three tests at the end of their three weeks' training. The first dealt with simple and straight-forward electrical aspects of diesel-electric locomotives: to score a mark, the trainee had to give the correct electrical term in answer to the problem posed. The second test was concerned with basic knowledge of electrical circuits and of their properties: this time the trainee was presented with questions offering a choice of answers, one of which he had to select. The third test dealt with the application of electrical knowledge in the diagnosis of electrical faults: here the testing involved a combination of the other two testing techniques.

---

**In the Swedish project,** the job of scribing was selected for the experimental study. Scribing is a part of the manufacture of, usually, single metal objects in which a worker transfers the object's profile to a metal blank with a sharp tool. The trainees chosen for the study were taken from a larger group undertaking a basic course for metal industry employees in two training centers. In all, 45 trainees participated in the project, 32 of them in two control groups, one trained by an instructor and the other by a programed self-study course. The remaining 13 were trained by the Discovery method. All of the trainees were divided into groups of younger workers under 30 years of age and of older workers 40 and older and into groups of more and of less than average ability as measured by a special test. The experiment ran for a week. Both control groups received three days of instruction, the Discovery group two days. On the fourth day a reproduction test was given in which all trainees scribed a nonadjustable spanner wrench from a drawing similar to one they had drawn under instruction. On the final day another test was given in which five new items were scribed. This final test was completed at only one of the training centers. The best results in the reproduction test were achieved by the younger workers in the able group who had learned through programed instruction and by the older workers in the able group who had been taught by instructor. Among the other groups, those who had been taught by instructor fared better than those who had learned by the other methods. The picture changed, however, when the criterion of learning changed to refer to comprehension, or the ability to apply knowledge to a different task. In the final test, the instructor-trained groups lost their advantage and were displaced by those trained by Discovery methods. These results suggest that the "best" training method may depend on the nature of the test and on the age and level of ability of trainees.

It is true that the range of existing knowledge stretched from complete ignorance to a reasonable understanding. But most of the trainees had only an elementary appreciation of the subject. The test scores naturally show a spread, but we are most interested in the media score. Any difference here is much less likely to be affected by differences in the individual composition of the groups. On all three tests, those trained by Discovery methods showed improvement except for the second electrical test with the younger men, where the results are similar to those obtained by the control group. In principle, these general improvements in scores might have been due to chance, but the probabilities were calculated and reveal that the improvement was real.

The fact that the older trainees in the Discovery group exceeded the performance of the younger trainees in the traditional group on one test and were at least as good on the other two tests does not mean that age is not all that important. The point is that although older trainees generally don't do as well in training programs, the use of a method of training that suits them compensates for the loss of learning efficiency that is due to age. Given a suitable method, the old will do as well as the young trained by that method and could do better than the young trained by traditional methods.

## Role of 'Hawthorne' effect

The evidence seems encouraging, but it may raise the question of whether the superior results gained by the Discovery group could not be attributed to the "Hawthorne" effect. The answer would appear to be no, for our experiments were not like introducing a new and stimulating set of conditions to a stable working group. For each of our trainee groups, these were the *only* conditions they knew. All the fuss surrounding the experiment may have stimulated them into doing well, but it could have stimulated the control group too. I don't think it was a question of novelty and of one group being insufficiently stim-

ulated. They were all keen to learn.

The Swedish project illustrates another major advantage of the Discovery method. Here we had 45 trainees, a fair proportion of whom were lumberjacks from the North. The project was concerned with scribing (being part of a general course in machine shop engineering). Scribing is the process of "scratching" the profile of a part to be cut on a metal blank. The work has of course to be done very accurately; it is a case of reading and interpreting drawing and using technique and understanding in choosing the right procedures.

## Training is task-centered

Trainees were taught to scribe a spanner from a drawing. Three different groups were trained by a traditional instruction method, a programed instruction method, and a Discovery method. On the intermediate test they had to scribe the same spanner without any help; in this the traditional instruction group figured best. But in the final transfer test at a later date, the trainees had to scribe new figures from drawings. This time the Discovery group did best, both in speed of performance and quality of work. I mention this case to illustrate the advantages of thinking about job training rather than task training. A great deal of

training in industry is task-centered rather than job-centered. This is a typical problem in industry. We train people in task A, but eventually we want them to do task B. So we devise a training program round task B only to find that task B is shortly to be transformed into task C. If trainees become proficient in task A, does it mean that they will be able to switch to tasks B and C when they come along? Should we measure effectiveness of training by how well they can do task A or by how easily they can transfer to tasks B and C?

It is quite possible that the immediate signs of progress in training are misleading. It is easy for a trainee to go through all the correct motions under close guidance, just as it is for him to give some verbal indication that he has "understood." But once he is on his own, there may be a real drop in his performance, especially if the circumstances are not quite the same as in training.

Industry is continually running up against people who progress in training but who disappoint afterwards. It can be quite alarming. This reminds me of a training scheme for process operators in a chemical factory that I heard about. All the trainees were shown charts of the process, had it all explained to them, and then were tested for their knowledge of

---

**The project in Austria** was hampered by a number of limiting factors. It took place at a training school operated by the Ministry of Social Affairs for men, especially building workers, who were out of work during the winter months, when the severe weather ordinarily causes a cessation of building work. The plan was to run two consecutive five-week courses with about 20 trainees in each course, of whom half would be over and half under 40. The trainees would be matched in terms of aptitude and intelligence. Actually, the weather was unusually warm during the winter of the project so that fewer men applied for the course and more dropped out than expected. The need to fit both courses into the winter season meant there would be no interval or breathing space between the courses. Only three days were available for formulating the design of the discovery program, which had to be applied without a manual and so was dependent on oral communications and notes. In the circumstances, the performance of the Discovery trainees showed a "fair measure of achievement." The Discovery method did not produce any evident gains in the practical work of the course, but it did produce significant gains on the theoretical parts of the final examination. It was the theoretical side which had posed the greatest problems for the older trainees. The improvement may be characterized as having raised the level of the poorer performers. The practical implication of this would indicate that with appropriate training methods, trainees can be brought into programs for which they would otherwise be thought unsuitable.

procedures. Shortly after one of them went onto the job, one of the vats exploded. It could have led to a serious accident. Apparently, he had been told never to let the thermometer reading rise above a certain critical figure. He removed the thermometer just in time!

## Can develop understanding

How can one tell in advance that a trainee is so completely lacking in understanding? Industry is often under pressure to accept people for training who might not be regarded as ideal material, especially in the case of redeployment within a firm following a no-redundancy agreement. But understanding can still be developed. However, this question of how you assess whether a trainee has understood is vitally important. If there is too much direct

guidance and instruction during training, it becomes very difficult to ascertain whether a trainee has understood or not, since his actions will broadly follow his instructions.

If you use the Discovery method from the outset, however, it can become evident whether a trainee is understanding. A feature of this method is that it gives little direct instruction. Even though the trainee uses cues, hints and the answers he receives in relation to his questions, he is still short of information. Any lack of competence to grapple with the task set is soon revealed, because he will have difficulty in proceeding. He is so dependent on his own resources that there is no way in which he can cover up.

If we assume, then, that Discovery learning works, how can we account for its advantages? First,

I should define *where* it has advantages before I say *why*. The evidence suggests that the best results relative to other methods are achieved with middle-aged and older learners and on tasks that demand the development of concepts and understanding. It would seem that in this field adults don't learn too well by passively following what they are told.

Secondly, adults are often handicapped in learning by the difficulty they experience in eradicating errors and misconceptions. But because the Discovery method reveals the trainee's progress and level of understanding to the instructor, his performance is easier to control.

Thirdly, learning from experience is easier for adults than learning from words; there is no stress on memorizing, hence this sort of learning is remembered.

There are, of course, disadvantages. A Discovery program needs to be designed for a limited group if it is to offer an appropriate challenge.

Another point is that because the Discovery approach is more concerned with fundamental understanding, the benefits are less evident in the short-term than in the long-term.

The Discovery method is a means of teaching which avoids expository instruction. The trainee is presented with tasks which engage him in the search for and selection of clues on how to proceed. The effectiveness of the Discovery method depends on the design of these tasks which have two aims: to provide an intrinsic means for unassisted learning and to provide the experience upon which insight into key relationships can be developed. If the method has something to contribute to industrial training, it does because, in our belief, it takes account of the natural way in which man uses his learning capacity. ∎

---

**In the United States,** color and number cues on machines in the machine shop were part of the training in the project which was set up in New Haven, Connecticut, under the auspices of Community Progress, Inc., in their West Street Skill Center. The Skill Center was well equipped and comprised a machine shop, electrical section and a data-processing room. Trainees were assigned to one of the three specialist courses for a period of 26 weeks, after which an attempt was made to place them in a job appropriate to their training. Because there wasn't enough time to prepare material applying the new experimental methods to the three full courses, appreciation courses were arranged for the trainees outside their main work. Four days a week were spent in the principal training activity and the fifth day in a short course in another training activity. The whole program was designed to operate in two stages of six months each separated by a one-month gap. In all, 242 trainees divided into 21 separate groups participated in the three different areas of activity. The outcome of the demonstration indicates that application of the Discovery method improved performance scores in both machine-shop work and data processing by between a third and a half. The electrical results did not reach the same measure of superiority as in the other two training areas, perhaps because the instructor approached his subject in a way that was singularly free from the shortcomings of the traditional method. As to the trainees themselves, within a month of the conclusion of the first stage, over 75 percent of the trainees completing the program had found suitable employment, most of them in jobs with better pay and prospects than they had ever had before. Three months later 70 percent were still on the job. Informal estimates of those working in the State Department Employment Service had predicted an ultimate placement of not more than 20 percent.

Pictures definitely seem to help in
training—and they need not "move"

# Using pictures improves training

If people are to be trained in some manipulative procedure, such as assembling components, it is customary to show them how the job should be done and combine that demonstration with actual practice by the trainees. If there are many trainees, it is generally most efficient to provide the demonstration in some standard, prepackaged form, such as a movie or pictorial book. The movie or book should, of course, be effective, that is, it should yield mastery of the assembly task in minimal training time and with minimum assistance from instructors.

Which demonstration materials are effective? The Human Resources Research Organization conducted an experiment for the Army to establish some effective general methods for developing and using demonstration materials. HumRRO used several versions of sound motion pictures and a pictorial programed book to compare methods of instruction on the disassembly and assembly of the M-73 machine gun.

An army training film was condensed to include only the segments that actually demonstrated disassembly and assembly. A revised version of the film was developed by showing it to novices, step by step, as they performed the task, and modifying the portions that viewers found difficult. Both the original and the revised films were adapted for showing either step by step or as a whole. The effect of showing the film twice (rather than only once) before practice was also explored. An optional introduction incorporating the "implosion" technique (as opposed to the standard Army introduction of naming the parts) was also prepared. The implosion technique is one in which the parts appear to pop suddenly into place, one at a time, to form the complete assembly.

These four variables, and all combinations, were compared experimentally with one group of 96 trainees to assess their effects and any interaction of these treatments. Another 48 trainees used a comparable pictorial book program which had been developed previously. All subjects practiced until they achieved one perfect trial without assistance.

When instruction began for subjects in the film groups, they first saw a two-minute introductory film. Then the subjects who were to view the film twice would view the whole disassembly/assembly film demonstration without interruption; then (a) the subjects in the subgroups who were to view continuously would have a second uninterrupted viewing, then their first practice trial, and (b) the subjects in the subgroups who were to view it step by step would have another viewing, interrupted for practice of each step, which constituted the first practice trial. The subjects who were to view the film once would view it continuously or step by step. With the book treatment, subjects did not see any film and used the book on their practice trial.

After the first practice trial, subsequent trials were run under test conditions (without the film, but with assists as required). Under the book conditions, however, if the subject needed an assist, he was allowed to continue using the book for that trial, since after his assist it would be impossible for him to meet the criterion on that trial. This practice seemed closest to normal classroom conditions, since the book can be managed on an individual basis, while movies are generally shown to the whole group.

During all trials, the experimenter provided correction or assistance only when the subject's

**Pictures definitely seem to help training, but, a study for the military finds, they need not be in moving form, such as films or videotape. Just how the pictorial techniques should be employed depends on management factors, volume costs and individual differences in trainees.**

performance indicated a need for such help. The contingencies for providing correction or aid were as follows: If the subject began to do something dangerous, or directly asked for help, an assist was provided immediately. If he was looking at or manipulating something relevant, something which might eventually lead to success, a rather long interval of several seconds would be allowed before the experimenter intervened. But if the subject were looking at or manipulating something irrelevant, or if he apparently gave up, only a few seconds would be allowed. The subjects did not seem to seek unnecessary help, since their objective was to perform the whole task without error and without aid, after which they would be released from the experiment.

The HumRRO researchers drew the following conclusions:

(1) The reliability of communication of a demonstration film may be increased appreciably by careful tryouts with novices and subsequent film revision. In a revision, the thoroughness that may be warranted will depend on how many trainees are expected, and other situational factors.

(2) When students see a film one step at a time as they perform the task, they require fewer assists on the first trial than students who see the film without interruption, yet on the second trial they need more assists (as the step-by-step guidance is withdrawn) than those who have had no such guidance. There is thus no evidence that such guidance (when assistance is available) saves time, and certain factors inherent in the guidance method place a limit on how rapidly a person can demonstrate mastery.

(3) The revised film, shown step by step, virtually eliminates the need for assists on the first trial. Thereafter, by appropriate methods of showing the film, assistance may be kept to a minimum.

(4) If the continuous viewing method is chosen in a situation where step-by-step viewing is considered especially awkward, an extra showing of the film at the start is likely to be worthwhile, in terms of both time and assists. (This is *not* true for step-by-step viewing.) If the film is developed like the revised one, many trainees will need no assists at all, especially if the film is shown twice.

(5) The pictorial book

**Four viewing methods: Army studies pictorial techniques in effort to improve training.**

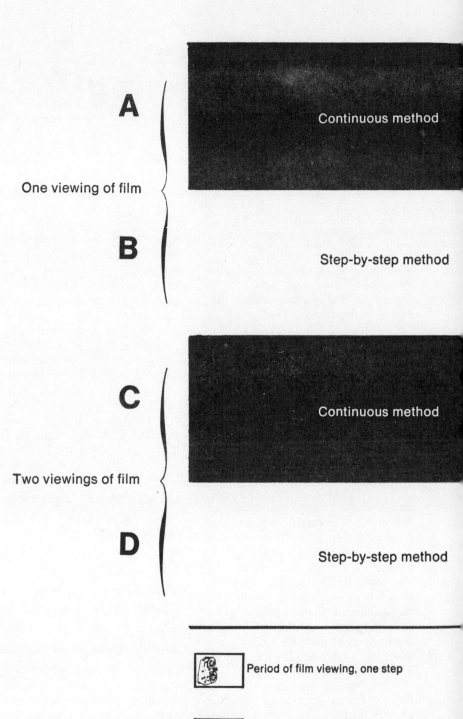

A

One viewing of film

Continuous method

B

Step-by-step method

C

Two viewings of film

Continuous method

D

Step-by-step method

Period of film viewing, one step

Period of hands-on practice, one step

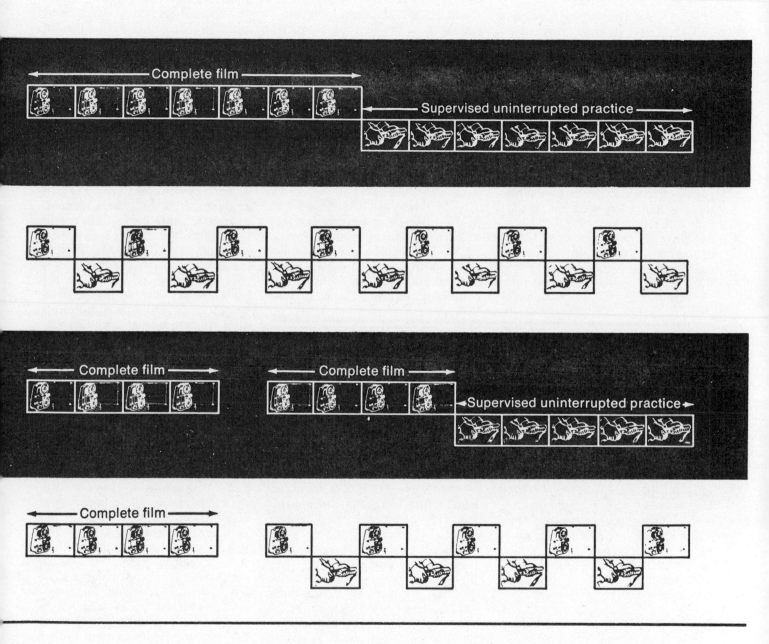

program does a very creditable training job, despite its lack of audio and its inability to represent motion; it was roughly comparable to the movie programs in time required, and comparable to the Army program in number of assists (but requiring significantly more assists than the revised film program).

(6) Developing a film through tryouts and revisions is promising as a research method, and in the experiment the development of the revised film yielded a coherent set of principles for producing demonstration films.

With reasonable extrapolation, the results of the experiment can be related to the sorts of problems likely to be encountered in designing practical training programs. Perhaps the first notable trend is that there were no significant differences between the methods (overall main effects) in terms of total instructional time required (including any demonstrations). All the training conditions insured that the great bulk of the student's

each step before proceeding with the next step. By having a few seconds of black leader between steps, this technique can be used conveniently with conventional projectors. Probably one would want a second showing step by step to reduce need for assistance but allowing the more able soldiers to anticipate (work somewhat ahead of) the demonstration, thus making it a self-test for them. If only an occasional assist were needed, it could perhaps be supplied by another student who understood the demonstration. The difficulty of the particular task would determine both the number of trials needed and various other details of the training procedure, matters which should therefore be worked out by trying each program with students.

There is a price to be paid for using step-by-step viewing and for developing a film empirically. The step-by-step presentation appears to start everyone at a fairly elementary level of learning; this is perhaps the best ex-

rapid, businesslike progress for all students, rather than with the ultimate in efficiency.

In some situations the step-by-step method may be considered needlessly clumsy. By use of a carefully revised film, one may still train with a rather small amount of assistance. When the film is viewed continuously, an extra viewing seems to save about as much practice time as it takes to show the film, at the same time sharply reducing the need for assists, though the extra viewing appeared to be a waste of time for the step-by-step viewers. The step-by-step method seems to be very useful in film development, even if the final film is shown without interruption.

The pictorial book program produced mastery in amounts of time generally comparable to those for the film conditions, and the number of assists was roughly comparable to that for the Army film conditions. Apparently, the disadvantage of the book in not presenting moving stimuli or coordinated audio directions is compensated for by its natural advantage of flexibility in use: (a) The subject is not forced to view a presentation for a fixed period whether he needs it or not; (b) he can review at will the points he is unsure of; (c) often he can take a book program to the job in situations where a movie would be awkward or impossible.

---

"The reliability of communication of a demonstration film may be increased appreciably by careful tryouts and subsequent revision. In a revision, the thoroughness that may be warranted will depend on the number of trainees and other factors."

---

time was spent on relevant activities; for instance, the Army film was severely edited, and only the actual demonstrations of the relevant task were retained. The assistance of the experimenter would insure that no great time periods were lost as a result of confusion. The data for assists, however, show many sharp differences, and the level of assistance given under many treatment categories is clearly excessive in relation to the general availability of instructors.

The very low number of assists when the revised film is viewed step by step demonstrates how reliably one can communicate this kind of skill by a demonstration film. In classroom practice, one might show a film step by step by allowing everyone to finish

planation of the fact that the step-by-step viewers did not seem to benefit from an extra viewing of the film before the step-by-step viewing (either in practice time scores or assist scores), since what they learned during the first viewing would duplicate the elementary sort of learning in the subsequent step-by-step viewing.

By the nature of the step-by-step treatment, such guidance does not allow a student to demonstrate his competence on that practice trial. On the other hand, step-by-step demonstration does apparently allow low ability subjects to learn tasks which by other training methods would be impossible. And in the perspective of general training practice, one generally is most concerned with

Although the revised film generally required fewer assists than the picture-guide book, especially under the step-by-step or the two-viewings treatment, the film was subject to a much more extensive development than the book, which was produced under a stricter production schedule. The pictorial programed books seem likely to become increasingly important as their techniques become further developed and for situations in which their unique advantages of flexibility are at a premium. **T**

*This article was prepared from the HumRRO Technical Report 71-12, "Comparison of Pictorial Techniques for Guiding Performance During Training," by Elmo E. Miller.*

If you've been encountering resistance to this technique, try this nine-step approach

# Making role plays pay off in training

by William F. Molloy

There is hardly a trainer today who hasn't been involved in a role-play situation. Yet, despite its initial popularity, role playing has become a threatening concept for many people. Even those who have never actually participated are frightened by stories of negative experiences. By developing a structured success format with controlled feedback, however, you can reduce initial resistance to role plays and make most effective use of this training tactic.

Role playing as a human relations training method came into its own when Dr. Jacob L. Moreno first introduced the methods of "psychodrama" and "sociodrama" prior to World War II.

Role plays subsequently were used to improve human interaction skills by having individuals carry out simulated discussions or assume a specified character whose behavior was to be imitated. It did not take long for the approach to spread to a variety of learning environments in an attempt to improve a wide range of human interactions.

But while the effectiveness of this training technique has not been seriously challenged, many role-play situations suffer from a lack of sound planning and preparation. This is a significant factor in the negative impact of role-play training on most supervisors and managers. In role play, they find themselves placed in situations in which they see themselves as doomed to failure and exposed to unbridled criticism from others. Such experiences can create a high anxiety level which not only inhibits learning, but seriously endangers an individual's self-esteem.

This need not be the case. An examination of present role-play approaches reveals several common characteristics which could be changed to produce a more meaningful learning experience. The key evolution is toward the development and practice of a specific skill. Here is a nine-step approach for making your role plays effective skill practices.

## 1 Start with specific behavioral objectives

Most role plays tend to be free-flowing, directionless discussions. Participants usually are given some general background information and asked to act out a solution to a problem, but no clear guidelines are provided on exactly what to say or do.

To target your role plays on specific skills, you should give learners specific behavioral objectives. One useful form is a progression of "critical steps." Participants are directed to conduct their discussion following a predetermined series of actions, a format which assures they will adhere to useful skill-building procedures within the framework of a realistic discussion.

Careful focus on a specific set of behavioral objectives reduces the anxiety level of participants, since they know exactly what is expected of them. It also probably represents a definite contrast to their past role-play experiences. One of the few studies conducted on role plays indicates that players tend to focus their observations more on their personal feelings than on the content of the situation. To alleviate this anxiety, focus participants' attention on the specific set of behavioral guidelines.

When participants must concentrate, not on their personal or professional anxieties, but rather on following critical steps in a logical sequence, they will be more confident in their actions—they will know what to do.

## 2 Make use of a positive model

Traditional role plays often do not provide participants with a complete understanding of the desired behavior. Without a model to follow, role players not surprisingly can be expected to do poorly and receive negative feedback. Effective skill practice, on the other hand, should be preceded by a positive model of the desired behavior. For example, participants might view a short modeling film showing an interaction that works. From this positive model, they see they can be effective by using the behaviors they observe.

## 3 Employ your own skills coaching for success

Many role plays provide a brief description of the situation, but leave participants to their own resources to interpret the data and develop a course of action. The introduction of coaching into this setting can greatly increase the likelihood that your learners will have a success experience.

Prior to beginning the exercise, take some time to thoroughly explain the object of the role play, the guidelines to be adhered to, and your own expectations and perspective. This coaching allows you to clarify issues and become aware of any misunderstanding of the material. It also helps participants focus their attention on the critical steps to be covered.

In your coaching, make sure you make use of this important opportunity to detect and alleviate any anxieties or apprehensions your participants may have. By coaching individual participants, you help ensure the success of the exercise to follow and provide a supportive model for others in the group.

## 4 Take special care to manage feedback

While most role-play manuals provide several general principles the trainer should follow, they do not sufficiently manage the feedback to participants. This management task is a crucial test for the instructor. A significant part of your role is to provide observations and insight to both target skill mastery and build participants' confidence. It's a delicate balancing act: you must manage feedback from observers to focus on how effectively the critical steps were used while maintaining participants' self-esteem.

Feedback can be enhanced by the guidelines observers are asked to follow. For one, insist on recording the exact conversation that takes place. Requiring observers to limit their feedback to the exact words used during the interaction eliminates the coloring of personal feelings and unconscious biases.

Secondly, instruct observers not to generalize or summarize. Instead of reporting, "He was not firm enough," or "She was hostile," make your observers list specific remarks: "Well, George, it's up to you if you want to start work at 8 a.m. or 8:30," or "You think I'm the cause of the problem, don't you?" Such remarks are fed back to the participant for each critical step followed to reinforce the use of the desired behaviors and illustrate how effectively the progression was followed. For example, "Pat, you effectively asked for the cause of the problem when you said, 'Can you help me understand why you're late getting those reports in?'"

## 5 Protect participants' self-esteem

Most role-play situations are followed by open feedback sessions. During these sessions, it is not uncommon for observers to make comments about the role play just witnessed, regardless of whether those comments are appropriate to the objectives of the exercise. This kind of feedback can have a negative impact on participants, especially if it is perceived as an attack on the individual's self-esteem.

For effective learning to occur, it is imperative that participants gain confidence in their ability to handle the situations being practiced. Feedback can never be allowed to overshadow the maintenance of an individual's self-esteem, and you must intervene immediately in feedback sessions, as well as in the actual skill practice if necessary, to protect your participants. Role-play exercises are not arenas in which people may be subjected to excessive negative feedback.

## 6 Broaden the experience with alternative positive behaviors

Feedback in most role plays often focuses on purely negative behaviors. It is not uncommon to hear observers say, "You blew it," or "You were really insensitive." This not only threatens self-esteem, but fails to provide specific behavioral information which could show the participant another way of handling the situation.

Observers should be encouraged to suggest alternative positive responses to role-play situations. This not only helps the participants in the exercise itself, but also helps the group focus on specific positive behaviors rather than general negative statements. An example of a statement offering an alternative positive behavior: "George, it would have been better had you said 'Mary, your production rate was down 5% last week,' rather than 'Mary, you're getting lazy.'" Such feedback provides the participant with an alternative set of words that might be more effective. It also sets the tone for observers to focus on a participant's positive, rather than negative, actions.

## 7 Prepare yourself to fulfill the role of instructor

Traditional role plays tend to let participants "sink or swim," followed by a discussion of the reasons for their fate. Such discussions can be expected to ramble when conducted without a trained moderator. Successful role plays require the presence of a specially trained instructor whose job it is to structure a positive experience for those involved and enhance the transfer of their newly acquired skills to the job.

As an instructor, you should be prepared to offer a number of services to your participants. You should be able to coach them to successfully handle role plays according to the critical step progression. You should be capable of guiding the participation of observers so discussion focuses on positive, growth-oriented outcomes. And you should be prepared to intervene in exercises that become disoriented or threaten to break down. While such intervention is obviously only for extreme situations, participants who begin to stray from the critical steps or flounder for direction need your protection.

Participants should be prepared for the eventuality of your intervention before beginning the role play, and everyone involved should understand that there is no implication of failure or need for diminished self-esteem if such action on your part is necessary. Knowing when and how to rescue your trainees from an unproductive exercise may be the most demanding challenge you face in conducting role plays.

## 8 Customize role plays to reflect realistic job settings

Quite often, role plays provide only general environmental descriptions to participants. When they deal with purely hypothetical issues, they fail to duplicate the real-life situations which can occur on the job. To be productive, then, you must make your role plays as realistic as possible.

One way to do this is to ask learners to prepare descriptions of situations they commonly encounter. The background they provide you in advance will help you create exercises which will benefit them. The more job-related the skills you practice, the greater the likelihood your participants will use those skills back on the job.

## 9 Focus attention on the process

Since role plays usually lack specific behavioral objectives, role players often have long discussions about familiar things. Not surprisingly, these sessions can bog down in detailed discussions unrelated to the *procedures* participants are trying to learn. For instance, when two supervisors in an electronics plant are asked to conduct a role-play discussion centered on motivating a poor performer, it is not uncommon that 90% of the discussion will focus on technical matters.

To practice and develop a skill, on the other hand, your learners need to focus on the process, rather than content of the discussion. Since the purpose of role playing is to acquire new skills, attention must be directed toward the desired behaviors, and not the setting in which discussion takes place. For this reason, the critical step progression needs to be well-defined and zealously followed to bring the discussion to a successful conclusion.

While role play has suffered from some negative stereotypes, there are many situations in which it can be an extremely positive and rewarding experience. By structuring the experience to emphasize skill practice, you will help alleviate the resistance and anxiety raised when role play is mentioned. And by utilizing the basic principles of role play in a more skill-oriented environment, individuals will have an opportunity to maintain their self-esteem and learn new solutions to problems. **T**

If your trainees haven't been part of a video role play before, here's one way to make sure that their first experience is successful

# Videotape roleplays without trainee trauma

A trainee's first experience with video role play can be traumatic. It's bad enough to make mistakes in front of one's peers...but to have them reviewed on instant replay is torture few people can endure. Many trainees never get full benefit from video-assisted instruction because they are too self-conscious to act as themselves in front of business associates.

Norman Tice, manager of sales training for Johns-Manville, has found a way to eliminate much of that self-consciousness. "The classroom is structured for 30 participants for daytime instruction," Tice explains. "We use six monitors controlled by a ¾-inch cassette deck to play back tapes. At night, four of these monitors convert to self-contained automatic role-play vehicles."

At the end of each workshop day, participants schedule themselves in pairs for half-hour cycles of role play during the evening hours. Usually all four units are engaged at the same time, but the participants aren't distracted because they're so involved in their own work they don't notice the other teams. Also, the monitors play through small remote speakers on the role-play table.

The key to this system is a table-top remote box that simplifies videocassette operation. There are only two knobs on the box, one for speaker volume and one labeled start. The person acting as sales rep pushes the start button to activate the camera and tape machine. The machine records automatically for seven minutes, then rewinds and plays back. After viewing the segment, the teams switch places and repeat the procedure.

Tice has found that the system works much better than set-ups where the instructor and/or equipment operators are present. "The participants evaluate themselves," he explains, "and tend to be more critical than any instructor would be. Also, we give them specific evaluation criteria during daytime sessions. The result of all this advanced planning," he adds, "is that participants get all the benefits of role play with little of the trauma associated with performing in front of an audience of peers." T

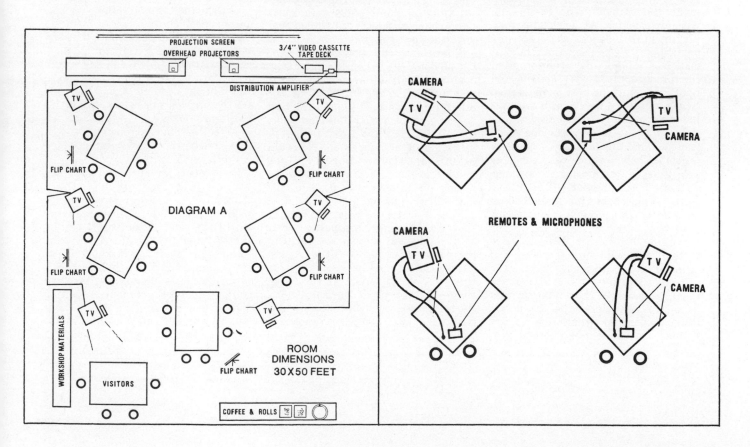

# Effective *informal* roleplaying

by Martin M. Broadwell

The word "roleplaying" is used with great abandon these days. But what, exactly, does it mean? Quite simply, it is a way to teach a new behavior, specifically in relating to another individual. Through roleplaying, we simulate troublesome relationships in the classroom, so we can practice before we get back to the job and face certain individuals in live situations.

There are many good how-to books about roleplay, so this isn't an attempt to educate, in a few paragraphs, the training world in this technique. But I think there are some missed opportunities to use roleplaying in informal ways. Let's consider these fast, simple, effective training devices after we mull over the question: Just what happens in a roleplaying situation?

Does the roleplayer play the real person, the imagined person, or the desired person? Probably some of each, but we don't know for sure. We do know, however, that roleplaying is more effective than having the instructor stand up and tell the students how they should act, hoping they'll make the transition on their own, without practice. At least with roleplaying, the students must actively participate. We've seen that the student in a roleplaying situation often can produce the proper actions and reactions, which he may have learned from a lecture, a movie, or a tape but has never actually experienced before.

Roleplaying often provides good feedback for the teacher, because it indicates how well certain concepts were grasped. No, it's not a guarantee that the new behavior will be transferred to the job, but it is an indication that such transference might occur. And that alone justifies using the technique. The more feedback we have in the class, the better the chance of transfer back on the job.

Feedback gives students a chance to react, to decide if they like the new model of behavior we're trying to foster. A parallel situation is when a trainee repairs or assembles or produces something in the classroom. While there's no guarantee that his or her success will be repeated on the job, we are better able to predict it will be. In other words, classroom feedback helps us gauge our success in imparting knowledge or, at least, information.

## Informal roleplaying

Informal roleplaying requires no structure, no written material, no stagesetting, no preplanning. We're talking about a situation that lasts for only a few minutes. It may occur between one student and the teacher, between several students and the teacher, or between several groups of students. Let's look at some examples.

The students are working on a short case study designed to assist them in dealing with an eager, ambitious employee who is often wrong but always fired up. The objective, among others, is to help the students describe the specific feelings of such an employee and to describe specific actions to overcome inherent hazards in dealing with him. Joe Miller is our ambitious young employee with the wrongheaded ideas. He has worked hard on a proposal that he thinks is great, but we can see it's not practical. Miller's solution has been suggested before by others, and has been tried and proved untenable. Now the class, working in small subgroups, must decide how the supervisor should deal with the young man.

After the third group has reported, it's obvious that the students favor opening with a statement like, "We'll just lay it on the line with you, Joe." In other words, we hear that each group is going to be pretty hard on poor, misguided Joe. But we're trying to teach a different approach. We could ask them, "How do you think Joe would react to this?" But if we're strong on roleplaying, it would be better if we just said, "Let's suppose I'm Joe. Now tell me what you have to say." Add that any class members can talk to Joe if they want to. The participants may have a little trouble getting into the supervisor's role at first, but we can make it easier for them—by keeping in character, offering information, maybe even raising a question that provokes a response. The goal is to get the group itchy to talk to Joe. We continue until the students see that they may have been heading down the wrong path. Not everyone will participate; nor will everyone learn the lesson. But a few will get some "ah-ha's," so it's worth it for them.

## Interpersonal relations

This same informal approach will be effective in situations other than supervisory or management training. For example, let's say we're training a group of nurses on hospital procedures. In the course of the training, several trainees have commented on the difficulty they're having with the staff at the radiology lab. "Everytime we go for a report on the work we've given them, we have to listen to a lot of guff about how hard we're making their jobs for them," they complain. Here's a good opportunity for an informal roleplay situation. When one of the nurses says something about the difficulty with the lab, an astute trainer might say, "Hey, why don't I play the part of the lab receptionist, and you come to me with a request." Thus the nurse/trainee gets a chance to practice how he or she will deal with the recalcitrant lab personnel the next time a sticky situation arises.

## Conclusion

With a little imagination, we can solve some of our tougher problems by letting the group participate in informal roleplaying. For instance, in a sales relationship, we can say to the group, "Count off by twos; the ones are the unhappy customers, and the twos are the harried sales clerk. See if you can figure out a way to approach the customer without increasing the anxiety, and, better yet, overcoming some of the tension."

Remember: every time a person plays a role appropriately, there should be positive reinforcement. A good argument for the teacher playing one of the roles is that there can be such immediate reinforcement for "good behavior." We'll know we've made this technique a habit when a coworker comes in and asks, "Are you going to get off Friday for the opening of deer season?" And we say, without missing a beat, "Tell you what, you be the boss, and I'll come in and say..." **T**

Reprinted from TRAINING, July 1977

*When the words you write must be heard to be understood, take care that you present them effectively*

# Writing for the eye and ear

by Judson Smith

**S**age advice from every lawyer in the nation is to "put it in writing." When something is written down, it lasts forever—it can be studied and stored and scrutinized. The spoken word, on the other hand, is worthless in court because it disappears as soon as it is expressed. What's worse, chances are whoever hears the words won't have the same sense of what they mean as the one speaking them.

Countless theories about effective communication fill textbooks with data and drawings about senders, receivers, communications paths and the like. But most people who write for the eye and the ear—for speeches, audio recording, films, videotape or audiovisual presentations— never consciously think about these things. Subconsciously, perhaps, their fingers are guided over the keyboard, but a spoken-word writer rarely refers to a thesaurus or dictionary, let alone a text on communications.

Think of verbal media as a foreign language. Can anyone enter a foreign country and immediately absorb, understand and communicate in the native tongue? Not likely. Nor can people instantly interpret and absorb highly sophisticated material presented in a foreign medium. But they can learn— some intuitively know— how to communicate on a basic level by using short words, lots of visual support, finding equivalent English words, and using almost childlike language and structure.

That's the way to write for the eye and the ear. To be understood, keep it simple, use short words, reinforce with visuals and follow some standard conventions, such as uncomplicated sentence patterns. Say what has to be said in a simple declarative sentence with an action verb, few or no polysyllables, and no confusing words.

Remember that people don't really translate what they hear into discrete words. Instead, they group words into "particles of meaning," phrases that convey a thought. In terms of verbal media, most of the particles of meaning that can be imparted well are emotional or feeling in tone, not intellectual. It would be difficult, for instance, for a trainer to illuminate all the details and procedures of a firm's benefit package through an audiovisual presentation, but not too tough at all to create a good feeling about that package if the AV presentation was accompanied by a booklet that explained the plan in detail and could be kept by the employee for ready reference.

## Writing begets rewriting

Revision is as important for the spoken word as it is for the written word. Most writers find they must get something down on paper, some barebones skeleton of the finished work, before they actually know what it is they are trying to say and what's wrong with the way they just said it. They have to "get it out of their system" in the first draft, then let it stew a bit.

It's far easier to build a framework that makes sense once the basic thoughts, particles of meaning, words and phrases are down on paper. The first draft often contains some interesting phrasing and insight, but needs support and substance in terms of order and focus. Revision and reshaping is simply a matter of fitting the thoughts into a usable format.

The basic rules, or at least suggestions, that will usually result in a decent product for the eyes and the ears are actually just common sense, but sometimes common sense falls by the wayside in the heat of writing. Here, for the nonsuperstitious, are 13 things to keep in mind as you write.

**1 Use active, not passive, voice.** Don't underestimate the power of an active verb. Even if the first draft must be passive, go back and recast in active voice. Passive voice says the subject has done something; active voice has the subject doing something. "The apple was eaten by Bill" is textbook passive. "Bill ate the apple" is active, and shorter, and the listener knows who did what to whom (or what) in an order that is easy to understand.

**2 Shorten everything.** Hemingway was a master at this. He'd write standing up, but edit sitting down. He'd cut everything not absolutely necessary. As a result, his sparse little books cut immediately to the core of the concept he was describing. It's better to die a little death at the typewriter or at the hands of a blue pencil when editing your "deathless prose" than it is to expire in a bomb blast at showtime.

The simplest way to cut a sentence is to go back to English grammar days and parse the sentence out. Find the subject and the predicate. Put those in simple word order and see how much, if anything, is lost. Add only those adverbs, phrases, clauses or other sentence parts that are absolutely necessary to enhance meaning. Cut long sentences into short ones, avoiding dependent clauses (like this one), and see if the writing doesn't read better.

**3 Break the rules.** If an American school child carries any rules into adulthood, they are probably rules about grammar, such as not using "ain't" and sentence fragments, and not repeating the same word in a sentence. In reality, people don't speak in complete sentences, yet they are understood. Write as you talk. (Like you talk.) Use implied subjects. Don't fear the pause...represented by those three dots. Fragment sentences when the fragment says it all. Actually, the punctuation of anything that is spoken rather than written is purely for the convenience of a reader. Take a look at what is popular in music and

Reprinted from TRAINING, March 1981

in magazines, things people buy because they are current. Popular communications forms are becoming far less rigid and structured. They are often sentence-less. Same for commercials.

**4** **Don't describe, amplify.** The classic example is the travelogue everyone yawns through. The traveler drones on about every nuance of the slide, even if those nuances are seen in the first second of viewing. "One picture is worth a thousand words" is trite and untrue, but there's no reason to speak a thousand words, or even ten, to describe what can be clearly seen. If you are writing "In this slide" or "As you can clearly see," chances are you are wasting valuable time that could be spent explaining what can't be seen.

**5** **Practice some verbal chauvinism.** Anglo-Saxon words are *magnifique*. If, when you write or read a word, you find a translation popping into your mind, use the translation. It will probably be shorter, have a more specific meaning, be clearer in tone and read better.

**6** **Use repetition.** People repeat themselves constantly. Spoken-word writers should, too. Follow that old rule: "Tell them what you are going to tell them. Tell them. Then tell them what you told them." Repetition works.

**7** **Write to reflect your audience's personality.** It's often considered bad form to use loose sentence structure and contractions (such as "it's"), but that's the way people talk. One way to include a proper amount of this informality is to use focus group interviews. If the task is to design an orientation program for factory workers, ask them what they think about the company. Then—within reason— use the words they use in writing your script. If they say, "I like workin' here 'cuz this's a company that cares a bunch, really does good stuff for us workers and like that," don't clean it up so much that your factory worker sounds like a displaced Ph.D. in English. Compromise: "This company cares. It really does good stuff for workers." Chances are the top brass will balk at "stuff," but workers won't.

There's another school of thought concerning cleaning up language, of course. This school says that the company is The Company, and should speak with a voice that is intelligent, reasoned and educated. There's something to be said for this, and your narrator should say it. Don't ask a stentorian-voiced narrator to say "stuff," but don't ask a semi-skilled employee who normally says "stuff" to say the firm offers "a complete benefit package and many fringe benefits of great value to those of us for whom the package was designed."

**8** **Write for one member of the audience.** Talk to one person, probably a composite, who represents the middle level of your audience. Consider several factors, including level of experience within the firm, age and education, sex, lifestyle and profession, geographic or fraternal taboos, and amount of involvement with the media you are using. Avoid colloquialisms and regional references and, if possible, avoid gender-specific structures.

The composite figure for this article, for example, is a training professional, probably a college grad with some post-grad work, in his or her mid-30s, with an urban background. Since TRAINING's readership is national, regional references shouldn't be used, and sexual stereotypes will not be allowed to pass unchallenged. Chances are the reader has an excellent command of the English language and is used to reading articles (thus a high degree of understanding and involvement with the medium). If you can distill the same sort of profile for every spoken-word writing assignment, it will help improve both style and word choice.

**9** **Use a narrative hook.** Look at the difference between an old movie, one that had a captive audience, and a made-for-television movie. In the boob-tube production, the grabber goes up front. If someone is going to get in trouble, it will be in the first few minutes. No suspenseful waiting for the action anymore. Here's a classic narrative hook: "Hell," said the Duchess. "Let go my leg!" It has excitement, royalty, violence, action and sex. You can just see a network executive buying a program that begins with that scene.

In training programs, it isn't usually possible to employ such a strong hook, but it is possible— and necessary— to grab the audience's attention early on. Maybe all it takes is a fast-paced beginning that uses music and some "happy face" shots of employees, or a narrator asking an almost unanswerable question. It is worth a great deal of time and effort to come up with a narrative hook that drags the audience into the presentation.

**10** **Don't climb too far up the ladder of abstraction.** This is a device to show the specificity of a noun. For example, "armament" is about as abstract as possible. "Gun" is more concrete, at least ruling out bows and arrows, rocks, slingshots, and other non-guns. And "Colt .45" is very concrete. Remember, keep it simple, clear and concrete.

**11** **Avoid number problems.** In rewriting, watch for the "him or her, he or she" problem. Don't say, "Everyone should have his or her day in the sun." Instead, say "People should have their day in the sun." Or avoid that cliche entirely. In some cases, varying the gender pronouns not only avoids the trap of "him and her," but also enhances listener attentiveness by keeping the audience a little off balance.

**12** **Watch your sentence context.** Avoid unconscious humor and poor use of gerunds. Many writers can't clearly state what a gerund is, but the problem of poor use of gerunds is obvious. "After climbing the mountain, the view was beautiful," is a glaring gerund problem. What's beautiful? And is it only beautiful because it climbed the mountain? Unconscious humor is harder to spot. Suppose you wrote a script for Planned Parenthood that said, "The problem only became apparent after pregnancy." You'd find the word "apparent" seemed fine on the printed page, and even when recorded, but had them rolling in the aisles at every viewing.

**13** **When you are done, quit.** This is difficult for every writer, but especially so in writing for the eye and the ear. There is a tendency to dot every "i", cross every "t" and never rely on the visuals to complete the message. But retention studies, not to mention introspective viewing of audiovisual shows, indicate that only a few key messages come out of most spoken-word scripts. If the audience walks away feeling the company is good, and cares, and does good stuff for its employees, an orientation program is probably pretty solid. If the audience thinks safety is a pretty good thing and individuals go back to the shop a little more wary of the machines, that safety program was a success.

The same idea works in written form, too. If this article leaves you with the impression that writing for the eye and the ear is different than writing for the printed page and that, basically, the keys are to write conversationally and simply, then the "particle of meaning" has been passed and it's time to quit. **T**

# Put 'believability' into video drama

**W**hile preparing videotape presentations for the Federal Prison System, Ed Harding's crew from Media Concepts, Inc., encountered some interesting training and production problems. Their solutions may help all trainers who must produce believable media packages under location conditions.

Harding's production company was hired to produce videotape materials that would help employees understand the workings of their own correctional facility, including how it connected with the surrounding community and the people inside and out of the prison. They had to seem real enough so that participants imagined themselves part of the work force, but they couldn't be shot at an actual institution.

Until Harding's Philadelphia-based firm was hired, the organization used a print hand-out that outlined a simulated institution. Although it described this fictional prison in great detail, participants had trouble making the transition from their actual position to this mythical place.

So Media Concepts produced a video documentary, complete with an on-camera news reporter doing an investigation on the simulated prison. The reporter interviewed the warden, other staff members and even prisoners. The trainee audience was exposed to people whose names would later come up in their sessions and also got some idea of the situations and conflicts they would deal with during subsequent course exercises.

Television news has a built-in credibility, Harding believes, and is familiar to most people. He felt that trainees would tacitly understand how to watch the program and would internalize the attitudes and information contained within the script.

Since trainees would be coming from institutions throughout the prison system, no actual prison settings were used in the tape. This helped eliminate the "guess where this was shot" distraction. For much the same reason, no actual prison employees were used. Harding went through the Prison System's file of prison photographs and then looked for non-prison locations that resembled actual penal institutions. A military barracks, for instance, served as the dormitory, and the grounds of a college campus looked like the landscape around a federal corrections institution.

Actors from several community theaters played the roles of employees. Here again, Harding used the System's picture file to guide his selection of actors according to existing employees' age, dress, grooming and other characteristics. One of the trainers, coincidentally, bore a striking resemblance to one of the actors used in the videotape. By adding a few small make-up touches, he was able to walk into the meeting room and participate "live" in a discussion of the attitudes espoused by the character played in the program.

As with most location productions, this one encountered disasters and lucky accidents. Harding found that the only way to cure an annoying video noise source was to wrap all equipment and cabling in aluminum foil, using most of a nearby supermarket's supply. The noise source—a local AM radio station—was being picked up by the video equipment because all the television cabling acted as a giant antenna; the aluminum foil shielded out this unwanted signl.

On the good side, a fortunate accident brought the production crew to a local college athletic field on the day after a heavy rain. Groundspeople, who were shoveling the field and sprinkling it with sand to make it playable, looked strikingly like prisoners. The sight of "inmates" in such an activity struck a responsive, realistic chord—at no cost for the "extras" in the scene.

Such unplanned events and meticulously planned set-ups came together in the form of several realistic training programs for the Federal Prison System. Because participants had little trouble believing that the scenes they were witnessing were from an actual prison, the training effect was enhanced. In fact, several trainees expressed interest in being transferred to this mythical institution, because it was so well run.∎

Reprinted from TRAINING, July 1979

# Here's why you should consider video-based learning

"**A**lthough trainers have used videotape for years as an instant replay device to improve role plays, to bring slices from the real world into the classroom and to train more effectively," says Walt Robson, "some still consider it an all-electronic version of the classroom projector. But videotape's unique features provide some tangible benefits. The challenge is to develop software that matches the sophistication of the hardware."

Robson, president of Innovative Media, Inc., a San Mateo, CA video production company, offers some classic examples of the misuse of video. He then offers some suggestions for using the medium more effectively.

The biggest problem is using video to make recordings of classroom lectures for distribution to the field. Robson says that training effectiveness may actually decline in this case, since the absence of the instructor eliminates the possibility of feedback. In addition, the instructor's absence can affect accountability; the trainees may not bother watching a long, boring lecture unless there's an instructor around.

Another problem is videotapes used as "learning experiences" but not integrated into the training design. "The medium is used as a gigantic information dump," Robson says, "but no reinforcement is built into the instructional design."

The problem with video as a tool for improving role plays is that many trainers use the medium *just* for this facet of the course. Trainees aren't given the chance to see positive behavior and to develop good role models. "We believe learning how to swim should precede being thrown into the water," Robson explains.

Given all those incorrect or inefficient uses of video, what positive ways exist to put the medium to work for training? Robson suggests integrating video into every part of the training process.

In a course recently designed by MR Communications Consultants, titled "Presentations That Work," each video module develops principles for in-house and sales presentations through two positive models. "Mary" depicts a person doing an in-house program, while "Jeff" must make a high-level sales presentation. Rather than watching one, long videotape, the trainees view several shorter clips at appropriate times during training. Each clip reveals principles and processes while stimulating discussion based on the behavior of Mary and Jeff.

During the second day of this course, attendees make a presentation to the class and video camera. Here, again, video is used somewhat differently than in normal applications. The morning session becomes an "on-camera" rehearsal, where the trainee makes mistakes and is evaluated by the class. But the afternoon performance, complete with changes determined by the rehearsal, is usually a positive experience. The trainee forgets the camera and concentrates on influencing the audience.

Robson has found this course to be highly effective; one client determined that presentation productivity increased by 23%. He believes that results such as these will cause more and more trainers to use the medium differently. "The trend is toward using the medium judiciously to make abstract concepts more concrete. It is a pivotal component in discovery-based learning and can stimulate discussion and interaction like no medium we have seen," he concludes.—J.S. **T**

Reprinted from TRAINING, November 1979

Among other advantages these training aids let the learner control instruction

# Using models, mock-ups and simulators

by Judson Smith

**W**hat do a 20-cent orange and a $200,000 computer have in common? Not much, it seems— unless the computer is painted orange. But, in training terms, both are simulators.

The orange has been used for decades to help medical personnel learn how to give injections without painfully pincushioning human subjects. And the computer is used to simulate real-life situations that would be economically unfeasible or hazardous to untrained personnel.

Both fit into the category of "simulator," since they approximate the real-life situation being learned. But one, the computer, is an active simulator, since it can be programmed to respond with feedback if the learner makes a mistake. The orange, on the other hand, won't squeal with pain if a shot is administered incorrectly, so it is a passive simulator, often called a model or mockup.

A model closely approximates some object, usually reduced in scale. A mockup, on the other hand, is often a same-size or larger device used to illustrate basic concepts or procedures by roughly approximating the real thing. The orange, then, is a mockup, since it has neither the texture, shape nor size of a human limb; it is simply a device used to illustrate the basic skills required to give an injection.

Given those broad definitions, the area of models, mockups and simulators covers a lot of ground and includes many items of interest to trainers. Rather than microscopically analyze each item, let's focus on applications and generalities of interest to all trainers.

The airlines are big users of mockups and simulators. From the basic stage of designing new aircraft, often done using precise models under carefully controlled wind-tunnel conditions, to the final steps of putting a qualified pilot and correctly scheduled passengers on board, models, mockups and simulators find extensive use.

The basic rationale is economic. "When you consider both the student-hour cost of a 747 pilot who makes $80,000 per year and the cost of dedicating an aircraft to training," explains Dennis Sullivan, director of instructional systems and training for the Canyon Research Group, "you can see why most airlines have invested in sophisticated simulators."

Through the use of such systems, Sullivan reports, actual airplane flying time has been reduced from an average of 13 hours to 1 hour for captains transitioning to newer aircraft. It's been calculated that it costs about $4,000 per hour to train an airline pilot in the cockpit. A full-scale simulator, on the other hand, runs about $400 per training hour. And, once initial programming costs are absorbed, computer simulation runs only about $40 per hour.

One such simulation, programmed on Control Data's "Plato" system, is in daily use at American Airlines' Flight Academy. The Plato terminal (Programmed Logic for Automatic-Teaching Operation) links by telephone to a Control Data computer in Minneapolis. The flight crew member, seated before a television-like console, types in requests for specific programs, and Plato displays required information on the screen.

In a typical program, the pilot is taken through an unfamiliar instrument panel, control by control. He or she is asked to identify each knob or meter by touching a sensitized probe to the object depicted graphically on Plato's screen. Right answers earn congratulations from the machine and the right to continue on to another control. Wrong answers start a learning process designed to teach the pilot how to identify the control and its purpose.

In the rarified atmosphere of aircraft operation, these simulations save not only money but lives. According to FAA figures, more pilots are killed in training flights than in actual operations. By using cockpit mockups and computer simulations, the airlines have reduced training accidents to almost zero.

A scaled-down version of computer simulation is now also being used by some private pilots or pilot candidates for the same safety and savings reasons. Companies such as Analog Training Computers and Pacer Systems now produce desk-top simulators that let learners "fly" at their own pace and at much less cost than if they were learning in the air with a rental plane and a Certified Flight Instructor.

These General Aviation simulators include mockups of a generalized instrument panel, plus computerized learning tools. The trainee plugs in tapes that either simulate actual take-offs and landings, for pre-training before flight to unfamiliar airports, or take the learner through a programmed course to teach new skills.

The advantages of such flight simulators are obvious. A cockpit, buffeted by wind and moving onward at several hundred miles per hour, is no place to develop a new skill or become familiar with a new airport— not when failures could easily lead to fatalities.

The airlines, however, must prepare for such failures. They do this with mockups and simulators, as well. At the American Airlines' Flight Academy, one building is solely devoted to the training of cabin crews. Within are exact replicas of airliner interiors, coupled to a computer console. The instructor can simulate any air emergency, including fires and ditching at sea (using a large pool). Although such emergency procedures are rarely required, it's good to know that all flight crews have experienced similar situations in training.

One major airlines estimated that

the millions of dollars it had invested in a training facility would be recovered in about five years. The company did it in two because of the increased cost of fuel and the release of aircraft back to revenue flying.

Training in the airline industry is highly controlled by government regulations, and airlines must continually send pilots and flight crew members back for updating. The success of simulators has many airlines considering doing *all* such updating or new-equipment training without using revenue-producing aircraft. They feel it is not only less costly but also far more effective and safer.

Airline ticket offices aren't nearly as hazardous as airliners, but computer simulation has still proved valuable in saving time and training effort in this area. Using the Boeing Computer Services' Scholar/Teach 3 system, for instance, TWA teaches personnel how to use their programmed airline reservation system and other air freight or load control systems.

BCS' ST3, like Control Data's Plato, gives the trainer several advantages over other learner-controlled instruction techniques. For one thing, these systems aid in training program management because they automatically monitor student enrollment and progress, as well as assigning students the correct curriculum. ST3, for instance, lists, by student, the answer given to each question in a given program. And a response report categorizes all student responses as "correct" or "incorrect," giving the training staff a measure of the course's effectiveness.

If a course, or section of a course, proves ineffective, most computer simulator programs allow "authors" to revise easily. In most cases, the computer command language is similar to basic English, and computer graphics can be generated easily with a sensitized pencil so updates and revisions can be incorporated at any time.

Of course, these same computer simulators can just as easily train personnel in more down-to-earth fields. Because mistakes during on-the-job training of technicians involved in nuclear or electric power plants can be just as disastrous as pilot error in an airliner, many companies use computer simulators to familiarize personnel with the operation and repair of generating stations and power grids. On Plato, for instance, an operator who mistakenly throws the wrong switch is suddenly confronted with a screenful of jagged lines and explosive words, a graphic demonstration of what would happen in reality if that switch were thrown.

Computer simulators are typically more versatile and less costly than models or exact mockups, but sometimes the subject being studied demands hands-on training with realistic devices. Many medical skills would fall into that category.

The example of the orange, familiar to any nursing student or intern, is still an accepted method for learning how to give an injection. But modern plastics and semiconductors have replaced the more traditional methods of supervised practice on patients for many other medical procedures. Insertion of catheters, for example, is a tricky procedure at best and not one to be undertaken by a novice. With the aid of a plastic model, medical people can now practice this technique on a "subject" that looks, feels and responds as would a human being.

Full-size replicas of the human body are also frequently used by health-care trainers. "Resusci-Anne," one of the most famous, is a willing victim on which procedures related to heart attacks are practiced. Other manikins can be stripped down, layer by layer, to uncover the inner workings of the body. Industrial trainers and educators also use these anatomical models to illustrate the effects of smoking, alcohol or other health hazards in an all-too-graphic way.

Some industrial machines are just as complex as the human body, and it is just as difficult to get under their "skin." For this reason, technical trainers often find plexiglass models extremely useful for explaining the inner workings of a device. Although such models are usually one-of-a-kind and, therefore, quite expensive, they provide every trainee with "x-ray eyes" to clearly view otherwise invisible parts and processes.

In the field of electronics, mockups and simulators are especially valuable. Submolecular particles just aren't visible as they move through wire or create differences of electric potential within solid semiconductor materials. By converting the actual circuit to a large-scale "equivalent circuit," electronic instructors are able to explain the mystical relationships between elements in a concrete, traditional manner.

It's fairly easy to understand why the U.S. Maritime Administration uses CAORF (Computer Aided Operations Research Facility) to simulate on a computer the conditions a tanker captain will face entering New York Harbor. It's just as obvious why oranges make better practice targets for student nurses than would a human being. Speaking of practice targets, it also makes good sense for law enforcement officers to learn fir-ing techniques against "quickdraw" simulated bad guys. But the use of models, mockups and simulators for most training applications are not quite so obvious.

Take something as basic to most large businesses as typing. Why use a simulator or mockup of a typewriter keyboard when the real thing is readily available? First of all, because a typewriter is a fairly complex device, consisting of several basic parts. When the keyboard is separated into number keys, alphabet keys and punctuation keys, trainees can learn in bite-sized steps rather than having to confront the entire board at once. By mocking up the carriage assembly, the trainer can point out features and be sure the entire class knows where he or she is pointing. Finally, typewriter repairs cost money, and it's all too easy for new typists to scramble the keys or strip the gears; by first learning correct procedures on a simulator or mockup, trainees can correct mistakes without damaging expensive equipment.

## Seeing the whole picture

The same theory holds true for every training procedure. When technical equipment is broken down into component parts and operators are trained on each part, the whole picture becomes clearer. By using large-scale mockups of small devices or small-scale replicas of large equipment, the trainee can grasp the total more easily.

Training time is valuable time, both in terms of the trainer's work and that of the employee away from production while learning. Devices such as computer simulators are usually learner controlled, so the trainer is freed from routine repetitive teaching tasks for individual counseling or instructional design. And the trainee who can schedule learning time to suit his or her own work schedule takes as much or as little time as required to learn effectively.

So, models, mockups and simulators make good sense for many training applications. They can save time and reduce hazards, let the learner control instruction and provide hands-on experience without pain, danger or lost production time. At the very least, they provide another form of learning reinforcement; at the most, they can help trainers illustrate and explain things that otherwise would be difficult or dangerous. So their worth is undisputable. The real challenge is to design or purchase models, mockups and simulators that fit an individual department's needs. **T**

When trainees aren't performing what
they learned— perhaps it's time to add more
elements that increase transfer of training

# Why they don't do
# what we train them to

by J. Regis McNamara

As the issue of accountability becomes more important in human resources development, the question of what training accomplishes becomes increasingly relevant. Of particular concern is the impact training programs have on individuals back on the job. In other words, how much transfer of training or generalization (terms used synonymously here) took place? Transfer of training effects can be considered to occur when the relevant aspects of behavior altered under one condition or in one setting carry over in some form to nontraining conditions or settings. Transfer occurs, then, when trainees do what you trained them to do, where and when you hoped they would do it.

A system I believe can assist trainers in developing programs with more transfer elements in them is based on the Training, Resource, Assessment, Intervention and Network System, or TRAINS. A TRAINS analysis begins with a thorough examination of all elements connected with the training experience.

## Training component analysis

The impetus for most training endeavors develops from the assumptions and models used in constructing a training experience. To analyze this component for transfer, the conceptual underpinnings of the training experience should be identified and assessed for their soundness in relation to achieving transfer objectives. A number of concerns related to this issue need be explored. The first question to pose is whether the training is derived from a *unimodal* or *multimodal* orientation. A management training program derived from behavior modification principles would be considered a unimodal system, whereas one that was jointly predicated on humanistic and behavioristic concepts is developed from a multimodal orientation. Unimodal systems are easier to deal with than those derived from a diversity of perspectives and viewpoints because of their greater theoretical integrity; also they usually have generated more extensive empirical evidence addressing the issue of external validity or generalization.

In unimodal systems, questions about what kind of discrepancies exist between the transfer procedures used to conduct a program and those implied by the theory are of particular concern.[1] An important associated issue is how discrepancies, when they occur, might influence the magnitude of desired transfer effects. For example, using a behaviorally based personalized system of instruction, more generalization in the use of concepts is achieved if the concepts are first defined, then elaborated on and finally worked through by learners using a concept formation program.[2] Failing to incorporate these elements into this type of instructional system may compromise generalization. For example, a program designed to enhance the counseling skills of trainees may be consistently derived theoretically. But its ability to change actual behavior in the counseling situation could be limited if the theory was developed to influence cognitive structures and attitudes of the counselee toward others.

Training is an eclectic field, where diverse orientations, philosophies and activities are accepted, and it is not unusual to encounter training programs that combine elements in ways that might seem, from a single perspective, unusual or perhaps even discordant. These multimodal systems pose vexing evaluation problems. When ideas from a social learning model, communication's theory and humanistic philosophy are tied together with the inspirational intuition of a program originator, an experiential tangle can be the end result. This is not to suggest that such a combination does not work from a participant's point of view, because it frequently does. It simply implies that the diverse orientations will contribute unevenly to the production of generalization effects. Whatever benefits might be evidenced from using procedures derived from one source probably will be compromised by adding less effective or counterproductive elements from another source. The synergism resulting from combining diverse theoretical orientations rarely enhances transfer effects, though the *chicken-soup, or the-more-ingredients-the-better, theory of training* asserts the opposite.

## Resource component assessment

Social factors and the physical training environment both influence transfer. The characteristics of both participants and trainers are one of these elements. One critical question pertaining to trainers is how much visibility, contact and influence they currently have and potentially will have in the post-training environment. To the extent that trainers are isolated from the rest of the organization, their ability to extend the gains made during training to other relevant organizational settings is unlikely to occur. If this situation exists, then it may be necessary to recruit, on a short-term basis, surrogate trainers from those settings to which the participants will return. By virtue of their continued presence around participants before, during and after training, surrogates are likely to provide relevant social support for the newly acquired behavior in the appropriate organizational setting. Even if trainers are well integrated into other aspects of organizational functioning, a variety of trainers should be employed to increase transfer possibilities.

Personal investment and a feeling of some ownership of training content by significant participating figures in the transfer environment also contribute to successful generalization. When individuals with social and administrative influence participate in the development of the goals and objectives of the training experience, they feel more committed to carry through on transfer objectives and influence others to achieve similar results.

Another critical factor to assess is whether there is considerable hostile, negative or unconstructive sentiment among the participants for any particular training experience. If there is, transfer will be minimal. If the critical mass of negative opinion is not neutralized or balanced by careful participant selection during training, then participants will either be uninfluenced by the transfer program or will attempt to undermine it by poor role modeling and verbal innuendo. This aspect is particularly important to understand when the program in question deals with potentially emotional or controversial subjects, such as race relations, social skills training or performance counseling.

Trainers and participants are bound together by the social climate created during training. A persistent problem that compromises transfer effects is the special emphasis placed on developing social and emotional response patterns that are most adaptive within the training program itself.[3] Too often, participants conform to the demands of training, because it is functional to do so. Once these demands are removed, other factors influence a person's response, such as work load, new organizational priorities and so on. Examination of the discrepancy that exists between the social climate created *during* training and that which exists in the primary work setting of the participant is important. Large discrepancies between the two social climates decrease the likelihood of transfer, while small discrepancies increase the possibility of transfer effects.

Similar training and transfer physical environments are also important. Two aspects of the training environment should be considered— the physical space provided for training and the resources contained in the training space. The more common and salient stimuli that exist in the training and transfer environment, the greater the likelihood that generalization will occur. One way to accomplish this is by "vestibule training": on-the-job problems or situations along with their physical characteristics are recreated in the classroom.[4]

## Assessment component analysis

All program assessment can be divided into two types— process and outcome. Process-oriented assessments are structured to collect information on what happens to people undergoing a training experience. And outcome approaches focus on the changes (both positive and negative) that happen to the individual and/or organization as a result of training. Both types of assessment are frequently used to evaluate the success of a training effort. Neither of these assessment techniques to promote and better understand transfer effects is used often enough.

There are several issues associated with the selection and use of assessment methodology. A fundamental concern associated with drawing conclusions from assessment is whether the instruments or procedures chosen will reliably detect change back on the job. Since assessment for transfer will, by definition be conducted some time after training and in an environment different from that of training, the procedures used must demonstrate situational relevance and temporal stability. Relevance is established by identifying whether the measures used to assess the beliefs, behaviors or attitudes during training are likely to detect these same characteristics in the transfer setting. The selection of particular dependent measures has differential utility for establishing outcomes related to transfer effects.[5] For instance, both video recordings and direct observations of selling behavior may be made during training. But when these same procedures are used in the field, in the presence of customers, the nature of the selling situation is likely to change so dramatically that an accurate representation of transfer to the field situation could not be made.

In order to strengthen transfer, special assessment procedures must be used. For example, an assessment strategy that can be used for both process and outcome purposes, as well as to promote transfer effects, is a self-monitoring data collection and feedback system. By recording their own behavior each day, individuals are motivated to change and progress, thus, positive change can be maintained in the transfer environment. Keeping track, in a diary, of the number of times employees are praised for their accomplishments reminds the supervisor to use principles of positive reinforcement taught during training. It also illustrates how dispensing such reinforcement affects improvement.

When self-monitoring systems are occasionally supplemented by means of external surveillance systems (which can corroborate or extend the information gathered by self-monitoring), even more sustained maintenance can be expected. One way to accomplish this is by having the employees also keep track of the amount of praise they receive from the supervisor. Periodic comparisons can be made to determine the correspondence between the two sources. The use of more automatic devices, such as television monitors, personal telemeters and electrical or mechanical counters, would also serve the same function.

Finally, we should consider the following factors when using assessment to promote transfer. First, how reactive are the procedures with the characteristic being measured? That is, will the mere process of having the behavior measured produce a predictable change in it? Second, are the cues associated with the assessment in the transfer environment obvious enough to remind individuals about their behavior? And is the feedback from the assessment delivered at appropriate intervals and in a practical way? And, third, are consequences provided to groups or individuals for meeting or failing to sustain adequate performance standards in the transfer environment? This last issue relates to the establishment of performance standards in the transfer setting and the creation of a motivational system that allows individuals to meet these standards. To the extent that much variation in transfer behavior is permissible, individually determined goals and reinforcement systems are acceptable.

## Intervention component analysis

The procedures and operations used during training to create generalization are critical to the transfer process. For instance, the diversity, variety and novelty of tasks, responses and problems presented during training assist transfer.[6] Providing an adequate number of informational stimuli, as well as teaching sufficiently varied responses to them, is important. An underused method for programming generalization is to do the training in a number of organizational settings. For example, subgroups can be simultaneously trained in different environments with appropriate sequencing between them until training is completed; or the whole group can serially pass through training presentations in different settings. Both these approaches increase the logistical problems of scheduling and staffing, but they increase the transfer effects by weakening the association between the behavior learned and the environment it was learned in.

Although immediate reinforcement for correct responding is usually the operation of choice to facilitate a learner acquiring a new response, intermittent and delayed reinforcement ultimately assure better generalization. Thus during the latter part of training, both feedback and reinforcement should be delayed over time and varied in their amount so that the learner will maintain a reasonable level of persistence. This thinning of reinforcement and feedback to small amounts and at lengthy or unpredictable intervals approximates the usual state of affairs in most organizational environments.

The use of cues and consequences to bring forth generalized responses and then maintain them in the transfer environment is important, too. Written and verbal instructions form the principal basis for most cueing (or signaling of what comes next) that exists in organizations. The development of a commitment to perform in the post-training environment can be fostered through the use of contingency contracts,[7] while the use of policy control procedures[8] can assure that the postraining behavior may be maintained through administrative means.

Consequences are those events that happen to a person after a behavior is performed. Positive consequences or reinforcement increases the likelihood that the behavior would be exhibited in the future; negative consequences or punishment decreases this likelihood. Those consequences that are useful during training— a passing grade in an examination or a certificate of attendance— may be entirely worthless in maintaining the behavior in the transfer setting. Therefore, it's important to identify payoffs in the transfer setting that are known to motivate employees effectively and to make these conse-

quences contingent on the transfer behavior.

The transfer effectiveness of the procedures used to promote facts, skills and concepts presented during training also must be established. Generalization of factual material involves the ability to recall pertinent information at a later time in different surroundings. An effective way to enhance recall during training is to provide the participant with a set of retrieval cues and plans for the material to be recalled. A mnemonic scheme based on a memorized list of words associated with information to be recalled would be appropriate here. The use of live or videotape models to simulate the behavior as it will occur in the transfer setting is essential for skill carry-over. For concept generalization, an approach combining guided and discovery learning seems applicable. Using these combined procedures, participants are initially taught about the task; later on, they are allowed, through trial and error, to find out the answers for themselves.

## Network component analysis

An examination of the arrangement and sequencing among the components in TRAINS is the focus in this part of the system. The adequacy of the linkages established between each component should be explored, with special attention being given to how each component complements and strengthens the influence of the other. The identification and removal of incompatible and counterproductive arrangements is of particular concern. The network analysis puts into perspective the entire transfer effort of the program and determines the effort's consistency and integrity. The network analysis finally attempts to balance transfer needs against other program and organizationally related factors, such as initial program learning, feasibility and

cost/benefit to the organization.

## Conclusion

Our knowledge of how to create transfer and generalization effects from training have reached a stage where formal recommendations for the use of such a technology is warranted.[9] The TRAINS system examines factors that have been identified as important in training programs. How widespread and effective the use of TRAINS becomes, however, will depend on two factors. First is the extent to which the ideas contained in TRAINS are incorporated into training programs. The second relates to the support this system receives from research that demonstrates its incremental benefit over other transfer systems and models.　∎

### REFERENCES

1. Leidecker, J.K., and J.J. Hall, "Motivation: Good theory— Poor application." *Training and Development Journal*, 1974, 28, 3-7.
2. Miller, L.K., and F.H. Weaver, "A behavioral technology for producing concept information in university students." *Journal of Applied Behavioral Analysis*, 1976, 9, 289-300.
3. Miller, F.D. "The problem of transfer of training in learning groups. Group cohesion as an end in itself." *Small Group Behavior*, 1976, 7, 221-236.
4. Luthans, F., and R. Kreitner, *Organizational Behavior Modification*, Glenview, IL: Scott Foresman, 1975.
5. McNamara, J.R., "Ways by which outcome measures influence outcomes in classroom behavior modification research." *Journal of School Psychology*, 1975, 13, 104-113.
6. Gagne, R.M., and L.J. Briggs, *Principles of instructional design.* New York: Holt, 1974.
7. Homme, L., A.P. Csanyi, M.A. Gonzales, and J.R. Richs, *How to use contingency contracting in the classroom.* Champaign, IL: Research Press, 1970.
8. Andrasik, F., J.R. McNamara, and D.M. Abbott, "Policy control: A low resource intervention for improving staff behavior." *Journal of Organizational Behavior Management*, 1978, 1, 125-133.
9. Stokes, T.F. and D.M. Baer, "An implicit technology of generalization. *Journal of Applied Behavior Analysis*, 1977, 10, 349-367.

# A trainer's glossary: Behavior modification

**W**hen Benjamin Franklin was a colonel of the Pennsylvania militia, he had a "training" problem. The soldiers weren't attending Sunday services. Rather than lay down the law or chastise the troops, Franklin turned over dispersement of the rum ration to the chaplin. Attendance was no longer a problem. When Franklin's parson began passing out the rum after Sunday services, he was practicing an art referred to variously as **positive reinforcement management, behavioral engineering, operant conditioning, behavior modification, contingency management,** or any of a dozen or so terms meant to describe the process of managing behavior through the systematic use of positive reinforcement.

Parents have always known that a behavior followed by certain consequences (sometimes incorrectly lumped together as "rewards") will continue to be exhibited until it is no longer reinforced. Grandma's law of "work first, then play" is as old as Adam.

What *is* new is the systematic and willful use of a number of "Grandma's laws," old and new, to control many aspects of behavior. The basic premise is that the consequences of a behavior shape the behavior. If the result is aversive, there is less likelihood that the behavior will be repeated; if the results of the behavior are favorable to the behaver, the likelihood of the behavior being repeated is increased. That may seem a complicated way to say good things increase behavior and bad things decrease behavior. But b'mod or operant conditioning isn't that simple. There are five consequences which can possibly follow any behavior. Each has a different effect on the possibility that the behavior will be repeated (see table).

There are some surprises in the table. For example, **punishment** doesn't have a predictable effect on behavior. This invariably is proved by research. Punishment is generally followed by emotional behavior, which neither increases nor decreases the chances that the target behavior will occur again. The only sure way to decrease a behavior is to follow it with an **extinction** procedure, i.e., by doing nothing. It seems so simple. Just pick the behavior you want to see promoted and go promote it. Not that easy. First, what is a reinforcer? Sure, rest for the weary, food for the hungry, activity for the bored, and liquid for the thirsty are all reinforcers, but they are also products of deprivation and we can't fool with **primary needs**.

Fortunately, **secondary reinforcers** are a possibility. When some neutral, non-reinforcing stimulus is repeatedly associated with a primary reinforcer, the formerly neutral stimulus takes on the ability to reinforce. Example: Money is used to purchase things which are primary reinforcers, so money becomes a reinforcer—as long as it still has purchasing power. But even the power of secondary reinforcement is limited, and the guideline for finding usable reinforcing stimuli is often best characterized by the maxim "different strokes for different folks and different ways on different days." Letting the behaver choose his own reinforcer—a process called contracting—is sometimes the only practical solution.

That leads us to a slight procedural problem. To reinforce a behavior, the behavior must occur. In some instances, we can simply wait until the target shows up and then make something "good" happen for the performer. Catch your kids being "good," pass out the positives, and, chances are, they will be "good" again. "Good" in this case defies definition; it's a matter of values and ethics, not technology. This waiting strategy is, alas, useless in many training situations. You can wait forever for your trainee to make his first computer program, but you'll never have anything to reinforce. Instead, you simply will have to reinforce the nearest approximation of the target behavior and then work toward the final target in a stepwise fashion. This is called **shaping.** It is pretty expensive in terms of time to be constantly reinforcing the target behavior. Fortunately, a process called **schedules of reinforcement** helps somewhat. A helpful surprise represented on the table is: A behavior which is only occasionally reinforced *after* it has been shaped into the desired form is more resilient to extinction (going away) than behavior which is reinforced after every occurrence. Don't be fooled, though: The reciprocal cost of getting a desired behavior where none now exists isn't cheap. Reinforcement isn't a something-for-nothing affair. You get when you give. If you stop giving, you eventually stop getting. Remember the story about the two canny rats in the Skinner box? One says to the other, "Look how well I've got this jerk trained. Every time I push the lever he serves up a meal." The only reinforcement system which lasts is the one based on mutual benefit. **T**

| CONSEQUENCE | CALLED | EFFECT ON POSSIBLE REOCCURRENCE OF TARGET BEHAVIOR |
|---|---|---|
| nothing | extinction | decrease in likelihood |
| something good occurs | positive reinforcement | increase in likelihood |
| something good withdrawn | punishment | unpredictable |
| something aversive occurs | punishment | unpredictable |
| something aversive withdrawn | negative reinforcement | increase |

Reprinted from TRAINING, June 1976

Don't stop at theory. Here
are specific steps

# Teaching daily work habits and patterns aids transfer

by Robert E. Kushell

**W**ith all the talk these days about MBO, very little thought or attention has been given to the daily habits and work patterns that ultimately affect the success or failure of a particular management plan. It's an unfortunate fact that most people have terrible work habits. They may be aware of what has to be done and may even think they are doing it, but a careful audit of their daily and weekly accomplishments reveals that much valuable time has been wasted on non-productive details.

Although much has been taught and written on business theory and practice, I know of no training ground where executives can learn the basic work disciplines: how to plan and organize their time effectively; how to develop the specific, small-scale goals necessary to the success of their long-range plans; and how to assess their productivity level accurately. As a result, many executives get bogged down in insignificant details and then wonder why certain production quotas or financial goals have not been met by year's end.

It was this premise that encouraged Dunhill to institute an expanded training program for both experienced and professional employment consultants and franchisees opening new branch offices. Years of observation and placement of middle management executives and technical personnel in a variety of industries have given Dunhill executives an understanding of the abilities and talents necessary for success in the corporate environment. It was only one

step further to the application of these observations and techniques to consultants in the 250-office Dunhill System itself.

The expanded training program, developed by Dunhill's Director of Training Joel Palmer, consists of a two-week intensive course required of all new franchisees, plus a follow-up, three-day management seminar. Since its inception one year ago, 51 offices from the Dunhill network have seen a 31% increase in total billings resulting from the management seminar alone. One year ago, only eight new offices out of 43 trained had billings during their first two months of operation. This past year, 25 offices out of 48 trained had billings during their first two months. Since most new franchise offices are managed by people who have never worked in this particular field before, the training is obviously effective.

The Dunhill training program focuses on the work habits, disciplines and procedures necessary for success in the recruitment business, but the techniques can be applied, by extension, to almost any industry. The program was developed originally because Dunhill executives realized that, like most franchisors, we were teaching franchisees what to do to run their new businesses but not really giving them the tools to do it. The problem was critical in the case of Dunhill franchisees, who, as personnel recruiters, work on a contingency basis. Fees are only generated when a successful placement is made. Therefore, successful decision-making abilities and effective work habits are crucial to success. But these are considerably harder to teach than the

concepts and mechanics associated with the running of a personnel recruitment agency.

Many of Dunhill's franchisees have pointed to the new training techniques as critical to their survival during their first year in business. In fact, the high failure rate of many new businesses in general is often due not to the lack of a bright idea or of motivation but simply because the new businessman may not have a working knowledge of how to run a business efficiently or how to organize his time and work efforts.

Almost all Dunhill consultants come out of corporate life. Although some have been quite successful, this is no guarantee that they will run a successful personnel recruitment business. Sometimes, quite the reverse is true. The underlying assumptions behind Dunhill's training program are that most new franchisees have little true understanding of time and priority, despite their corporate backgrounds; that they have little, if any, formal discipline for daily planning; that they may have difficulty distinguishing between what they like to do and what they must do to accomplish their goals; and that they may have fundamental difficulties replacing old work habits with new.

The training program begins with an evaluation of the long-range goals of the new Dunhill owners and then asks them several questions. Why do they want to operate their own business? What sacrifices do they expect to make? What tangible returns do they expect over the next 10 years? And so on. These questions are, of course, very open-ended.

The next step is for new franchisees to learn how *to establish realistic, shorter-range goals with meaningful benchmarks for success.* This is one of the keys to the success or failure of any business plan. Long-range goals have little place, if any, in the world of the new, unrooted business. The battle is fought and won or lost in the setting and reaching of a multitude of short-range goals.

To establish realistic concrete goals, franchisees calculate exactly how much money they must generate yearly to make their fledgling business a success. They are then asked to break down this figure on a monthly and weekly basis, so that they will have a specific idea of how much revenue must be forthcoming at all times to meet their financial requirements. After this is done, they learn to calculate how much and what kind of preliminary work (phone calling, interviewing, etc.) it will take to generate one job placement (the successful

Reprinted from TRAINING, November 1979

bringing together of candidate and employer) and how to keep this information up-to-date based on fluctuations in the market. These calculations provide franchisees with a series of realistic daily, weekly, monthly and yearly goals.

Once these realistic goals have been set, new franchisees are taught how to *formulate specific, step-by-step plans to carry out these goals.* A series of simple log sheets helps accomplish these ends. A daily log sheet has space for listing each phone call and its results, as well as for a summary of the day's transactions. Weekly, monthly and yearly log sheets summarize important transactions, indicate what has been accomplished and what must be accomplished by which date in order to meet certain goals. These log sheets take no extra time to keep, are easy to read and reveal the status quo at a glance.

Based on the information listed in the log sheets, franchisees are shown the importance of constructing a *realistic, attainable daily plan* for *every* working day, listing what must be done and when. This daily plan is integral to the success of the training program, and trainees are given a specially designed desk diary to help them organize their activities within specific time frames. Standard rankings of daily priorities are preprinted on each diary page so that items can be listed in their order of importance. Items of the highest priority are tackled first thing in the morning. These are the activities that are most critical to accomplishing specified goals.

Learning how to *control task interference* is as important to the new franchisee as is establishing priorities. It is one thing to set up a list of daily tasks that *must* be accomplished and quite another thing to accomplish them. No day is without its interruptions, and these often can be fatal to the success of any pre-planning.

Controlling task interference can mean different things to different people. For some, it means making sure the telephone doesn't ring in their office and that messages are taken, unless an important call is expected. For others, it may mean scheduling regular daily appointments with colleagues or subordinate department heads in order to prevent people from wandering in and interrupting with random questions.

The key thing franchisees are taught is that, once a daily plan has been established, it must not be deviated from, as long as it is deemed realistic and attainable. No matter what else piles up on the desk, the pre-established tasks take first priority.

One specific trick taught in the sessions is to open mail only during "down time" (non-productive work periods such as lunchtime and late in the day). When mail is opened, immediate decisions must be made. Does something warrant enough attention to be included in tomorrow's daily plan? Does something warrant attention at all? This structure constantly forces the new franchisee into a decision-making mode that eventually becomes automatic.

Since the telephone call is the basis for all personnel placements, franchisees are taught to make chain telephone calls during the prime morning and afternoon hours, using other times for less critical tasks. This one simple technique alone is responsible for Dunhill's high rate of placement, compared with similar personnel networks.

Once they have mastered these techniques, franchisees are shown how to *audit themselves every evening* to assess their success. The franchisee meets respectively with each member of his staff to go over the day's activities, asking such questions as, "Was the daily plan completed?" "If not, why not?" "How might better control and handling of 'new' items be accomplished?" "How might problems be made non-recurrent?" "If the plan was completed, what were the results?" "Were they as planned?" "If not, why not?" The franchisee is encouraged to have one of his staff members audit him in return, rather than attempting the procedure himself.

Trainees are taught how to handle the daily audit through special role-playing sessions where they analyze sample problems. Once mastered, the whole technique should take no more than 10 to 15 minutes per session.

In addition to this audit, trainees are taught to construct a new daily plan for the following day before they leave in the evening. This plan must be submitted and approved by their manager before enacted . This is the time to establish the following day's priorities based on the accomplishments of today. What must be done so that weekly goals can be met? If the end of the month is near, how close are those goals to completion? These questions should all be considered when the evening plan is drawn up. Without such a daily plan, the work day becomes a formless mass of confused detail.

In addition to being taught numerous work disciplines, trainees are placed in an environment that exactly duplicates their future offices. Videotape is used to help them observe work routines and identify problem areas. The actual tasks performed during training sessions are those that the trainee will continue to perform once he has established his own business. Thus, all telephoning during this time is done in the geographic locale where the new branch will be located. To minimize "real-world" shock, the Monday following the last day of training becomes nothing more than an extension of those activities undertaken during the past two weeks.

Once a newly franchised office has been opened, periodic visits by Dunhill staff specialists enable the fledgling entrepreneurs to review what they have learned, ask questions and take stock of their successes. Regional seminars also provide a forum for exchanging ideas and assessing successes.

The basic assumptions and techniques underlying Dunhill's training program can be implemented easily and to great advantage in almost any corporate environment. The guideposts to working effectively are simply: *establish short-range, realistic goals; formulate a plan to carry out the goals; control task interference;* and *audit success daily.*

Many executives have a clear sense of overall goals, but they neglect to break down these goals to their simplest elements and ask such questions as: What production deadlines must be met this week to achieve year-end quotas? What must I do today, this morning, to make that happen? Many executives rely on random notes to jog their memory, but this doesn't structure a day. A simple matter such as scheduling brief end-of-the-day appointments with colleagues can drastically eliminate uncalled-for interruptions and increase working efficiency. Used routinely and conscientiously, the written daily plan and the daily audit are also invaluable executive tools.

The significant increase in the number of placements Dunhill achieved over the past year, coupled with the entire system's outstanding success in the personnel recruitment industry, are not surprising when viewed as the partial outcome of this intensive training program. The *techniques* may seem obvious to some; but it is the *discipline* that most executives fail to exert over themselves and their staff. It is this discipline and the flexibility to implement new ideas that can make the difference between the success or failure of business goals. **T**

Disregarding the post-training
environment is asking for trouble

# Keeping supervisors
# from sabotaging
# your training efforts

by Joseph Spinale

**W**ell-designed training efforts
that meet specific objectives
and produce the desired behavioral changes can prove to be ineffective or even counter-productive unless the organization considers the
supervision style the new trainee will
encounter back on the job. The trainer,
then, is responsible for defining the
parameters of the supervisory behavior the trainee will experience; and
this will ensure that the training will
result in behavior that meets supervisor expectations.

In order for the trainee to maintain
and strengthen newly learned behaviors, these behaviors must be positively reinforced back on the job. In
many occupations, the supervisor provides the main source of reinforcement
of the newly learned skills. This is particularly true of human relations
skills: the trainee may tend to adopt
and emulate the behavior of the
supervisor, regardless of what he
learned in the training situation.

In some cases, supervisors should be
pretrained so the necessary climate for
maximum reinforcement of training
objectives can be established. The nature of the industry and/or the organization, on the other hand, may require
that training complement existing
supervisory behavior, particularly if
that behavior produces desired organizational results. If the trainer
fails to consider this situation, the
trainee may receive contradictory
messages from training and supervision, and the organization may experience alarming levels of turnover.

A recent study, conducted in one of
the major fast-food organizations,
supports these conclusions. The original intent of the study was to measure
the relationship between satisfaction
with various dimensions of the job of
restaurant manager and an individual's value orientation toward

work in general. The hypothesis was
that certain occupations provide certain kinds of satisfactions. These satisfactions, in turn, appeal to individuals
who value the kinds of rewards and
reinforcements available on the job.

Everyone's value system develops
through a psychological process which
begins in early childhood, and is fairly
well established by the time an individual enters the work force. If an
organization is able to identify the
kinds of satisfactions available in a
particular job and the types of individuals who will respond to these
satisfactions, then it should improve
its ability to fit the person to the job
and, thereby, reduce turnover.

A hundred fast-food restaurant
managers who were assigned to units
in one of nine different geographical
regions participated in the study. A
different supervisor was responsible
for each region or area; in general,
there were 10 or more managers per
supervisor. Each manager completed
two separate questionnaires: one was
designed to measure satisfaction with
various dimensions of the job, and the
other measured aspects of the value
system associated with the individual's attitudes about work in
general. The resulting data were computer processed and statistically
analyzed. (Both questionnaires were
factor analyzed and a multiple regression performed between the resulting
factors.)

## Supervisors are key

Interestingly, the strongest multiple
correlation (describing the relationship between all the work-value factors combined and a specific job-
satisfaction factor) was satisfaction
with supervision ($r = .74$, $p < .01$).
Since the study was conducted with
managers who reported to nine different supervisors, this result would tend
to suggest two things. First, the

supervisor apparently is the source for
much of the satisfaction (or dissatisfaction) that occurs with this particular occupation. Secondly, it seems that
supervisors in this organization tend
to behave in some uniform way, since
similar management personnel tend
to respond to different supervisors in
similar ways.

The implications for training become clear when one examines the factors that contributed to this significant relationship. Those managers
who tended to be satisfied with the
kind of supervision they received were
those who considered their jobs a way
of life and had settled down in their
chosen occupation with career objectives. They had accepted the job for
what it offered and were willing to
work within its defined scope. Managers who tended to be dissatisfied with
supervision, on the other hand, were
typically those who valued creativity
or the ability to be innovative in their
work; they valued achievement in
terms of positive feedback and reinforcement from their supervisors.

From a training point of view, these
results help explain a phenomenon
that the organization's training department had been experiencing for
some time. Certain managers who left
the week-long management development seminar reported that some of
the skills and behaviors they had developed in the training situation were
not supported by the policies or actions
of their supervisors in the field. When
these managers tried to apply these
skills in dealing with their employees,
their actions were considered suspect
by their supervisors. In other cases,
certain managers felt compelled to use
one set of skills in dealing with their
employees and another set when dealing with their supervisors. The resulting confusion and frustration contributed to the high rates of turnover
among managers in the period immediately following the management
seminar.

In addition, a kind of self-perpetua-
ting cycle was established. Since those
managers who were satisfied with
their jobs were dealing successfully
with the existing supervision style,
they generally were able to maintain
the most satisfactory relationships
with their supervisors. Since the
supervisor is largely responsible for
determining who is eligible for promotion into supervisory ranks, they
usually selected those who were satisfied with the existing situation, required minimum feedback and reinforcement, and were not inclined to be
particularly creative or innovative in
their work.

This sets up an interesting and challenging dilemma for the trainer. Training objectives are being met, and managers are developing behaviors consistent with the desires of the organization. Supervisors, on the other hand, are behaving in a way that virtually negates training results, even while giving verbal support to the methods and objectives of the training department. In some cases, effective training actually was establishing no-win situations for both managers and supervisors. Supervisors were not deliberately behaving in ways that would sabotage training efforts, but they were responding in ways that had proved successful for them in the past. They had survived and been successful in the system by adhering to certain methods of behavior. And these entrenched behavior patterns had been rewarded with promotion. While these

supervisors gave lip service to what the organization promoted as improved methods of restaurant management, they actually continued to use tried-and-true methods with which they felt more comfortable.

Depending on the objectives of the organization, the trainer in this situation has various options. One obvious alternative is to provide the supervisor with intensive training first, while ensuring that the next higher level of management not only supports this behavior change but reinforces appropriate responses by the supervisor. In addition, the current state of affairs should be presented to the supervisor openly and honestly so that he becomes more aware of the significance of his own behavior.

An alternative approach simply would be to revise current manager

training to be more consistent with existing patterns of supervisory behavior. Training effectiveness should increase dramatically in this instance since the trained behaviors will be more naturally reinforced by the supervisor back on the job. In any case, any alternative must be considered in light of specific organizational objectives and in relation to desired job performance levels and results.

The point is, training objectives must always be consistent with the kinds of behavioral reinforcements available from the immediate supervisor once the trainee returns to the job. Obviously, any training effort that promotes behavioral change that is inconsistent with the existing supervision style will subtly be sabotaged and prove to be either ineffective or, worse yet, counterproductive. **T**

---

# Link classroom learning to on-the-job experiences

**B**y designing course assignments that link the classroom to the trainee's work environment, Toronto General Hospital transformed a routine in-house supervisory training program into one that is tailor-made for its participants.

TGH's Employee Services and Education Department has been conducting this supervisory skills program (two-hour sessions for 12 weeks) for three years. The course is so effective and popular that TGH now accepts trainees from six other area hospitals.

Central to the course's success is the close and dynamic trainee/supervisor relationship set in motion during the two-hour discussion sessions. After each session, attendees receive assignments that are to be completed

in their respective department settings, with the cooperation of their co-workers and supervisor. This arrangement brings the participant's bosses immediately into a teaching partnership with the TGH education department. For TGH's HRD program, this student/mentor relationship has become the key component of this unique program.

A sample supervisory skills assignment is this one on "Problem Solving and Negotiation":

It appears that there have been an increasing number of complaints about your department from within the hospital. Your director believes that it is not so much the way the department is operating as the fact that people seem unclear about the service you are offering. Other departments are making inappropriate requests (in type and frequency) of you and your people. You cannot have more money, more help, or, of course, more time. The director wants to know how you are going to handle the situation. (The manager has delegated the matter to you because, for three or four weeks, he is

going to be tied up with the hospital's "Operation Austerity.")

Each week, participants receive similar course assignments and complete them under the tutelage of their superior. The payoff, according to TGH trainers, is that participants and their managers have enjoyed a spillover from this new learner/coach relationship into their day-to-day dealings. In general, both parties have found the trainees role expanding on the job as they demonstrate capacities each week and as their supervisors trust them with more discretion and responsibility.

TGH trainers report that because this strategy has been effective with supervisory training, it probably could be used in other areas, such as clinical or professional development, as long as the key student/mentor relationship could be established. — Pam Smith **T**

Reprinted from TRAINING, November 1979

Trainers can ensure that skills learned in the classroom are used on the job

# Making sure your supervisors do on the job what you taught them in the classroom

by James C. Robinson
and Linda E. Robinson

The real measure of success of any type of supervisory training is not the amount of learning that takes place in the classroom but the extent to which supervisors continue to use the new skills back on the job. The new training technologies of the 1970's have proved to be highly effective in improving supervisory skills in the classroom. A disturbingly large amount of evidence indicates, however, that the amount of skill actually transferred to the job is still disappointingly low.[*]

What can you, as a trainer, do to ensure that the skills you teach will be transferred to the job? Fortunately, a great deal. In recent years, specific methods for increasing the amount of skill transfer in supervisory training have been identified. Because all these methods are within the direct control of the trainer or the line manager, you can use them in conjunction with your supervisory training programs to increase skill transfer.

## Prior to training

If supervisory training is to be successful in changing on-the-job behavior, two essential issues must be satisfied before the training begins. First, the supervisors' needs must be identified. Additionally, management must be prepared to support on-the-job use of the new skills to be taught. Therefore, the trainer's pre-workshop responsibilities include conducting a thorough needs analysis and obtaining management support for the classroom training and for the supervisors' use of the skills on the job.

Adults are more motivated to learn when they see that the skills being taught have immediate application, will enable them to overcome problems, and will have a "pay-off" in the real world. For example, supervisors will be more motivated to learn the skill of handling an employee complaint than the skill of effective listening. The former solves a specific supervisory problem, while the latter is "nice to know."

By conducting a thorough needs analysis prior to training, you can help ensure that the skills selected for the program are those of greatest "need" to the supervisors. In other words, the supervisors should consider the skills selected relevant to their problems and success on the job; communicating performance standards and negotiating performance goals are examples of such skills. While the proper selection of skills to be taught is no guarantee that skill transfer will occur, teaching skills for which the learners perceive no need is definitely a waste of time.

Supervisors will do those things their managers and the organization consider important and that are tied to the reward system. For example, when an organization introduces a new budgeting process, management must actively support the process, or it will fail. Likewise, when supervisors are learning new supervisory skills, management must actively support the use of the specific supervisory skills on the job.

Management support will result only if management sees that the proposed training will produce specific benefits. For example, in a new budgeting process, the pay-off is improved planning and better management control. In supervisory training the pay-off can be increased productivity, improved products and better employee/supervisor communications. In each case, management must see specific benefits before it will support the training totally.

To gain management support, the trainer must give managers the opportunity to determine whether or not improved supervisory skills in these areas will provide a return on investment to the organization. Managers must also decide if they are willing to provide the required time, money and support essential to the success of the training endeavor. Obtaining the support of management prior to training can require a considerable time investment by the trainer. But the pay-off will be substantial in terms of long-term use of the skills on the job.

## During training

The trainer controls the classroom learning experience. If the objective of the learning experience is to increase skill transfer and if the classroom training is designed to meet that objective, the extent to which supervisors actually will use the skills on the job will be considerable.

1. **Develop skill mastery.** Developing skill mastery in the classroom is essential. Until supervisors can successfully utilize the new skills in the classroom, they probably won't attempt to use them on the job. First attempts at using a skill are often discouraging because a person feels awkward and unsure. It is unrealistic, then, to expect a supervisor to utilize a skill such as conducting a performance appraisal if he or she has not previously mastered that skill in the classroom. The trainer can help supervisors master skills in the following ways.

- Demonstrate effective use of the skills. Allowing supervisors to learn by trial and error is neither cost effective nor efficient. Without an appropriate model, supervisors may stumble upon a better way of handling a situation, but this is unlikely. A person could not begin to fly an airplane without first observing an experienced pilot. Likewise, supervisors must see the correct way of handling a situation before they can develop the skills to do so themselves. Supervisors who witness an adequate demonstration of what they should be doing, rather than what could go wrong, will make fewer initial errors in

*Byham, W., and Robinson, J. Interaction modeling: A new concept in supervisory training. *Training and Development Journal*, 1976, 30(2), 20-33.

using the skills. Once they see that the new skills do work, training time will be reduced.

- Provide sufficient opportunity to practice the skills. But just seeing someone demonstrate the correct way of doing something isn't enough. Supervisors need an opportunity to practice the demonstrated skills often enough to become proficient at using them.
- Provide immediate feedback on effective and ineffective use of the skills. Positive reinforcement and suggestions for improving while practicing newly learned skills will increase the probability that supervisors will continue to use effective behaviors and that ineffective behaviors will gradually diminish. Effective football coaches provide specific feedback to the players immediately after each practice session. Likewise, the most effective supervisory trainers are those who provide specific feedback to the supervisors immediately after each skill practice.
- Strive for "overlearning." The more supervisors practice correct behaviors, the more likely they will be to apply the skills appropriately on the job. It's not difficult to use skills correctly in the comfort of the training room. Back on the job, however, anxiety or stress may inhibit use of the skills. For example, when supervisors learn the skill of introducing change to their work group, they often are able to handle this task with little difficulty — in the classroom. But when supervisors actually introduce on-the-job changes and employees raise difficult questions, the stress of the real-life situation can make supervisors nervous and ineffective. Supervisors who have overlearned skills in the classroom will be more likely to use them effectively under stressful on-the-job conditions.

2. **Build confidence.** Supervisors who develop confidence in their ability to use the new skills successfully will be more likely to use those skills on the job. But, too often, supervisors leave training programs feeling that the new skills are even more difficult and complicated than they had envisioned at the beginning of the program. The trainer can counter this by building supervisors' confidence through the following approaches.

- Coach for success experiences. Supervisors' confidence must be built through a series of successes rather than failures. Before the start of each skill practice, the trainer must discuss the situation

to be handled to make sure the supervisor understands all the issues and information involved. In addition, the trainer must coach the supervisor on how to use the skills being learned so he or she can deal effectively with the situation in the skill practice exercise. This coaching assures that each skill practice attempt will result in a success, rather than a failure, experience for the supervisor.

- Provide an opportunity to practice using the skills in increasingly difficult situations. The trainer should structure the learning experience so that each practice situation becomes increasingly difficult to handle. As supervisors discover that they can successfully handle the more difficult situations, particularly those they previously had been unable to handle effectively, their confidence in their ability to use the skills will increase.

3. **Apply skills immediately.** The shorter the time between the training and the actual on-the-job use of the skills, the greater the probability that supervisors will continue to use those new skills. To facilitate immediate skill transfer, the trainer should gain the supervisors' commitment to use the skills.

While in the classroom, the supervisors should describe a situation in which they will use the new skills as soon as they return to the job. Once a supervisor has verbalized to his or her colleagues that he or she intends to handle a particular situation, the probability of actually doing it increases. For example, if Supervisor Smith indicates that he intends to handle a work habit problem with Employee Jones, Smith will feel more committed to tackle that problem.

The probability of skill transfer can be increased by having supervisors practice handling specific on-the-job situations in the classroom before applying the skills in real life. This rehearsal often provides the extra measure of confidence needed to confront a particularly difficult problem on the job.

The trainer also should follow up on skill use. In subsequent class sessions, time should be set aside to review the supervisors' experiences in using the new skills on the job. This provides a non-threatening environment in which supervisors can share their successes and discuss how to overcome the problems encountered in applying the skills.

When other supervisors hear that Jones did change his poor work habit after Smith discussed it with him, they will feel that they, too, can

handle similar situations themselves. Those supervisors who had difficulty using the skills on the job can be coached by those who handled similar situations successfully. This mutual sharing of success experiences and coaching in problem areas will increase the use of the skills on the job.

### After training

The success of supervisory training depends both upon the effectiveness of the classroom training and the reinforcement received on the job. Therefore, supervisors must be rewarded for using the skills on the job. This reinforcement can come from several sources, and, in each case, the trainer can increase the probability of it occurring.

1. **Self-assessment.** As supervisors begin to use their new skills on the job, the most readily available source of feedback and reinforcement is the supervisors themselves. Therefore, they must be able to assess their own effectiveness and then make the necessary adjustments for using the skills in the future. When supervisors determine that they have used the skill well, that behavior is reinforced. When supervisors judge that they used the skill ineffectively, they must be able to correct their behavior for future applications.

The trainer can help supervisors accurately assess their own skill levels by teaching them to discriminate between their effective and ineffective use of the skills. Often, supervisors don't know the difference between effective and ineffective behavior in handling a specific situation. They first must be provided with an effective model so they will have a standard with which to compare their own skill level. As supervisors observe others, as well as assess themselves in skill practices, their ability to distinguish between effective and ineffective behaviors gradually will increase.

Trainers also should encourage supervisors to assess their own skill level continually when they use the skills back on the job. To maintain skill proficiency, a person continually must analyze how he or she is doing compared with the established standard. Just as athletes compare their actual performance after each game with what they wanted to do, the good supervisor must analyze how a situation actually was handled compared with what he or she wanted to do. The supervisor then can determine what should be done differently next time.

2. **Peer reinforcement.** Supervisory training shouldn't be limited to new

supervisors or to those "who really need it." When only some supervisors learn new skills, they return to work with peer supervisors who may lack those skills. The reinforcement the trained supervisors receive from their peers will be directed primarily toward those skills that all the supervisors have in common. Consequently, the newly learned skills may receive no reinforcement and gradually may be extinguished.

The trainer can increase the likelihood that peer supervisors will reinforce each other's use of the new skills by having *all* supervisors within a functional group participate in the training. That way, supervisors who have successfully applied the skills will receive recognition from their peer supervisors. And supervisors who have been reluctant to use the skills will be encouraged to do so when they hear about other supervisors' successes.

3. **Management reinforcement.** If transfer is to occur and skill usage continue, supervisors must also receive reinforcement from their bosses for using the new skills. The trainer must make sure that managers assume three essential roles in reinforcing the skills their subordinate supervisors have learned in the classroom.

• Manager as a coach — Skill transfer will occur more often when managers coach their subordinate supervisors on how to use the newly learned supervisory skills. Unless managers are thoroughly familiar with the new skills, however, and can discriminate between effective and ineffective supervisory behavior, they will not be effective coaches. Therefore, the trainer must teach managers what specific skills the supervisors will be using. Once managers develop a thorough knowledge of these supervisory skills, they can coach their supervisors on how to use them on the job.

• Manager as a reinforcer — Managers may understand the theory of reinforcement but not be effective reinforcers, because they haven't been trained how to reinforce. For reinforcement to be effective, it must be directed toward specific behavior. Thus, managers must be trained to discriminate accurately between effective and ineffective behavior, as well as to utilize appropriate methods to reinforce the use of supervisory skills on the job. Trainers should provide managers with sufficient opportunities to develop the skills of discriminating between effective and ineffective supervisory behavior and of reinforcing effective supervisory behavior on the job. Thus, a manager will be able to recognize when a supervisor is correctly handling a situation, such as an employee's poor work habit, and positively reinforce the supervisor for doing so.

• Because managers are the most visible models for their subordinate supervisors, supervisors will tend to imitate their behavior. Consequently, to increase the probability that supervisors will use their new skills on the job, their managers must utilize supervisory skills compatible with those the supervisors learned in the classroom. In the classroom, for example, supervisors may learn to handle employee complaints effectively by listening to the employee and getting complete details about the complaint. When the supervisor then brings a complaint to his or her manager, he or she expects the manager to listen to all the details about *that* complaint. If the manager fails to do this, the supervisors will feel it's a waste of time to use those skills when handling complaints with his or her subordinates. The trainer must make managers aware of their impact as models upon their subordinate supervisors. In addition, the trainer must provide managers with classroom experiences that will enable them to develop the skills necessary to fulfill their roles as positive models.

## Summary

Training provides skills, information, knowledge and the potential for successful application on the job. But only the actual transfer of those skills to on-the-job situations demonstrates the success of the training. And reinforcement of the use of skills on the job determines whether or not the acquired skills will be used in the future.

Trainers have the opportunity and the responsibility to use methods in the classroom that will increase skill transfer on the job. Through these methods, trainers can increase skill transfer, thus assuring on-the-job application of the potential developed in the classroom. **T**

# Reinforcement of learning has big payoff

by Peter Jones

It's time to take a hard, cold look at a classic training problem: How do we, as trainers, make sure that trainees employ their newfound knowledge and skills in actual on-the-job situations. How, in other words, do we ensure that training is a useful, not a wasteful, commodity? It's not easy. But strides are being made in the right direction.

After all, we've already come a long way toward eliminating one of training's original stigmas—that classroom sessions were irrelevant and meaningless in terms of nuts-and-bolts performance. Once we admitted to ourselves that *this* problem existed, it didn't take us long to tailor training sessions around knowledge and basic skills based on everyday situations our trainees faced. We began by developing better job descriptions, task analyses, behavioral objectives, and so on. Designing relevant course content is still hard work, of course, but nearly everyone recognizes it can be done and done well.

Once we started paying more attention to the worker in his job environment, we realized that the environment often has built-in obstacles that prevent the trainee from applying the knowledge and skills we helped him gain. So we began to think of effecting changes in job environments as part of our training job.

For many of us, this hurdle seemed more difficult to surmount than creating relevant course content. After considerable thought, discussions and research, we began to develop techniques to make these types of changes. But a lot of developmental work remains to be done in this area. In fact, it's unlikely that we will ever reach the stage where job environments always, or even often, produce ideal situations.

But that's no reason to give up. In our search for a solution, let's look in the classroom. This area has been thoroughly examined by practically everybody, but we'll do it a little differently this time. Ignoring everything up to the point where the student actually does what we've worked so hard to get him to do, we'll concentrate on how the trainee is rewarded, or not rewarded, for his response. Specifically, we'll consider how often this reinforcement occurs. Psychologists tell us that the frequency of reinforcement determines how fast the trainee will learn and how long he will remember a fact or perform a skill; they describe how often a reinforcement is delivered in terms of reinforcement schedules.

Basically, there are five kinds of reinforcement schedules. The one most commonly used in our business is probably the Continuous Reinforcement (CRF) schedule. Learning occurs faster with this schedule than with any other. Unfortunately, the CRF schedule also has the lowest retention rate. That means the trainee stops doing a learned behavior quickly if he stops receiving reinforcements for performing that behavior.

While trainers may use the CRF schedule frequently, the rest of the world marches to the beat of a different drummer. With any job there are periods of time when the employee receives no reward, feedback, or reinforcement of any kind. This erratic delivery of reinforcements is called the Variable Interval (V.I.) schedule. Psychologists usually agree that the V.I. schedule offers the slowest learning acquisition and the longest retention rate.

Hence, the problem. We take a trainee and put him on a schedule (CRF schedule) which has fast learning acquisition and low retention and then put him back in the real world, which is probably operating on the V.I. schedule of infrequent reinforcements. Nine chances out of ten, he will stop doing the learned behavior before he receives any feedback. Knowing this, how can we expect a trainee to take those newly learned skills back to his work environment and continue to use them?

One answer could be to start the learning process by using a Continuous Reinforcement schedule and convert to a Variable Interval schedule before the training is completed. But this answer raises some tough questions. How do we get each trainee to respond that many times in an abbreviated training session? How do we keep track of when the reinforcement is to be delivered and when it's not?

Another possibility is to train the trainees' supervisors in the art of delivering reinforcements. Now they can convert the trainee from the Continuous Reinforcement schedule used in the training session to the Variable Interval schedule their job environment requires. But this solution also poses problems. How do we get management to agree with us? How can we be sure the supervisors will do what they've been trained to do? Do we have to train the supervisor's supervisors?

Obviously, there is no panacea for the problem at hand. Even finding solutions which only create manageable problems is difficult. But then finding techniques to develop relevant course material and techniques to change job environments wasn't easy either. The initial reaction for many of us might be to declare this an impossible task, while some of the more stalwart members of our profession may accept the challenge. Somebody must if we ever want to reach the point where trainees are actually using the knowledge and skills they gained in our training. **T**

| Reinforcement Schedule | Topographical Description |
| --- | --- |
| Continuous Reinforcement Schedule (CRF) | Reinforcement is received after each appropriate response (i.e. response . . . reinforcement . . . response . . . reinforcement . . . etc.). |
| Fixed Ratio Schedule (FR) | Reinforcement is received only after a certain number of appropriate responses (i.e. 5 responses . . . reinforcement . . . 5 responses . . . reinforcement . . . etc.). |
| Variable Ratio Schedule (VR) | Same as the FR Schedule listed above but the number of responses before a reinforcement is received varies (i.e. 5 responses . . . reinforcement . . . 2 responses . . . reinforcement . . . 7 responses . . . etc.). |
| Fixed Interval Schedule (FI) | Reinforcement is received after the first appropriate response is made after a certain time period has elapsed (i.e. response . . . reinforcement . . . 2 hour time-out period . . . response . . . reinforcement . . . 2 hour time-out period . . . etc.). Any responses made during the time-out period are completely ignored. |
| Variable Interval Schedule (VI) | Same as the FI schedule listed above except the time-out periods vary in length (i.e. 2 hour time-out period . . . response . . . reinforcement . . . 5 minute time-out period . . . response . . . reinforcement . . . 1 day time-out period . . . etc.). |

If you're not sure your trainees
are applying on the job what
they've learned in training,
perhaps a checklist can help

# Using checklists as an aid to transfer of training

by Don Joinson

**T**raining for transfer is essential if training is going to attain lasting balance-sheet respectability. If a training manager wishes to claim professional status, he must learn to mistrust end-of-course test scores as a valid criteria of the success of his training design. The only truly valid criterion is the extent to which trainees actively and accurately use on the job the behaviors they have learned in training.

How do you measure transfer? How do you design training to maximize the chance of transfer? These are both troublesome, but intriguing, questions. For our purposes here, we're going to focus on one small, but crucial aspect of the second question. The core answer lies in extensive simulation practice, ideally practice that continues until the learner feels comfortable, capable, and confident in making the learned responses to the stimulus situation.

Recent experience shows that the humble checklist provides an excellent transfer aid. At the end of the formal training course, the learner takes with him a step-by-step checklist of how he should apply his newly acquired concepts and ideas. And he makes a commitment to check his performance at specific intervals.

The checklist becomes, in effect, an over-learning schedule. It represents controlled learning by doing, with every rehearsal helping to consolidate and reinforce the behavioral se-

quence. After five or six such rehearsals, the checklist is withdrawn. The procedural chain of responses will have become a well-established behavioral pattern, and that elusive "transfer" will have been attained.

## Contents of the checklist

A typical checklist, shown in Figure 1, comes from the supplementary material to a training-the-trainer program in the area of learning objectives, where transfer failure is notorious.

Trainers in training accept the concept of measurable objectives, and post-test analyses show us they can understand and describe the need to specify terminal performance in measurable terms, to specify the standards for such performance, and to state the conditions applicable to satisfactory demonstration of the performance. But, having learned how to write such objectives, some trainers still don't write them.

Instead, they will incorporate a film into a program "because it always gets a good reception." And they will run a mediocre supervision or sales training course "because it seems to meet our needs." Meanwhile, the concept of behavioral training objectives lies, dormant and unrealized, at the back of their collective skull.

We believe the solution to this transfer resistance may be extensive simulation practice, supplemented by the follow-through aid of the checklist. Simulation practice shows the impor-

tance of objectives (from a ten-minute lecturette to a whole semester of integrated learning activity) and helps develop the habit of constructing specific behavioral objectives for *every* designed learning activity. The checklist, a "process reminder" step-by-step aid, consists of 12 prime questions related to specific objectives.

Each question is so phrased that a "Yes" answer will signify that the original learning objective is being met in full. Wherever a "No" or "Partly" or "Not Sure" answer is recorded, the learner should check the "Action" column and commit himself or herself to remedy the deficiencies.

## Build your own checklists

As an alternative to providing ready-made checklists and devices as transfer aids, why not have trainees design their own as the concluding exercise to a formal instructional course? We constructed such a checklist-building module as the final exercise in a two-day time-management training package, "The Time Machine," and found it has a significant effect on assisting transfer.

The training group receives guidelines in checklist construction and a sample checklist as a working model. The group then divides into teams, each of which develops a series of checklist questions for such areas as time-budgeting, delegation, handling paperwork, self-organization, and use of clerical support staff.

Later, the checklists are displayed, discussed, and synthesized into a commonly acceptable version. The course leader then has the final versions printed and distributed to members of the training group. Significantly, transfer tests and field surveys have shown the commitment to a series of self-developed checklists to be extremely high. **T**

# Sample checklist on following page

## Figure 1.

| Use the checklist as an essential step in your instructional design procedure. Whenever you check any column other than YES, also check the ACTION column. Ensure that appropriate action follows. | YES | NO | PARTLY | NOT SURE | ACTION |
|---|---|---|---|---|---|
| 1. Have I stated exactly what the learner will be able to do as a result of successful completion of the learning? | | | | | |
| 2. Have I stated the desired standard to which the learner will be able to carry out the desired end performance? | | | | | |
| 3. Will it be possible to measure precisely that the learner can perform as required to the standard required? | | | | | |
| 4. Have I specified what the learner will be allowed to use while he demonstrates he has reached the learning objectives? | | | | | |
| 5. Have I specified what the learner will NOT be allowed to use while he carries out the desired end performance? | | | | | |
| 6. Is all the above expressed in clear, concise, specific, and measurable terms as a Statement of Learning Objectives? | | | | | |
| 7. Have I tested the Statement to ensure that it accurately and completely communicates the learning objectives to the learners? | | | | | |
| 8. Have I divided each major learning objective up into a series of goals that may be used as reliable progress markers? | | | | | |
| 9. Have I checked that the objectives provide adequate challenge to the learners, without appearing too difficult of attainment? | | | | | |
| 10. Have I verified that I have, or will be able to obtain, all the resources needed to assist in objective attainment? | | | | | |
| 11. Have I constructed a post-test which will adequately sample learner performance for each of the learning objectives? | | | | | |
| 12. Have I constructed a transfer test which will adequately measure how well (if at all) the learning is putting learned skills to work on the job? | | | | | |

© INSTRUCTA PTY. LIMITED

Learn from these survey results

# Training for survival back on the job

by Don M. Ricks

Following their training, people should return to a work environment where their new performance skills will be recognized and rewarded. Trainers know that. Trainers also know that such an environment can be cultivated by including managers in the planning stages of training so that they become committed to looking for and supporting the subsequent results.

But trainers in many organizations know some other things as well. They know, for instance, that a promising program can wither on the vine while months are spent searching for a "convenient" time for a group of managers to get together. They know that some managers have vaguely defined and ambivalent notions about training and are unwilling to discuss them openly. They know that some managers view training not as the road to improvement but to preservation — a way of perpetuating whatever level of mediocrity has become established as "the way we always do it." And to others, training, like janitorial services, is a necessary but essentially nonproductive part of organizational life, something best left to those who are interested in that sort of thing.

So while the average trainer may enjoy reading articles on the systematic design of programs — the ones with the diagrams of boxes and arrows arranged into neat feedback loops — he or she knows that "real life" is very different. A lot of guessing has to be done concerning what results managers actually expect from training. Programs have to be designed or acquired in spite of unrealistic budgetary and constraints. Schedules have to be negotiated to assure that the training does not conflict with the important activities of the organization. And then trainees, having been put through the best program that management could be talked into approving, are sent back to work environments where their new skills, hardwon and still a bit tentative, are vulnerable to the clumsy criticism of the uninformed and the neglect of the indifferent.

We recently concluded a study that illustrates how little encouragement trainees can often expect "back at the office." From the records of writing workshops conducted, over an 18-month period, for a wide range of corporate and governmental organizations, we selected 150 people. The selection was random except for one variable: on the basis of their pre-course writing style scores, 75 people were chosen as the Study Group and another 75 as the Comparison Group.

The Study Group consisted of people whose pre-course scores indicated that they had entered the workshop with either "fair" or "deficient" stylistic skills. In other words, a substantial number of them could be expected to improve sufficiently to attract the notice of their superiors. The Comparison Group was made up of people whose pre-course scores indicated they entered the workshop with "good"

stylistic skills. So any improvements they took back to work were not likely to cause much comment.

The records on these people contained the pre-/post-follow-up scores from their writing style tests and their responses to a course critique form, completed four weeks after each workshop, that included questions about post-course feedback. In short, we were able to determine who had improved by the end of the workshop and who had retained that improvement until the follow-up testing point, as well as who had received feedback on their writing after the course and the nature of that feedback.

**Q. Did the trainees receive post-training feedback from their superiors?**

**A.** Some did, but not nearly as many as we would have liked. Exactly one out of three (only 50 of 150) people indicated that something had been said to them about their writing during the four weeks following the workshop.

**Q. Was the feedback that was received consistent with measurable improvements in writing ability?**

**A.** Apparently not. The above ratio applied (with only one percentage difference) to both groups. That is, one of every three people received post-training feedback, whether they were in the Study Group (which was expected to show visible improvements) or the Comparison Group (which was not). Moreover, the ratio held true within the Study Group itself. Of the 75 people in the group, 63 (84%) had achieved measurable improvement on the post-score test. Yet their feedback rate was only slightly higher that that of the 12 people whose test scores indicated no measurable improvement.

**Q. Did post-training feedback from superiors affect the permanent acquisition of skills?**

**A.** Again, apparently not very much. Of the 40 people in the Study Group who achieved measurably improved scores on the four-week follow-up test, only a moderately higher percentage (37.5% vs. 33.3%) indicated that they received feedback. In fact, the data contained one real surprise. Nine people who had pre-tested in the "deficient skills" range achieved "marked improvement" (a level of change that produces an almost new writing style) on the follow-up test, yet *all* of them indicated that no one had commented upon the improvement.

## General conclusions

At this point, we had to arrive at three general conclusions:

1. We could expect the managers of

only one-third of our workshop participants to provide post-training feedback.

2. Those managers would provide feedback whether or not the individual actually improved.

3. The feedback would have little effect on whether the individual retained his/her improvement.

Then we turned to the critique form responses of those people who had indicated that they had received feedback Of the 50 people, 40 characterized the feedback as "positive," and the written explanations of several suggested that their superiors had offered explicit comments on specific improvements. Of the remaining ten, none indicated the feedback was "negative," six said "mixed" (managers wondered if their writing had become "too direct"), and four checked the disturbing answer, "indifferent." (One written explanation: "Change was noticed but no reaction was evident.") On the surface, these figures suggested the conclusion that, of our participants who would receive feedback, 80% were likely to get positive responses, and the remainder would at least have a chance to discuss their training with their superiors.

But when we examined the written comments, another variable appeared. Nine of those 40 "positives" looked very much like *self-feedback*. Some examples: "My director signs my letters as I compose them; seldom now does he request changes"; "I received fewer inquiries as to what I have said and wanted in my letters and memos"; "I've been given more letter- and report-writing duties. The result has been great." In other words, these managers apparently did not *say* anything. But their behavior relative to the trainees' writing changed, and the trainees interpreted that change as evidence of their own improvement.

In short, the study suggested that our trainees, when they return to work, are pretty much on their own. Only a few will receive direct, positive encouragement to continue working at improving their writing. The rest will have to depend upon whatever self-teaching and self-feedback skills they gained in the course.

## Implications for training

What do the results of this small study suggest for training generally? One pessimistic interpretation is that, except where it is feasible to prepare a receptive post-training environment, those who design workshops should assume that their trainees will return to a work situation in which few will understand what they are trying to do, fewer will care and some will feel threatened. On the other hand, the study also demonstrates that people can improve in a non-supportive work environment. Substantial numbers of the people did upgrade their writing skills, demonstrably and permanently, in spite of receiving little or no post-course feedback.

The key to training people for survival in the post-training environment is, of course, that foundation concept of adult learning — self-direction. Programs designed to provide people with the opportunity to define what skills they need, to measure their own strengths and deficiencies, and to set their own learning objectives will give them the tools they need to improve their performance in the absence of post-training support from others. The most positive result of our study was to illustrate, once again, that training is not something done *to* people, whether by the trainer alone or in collusion with management. It is something done *by* the individuals, who are the sole masters of their environment. ∎

The body of knowledge on the subject
is just beginning to accumulate, but
there are some truisms (we think)

# 30 things we know for sure about adult learning

by Ron and Susan Zemke

**W**e don't know a lot about the mechanisms of adult learning. At least, not in the "What are the minimum— necessary and sufficient— conditions for effecting a permanent change in an adult's behavior?" sense of knowing.

In that, we're not alone. Dr. Malcolm Knowles came to much the same conclusion in *The Adult Learner: A Neglected Species*. Eight years ago, he equated his efforts to summarize what was then known about adult learning to a trip up the Amazon: "It is a strange world that we are going to explore together, with lush growth of flora and fauna with exotic names (including fossils of extinct species) and teeming with savage tribes in raging battle. I have just made a casing-the-joint trip up the river myself, and I can tell you that my head is reeling." Today Knowles says, "The river is much tamer. We are beginning to understand what we do that works and why it works." But as we listen, we have the distinct impression that what our point man Knowles sees as tame travel can still be white-water rapids for the rest of us.

While there are hundreds of books and articles offering tips and tricks for teaching adults, the bulk of that knowledge is derived from three relatively limited spheres. The first is "My life and times in teaching," wherein one teacher/trainer of adults shares his or her career's accumulation of secrets with others. Though intriguing and interesting, this literature focuses more on teacher survival than anything else, and while we learn much about living, we learn relatively little about learning.

The second common source is the "Why adults decide to study" research. Here we learn some interesting, even fascinating, things about the conditions and incidents that motivate adults to engage in a "focused learning effort." But in most of this research, the adult seems assumed to be a learning machine who, once switched on, vacuums up knowledge and skill. It is more indicative than instructive, suggestive than substantive. A cynic would call this body of knowledge about adult learning a form of market research.

The third source is extrapolation from theory: both adult learning theory and research and that derived from work with children and nonhuman subjects. The adult learning theories in question are really holistic treatments of human nature: the Carl Rogers/Abraham Maslow sort of theory from which we can only infer, or guess at, rules of practice. "Would you rather learn from a lecture or a book?" or "On your own or with direction?" are interesting questions, but ones that beg the issue of results or learning outcomes. A trainee may prefer listening to lectures but learn best by practice and application exercises.

The nonadult theory and research is a broad lot— everything from child development studies to pigeon training. The tendency seems to be to draw guidance from the B. F. Skinner/behavior modification/programmed instruction, and the Albert Bandura/behavior modeling/social learning schools of thought. While both schools are generating research and results, they are still shorter on proven practices than pontification and speculation. No single theory, or set of theories, seems to have an arm-lock on understanding adults or helping us work effectively and efficiently with them.

Still and all, from a variety of sources there emerges a body of fairly reliable knowledge about adult learning—arbitrarily 30 points which lend themselves to three basic divisions:

● Things we know about adult learners and their motivation.
● Things we know about designing curriculum for adults.
● Things we know about working with adults in the classroom.

These aren't be-all, end-all categories. They overlap more than just a little bit. But they help us understand what we are learning from others about adult learning.

**Motivation to learn**

Adult learners can't be threatened, coerced or tricked into learning something new. Birch rods and gold stars have minimum impact. Adults *can* be ordered into a classroom and prodded into a seat, but they *cannot'* be forced to learn. Though trainers are often faced with adults who have been sent to training, there are some insights to be garnered from the research on adults who seek out a structured learning experience on their own; something we all do at least twice a year, the research says. We begin our running tally from this base camp.

**1** Adults seek out learning experiences in order to cope with specific life-change events. Marriage, divorce, a new job, a promotion, being fired, retiring, losing a loved one and moving to a new city are examples.

**2** The more life-change events an adult encounters, the more likely he or she is to seek out learning opportunities. Just as stress increases as life-change events accumulate, the motivation to cope with change through engagement in a learning experience increases. Since the people who most frequently seek out learning opportunities are people who have the most overall years of education, it is reasonable to guess that for many of us learning is a coping response to significant change.

**3** The learning experiences adults seek out on their own are directly related— at least in their own perception— to the life-change events that triggered the seeking. Therefore, if 80% of the change being encountered is work related, then 80% of the learning experiences sought should be work related.

**4** Adults are generally willing to engage in learning experiences before, after, or even during the ac-

Reprinted from TRAINING, June 1981

tual life-change event. Once convinced that the change is a certainty, adults will engage in any learning that promises to help them cope with the transition.

**5** Although adults have been found to engage in learning for a variety of reasons— job advancement, pleasure, love of learning and so on— it is equally true that for most adults learning is not its own reward. Adults who are motivated to seek out a learning experience do so primarily (80-90% of the time) because they have a use for the knowledge or skill being sought. Learning is a means to an end, not an end in itself.

**6** Increasing or maintaining one's sense of self-esteem and pleasure are strong secondary motivators for engaging in learning experiences. Having a new skill or extending and enriching current knowledge can be both, depending on the individual's personal perceptions.

The major contributors to what we know about adult motivation to learn have been Allen Tough, Carol Aslanian and Henry Brickell, Kjell Rubenson and Harry L. Miller. One implication of their findings for the trainer is that there seem to be "teachable moments" in the lives of adults. Their existence impacts the planning and scheduling of training. As a recent study by the management development group of one large manufacturer concluded, "Newly promoted supervisors and managers must receive training as nearly concurrent with promotions and changes in responsibilities as possible. The longer such training is delayed, the less impact it appears to have on actual job performance."

**Curriculum design**

One developing research-based concept that seems likely to have an impact on our view and practice of adult training and development is the concept of "fluid" versus "crystallized" intelligence. R. B. Catell's research on lifelong intellectual development suggests there are two distinct kinds of intelligence that show distinct patterns of age-related development, but which function in a complementary fashion. Fluid intellect tends to be what we once called innate intelligence; fluid intelligence has to do with the ability to store strings of numbers and facts in short-term memory, react quickly, see spatial relations and do abstract reasoning. Crystallized intelligence is the part of intellectual functioning we

have always taken to be a product of knowledge acquisition and experience. It is related to vocabulary, general information, conceptual knowledge, judgment and concrete reasoning.

Historically, many societies have equated youth with the ability to insatiably acquire information and age with the ability to wisely use information. Catell's research suggests this is true—that wisdom is, in fact, a separate intellectual function that develops as we grow older. Which leads to some curriculum development implications of this concept:

**7** Adult learners tend to be less interested in, and enthralled by, survey courses. They tend to prefer single-concept, single-theory courses that focus heavily on the application of the concept to relevant problems. This tendency increases with age.

**8** Adults need to be able to integrate new ideas with what they already know if they are going to keep—and use—the new information.

**9** Information that conflicts sharply with what is already held to be true, and thus forces a re-evaluation of the old material, is integrated more slowly.

**10** Information that has little "conceptual overlap" with what is already known is acquired slowly.

**11** Fast-paced, complex or unusual learning tasks interfere with the learning of the concepts or data they are intended to teach or illustrate.

**12** Adults tend to compensate for being slower in some psychomotor learning tasks by being more accurate and making fewer trial-and-error ventures.

**13** Adults tend to take errors personally, and are more likely to let them affect self-esteem. Therefore, they tend to apply tried-and-true solutions and take fewer risks. There is even evidence that adults will misinterpret feedback and "mistake" errors for positive confirmation.

Dr. K. Patricia Cross, author of *Adults As Learners*, sees four global implications for designing adult curriculum in Catell's work. "First, the presentation of new information should be meaningful, and it should include aids that help the learner organize it and relate it to previously

stored information. Second, it should be presented at a pace that permits mastery. Third, presentation of one idea at a time and minimization of competing intellectual demands should aid comprehension. Finally, frequent summarization should facilitate retention and recall."

A second neat new idea that impacts curriculum design is the concept of adult developmental stages. Jean Piaget, Lawrence Kohlberg and others have seen children as passing through phases and stages for some time. It is only recently, thanks to Gail Sheehy, Roger Gould, Daniel Levinson and others, that we've come to acknowledge that there are also adult growth stages. A subset of this concept is the idea that not only do adults' needs and interests continually change, but their values also continue to grow and change. For that insight, we can thank Clare W. Graves and his pioneering work in value analysis. The implications, though still formative:

**14** The curriculum designer must know whether the concepts and ideas will be in concert or in conflict with learner and organizational values. As trainers at AT&T have learned, moving from a service to a sales philosophy requires more than a change in words and titles. It requires a change in the way people think and value.

**15** Programs need to be designed to accept viewpoints from people in different life stages and with different value "sets."

**16** A concept needs to be "anchored" or explained from more than one value set and appeal to more than one developmental life stage.

A final set of curriculum design guides comes from the research on learning media preference. Researchers have for years been asking students if they preferred learning XYZ from a book, a movie experience or another person. Though there are limitations to the value of this sort of data, enough of it is accumulating to be of some help to the design effort.

**17** Adults prefer self-directed and self-designed learning projects 7 to 1 over group-learning experiences led by a professional. Furthermore, the adult learner often selects more than one medium for the design. Reading and talking to a qualified peer are frequently cited as good resources. The desire to control pace and start/stop time strongly affect the self-directed preference.

**18** Nonhuman media such as books, programmed instruction and television have become popular in recent years. One piece of research found them very influential of the way adults plan self-directed learning projects.

**19** Regardless of media, straightforward how-to is the preferred content orientation. As many as 80% of the polled adults in one study cited the need for applications and how-to information as the primary motivation for undertaking a learning project.

**20** Self-direction does *not* mean isolation. In fact, studies of self-directed learning show self-directed projects involve an average of 10 other people as resources, guides, encouragers and the like. The incompetence or inadequacy of these same people is often rated as a primary frustration. But even for the self-professed, self-directed learner, lectures and short seminars get positive ratings, especially when these events give the learner face-to-face, one-to-one access to an expert. Apparently, the adult learner is a very efficiency-minded individual. Allen Tough suggests that the typical adult learner asks "What is the cheapest, easiest, fastest way for me to learn to do *that*?" and then proceeds independently along this self-determined route. An obvious tip for the trainer is that the adult trainee has to have a hand in shaping the curriculum of the program.

### In the classroom

We seem to know the least about helping the adult maximize the classroom experience. There are master performers in our trade who gladly pass along their favorite tips and tricks, but as Marshall McLuhan observed, "We don't know who discovered water but we can be pretty sure it wasn't a fish." In other words, the master performer is often a poor judge of how one becomes a master performer. There certainly are volumes of opinion and suggestion, but by and large they rest more on theory than hard data. Ironically, some of the strongest data comes from survey studies of what turns off adults in the classroom. Likewise, there is a nicely

developing body of literature on what makes for good and bad meetings that has implications for training:

**21** The learning environment must be physically and psychologically comfortable. Adults report that long lectures, periods of interminable sitting and the absence of practice opportunities are high on the irritation scale.

**22** Adults have something real to lose in a classroom situation. Self-esteem and ego are on the line when they are asked to risk trying a new behavior in front of peers and cohorts. Bad experiences in traditional education, feelings about authority and the preoccupation with events outside the classroom all affect in-class experience. These and other influencing factors are carried into class with the learners as surely as are their gold Cross pens and lined yellow pads.

**23** Adults have expectations, and it is critical to take time up front to clarify and articulate *all* expectations before getting into content. Both trainees and the instructor/facilitator need to state their expectations. When they are at variance, the problem should be acknowledged and a resolution negotiated. In any case, the instructor can assume responsibility only for his or her own expectations, not for that of trainees.

**24** Adults bring a great deal of life experience into the classroom, an invaluable asset to be acknowledged, tapped and used. Adults can learn well—and much—from dialogue with respected peers.

**25** Instructors who have a tendency to hold forth rather than facilitate can hold that tendency in check—or compensate for it—by concentrating on the use of open-ended questions to draw out relevant trainee knowledge and experience.

**26** New knowledge has to be integrated with previous knowledge; that means active learner participation. Since only the learners can tell us how the new fits or fails to fit with the old, we have to ask them. Just as the learner is dependent on us for confirming feedback on skill practice, we are dependent on the learner for feedback about our curriculum and in-class performance.

**27** The key to the instructor role is control. The instructor must balance the presentation of new material, debate and discussion, sharing of relevant trainee experiences, and the clock. Ironically, we seem best able to establish control when we risk giving it up. When we shelve our egos and stifle the tendency to be threatened by challenge to our plans and methods, we gain the kind of facilitative control we seem to need to effect adult learning.

**28** The instructor has to protect minority opinion, keep disagreements civil and unheated, make connections between various opinions and ideas, and keep reminding the group of the variety of potential solutions to the problem. Just as in a good problem-solving meeting, the instructor is less advocate than orchestrator.

**29** Integration of new knowledge and skill requires transition time and focused effort. Working on applications to specific back-on-the-job problems helps with the transfer. Action plans, accountability strategies and follow-up after training all increase the likelihood of that transfer. Involving the trainees' supervisor in pre-/post-course activities helps with both in-class focus and transfer.

**30** Learning and teaching theories function better as a resource than as a Rosetta stone. The four currently influential theories—humanistic, behavioral, cognitive and developmental—all offer valuable guidance when matched with an appropriate learning task. A skill-training task can draw much from the behavioral approach, for example, while personal growth-centered subjects seem to draw gainfully from humanistic concepts. The trainer of adults needs to take an eclectic rather than a single theory-based approach to developing strategies and procedures.

Study of the adult as a special species of learner is a relatively new phenomenon. We can expect the next five years to eclipse the last fifty in terms of hard data production on adult learning. For now, however, we must recognize that adults want their learning to be problem-centered, personalized and accepting of their need for self-direction and personal responsibility. When you think of it, that's quite a lot to work with right there. **T**

# New research on adult "styles"

**M**ost trainers know that STYLE is one of the hottest buzz words for 1977. There's a renewed interest in leadership style. There's a communication style, conceptual style, and behavioral style.* Confused by all this stylish babble? You needn't be, as the concept behind it is pretty straightforward.

Suppose you have two teenagers, Susan and Sam. Susan moves slowly and languidly. When she speaks, she does so evenly and quietly. When Sam walks, he runs. He speaks at a machine-gun pace and often with .45 caliber concussiveness. His tone and volume run radio-dial ranges. Sam and Susan are different.

A personality theorist would look at them and wonder about the antecedents of their behavior and their cognitive structures. Was Sam punished for being idle as a tot? Was Susan scolded for making noise as a baby? What pathologies might they develop as they grow into adulthood?

### Different learners, styles

Style theorists, on the other hand, would ask how Frenetic Sam and Dreamy Susan live together in the same house without producing a constant state of undeclared sibling warfare. Could Sam and Susan ever learn to work together? Where do their differences complement; where do they collide?

Personality theorists are interested in the whole person—all the interests, attitudes, temperaments, needs, physiology, aptitudes, and morphology which they consider necessary to fully describe and explain a person. Those who study style have different fish to fr  They try to:

1. determine and codify those observable behavioral aspects of individuation referred to as Style;

2. develop a theory of interpersonal one-to-one relations and communications based on style differences;

3. determine and codify interpersonal style factors which lead to effective and ineffective interpersonal relations and communications; and

4. develop a body of knowledge which will yield a technology for improving interpersonal relations and communications utilizing the concept of style.

### Are you a relational?

Now a group of adult education researchers from the Ontario Institute for Studies in Adult Education have added a fifth concern—developing a theory of differential instruction based on cognitive style differences between learners.

Researchers Richard W. V. Cawley, Sheila A. Miller, and James N. Milligan have done preliminary work that supports the conjecture that there are a limited number of cognitive styles among adult learners. Their research indicates that these styles are pretty evenly distributed in the population and, therefore, may be critically important to understand in the design of training for adults. Based on research conducted with a small group of graduate students, Cawley, Miller, and Milligan are convinced that there are at least two major cognitive or adult information processing styles: the *Analytical* and the *Relational*.

The *Analytical* learner is field-independent and able to select relevant stimuli imbedded in a larger context. Analyticals seem able to resist interfering signals when working on technical tasks. They have long attention spans, are highly reflective, and can concentrate deeply. In tasks, the Analytical prefers complexity. In learning environments, he or she prefers the formal learning situation, sees the instructor strictly as an information giver, and conceptualizes learning as a non-social experience.

The *Relational* learner is field-dependent. He or she sees things in global terms and tends to understand learning experiences as wholes or Gestalts. A short attention span, distractability, and hyperkinesis characterize the *Relational*. Simple tasks and concepts appeal. The Relational values learning which is centered in the self, has relevance for his or her life, relates to his or her feelings, ties into other, prior experiences. The Relational prefers the informal learning setting and sees the instructor first as a person, then as a facilitator of learning.

### Ah, congenial company

Two supplemental findings tend to tie Cawley's, Miller's, and Milligan's work with other style research. First, they noticed that the Relationals who had difficulty with one particular analytically oriented test tended to be apologetic for taking so much time and doing so poorly. The Analyticals, on the other hand, responded to a similar situation without apologies.

The second incidental finding pertained to the life styles of the graduate students studied. Analyticals tended to live alone, while the Relationals tended to live with a group or in a family. The Analyticals believed that a family obligation would detract from the tasks of student life and interfere with the goal of attaining a graduate degree. The Relationals rationalized their life-style selection thusly: You only go around once in life, and without congenial company, the trip is not worth taking.—Reported in "Cognitive Style and the Adult Learner," *Adult Education*, 1976, Vol. 26, No. 2. **T**

Reprinted from TRAINING, May 1977

# Understanding trainee communication styles: Different strokes for different folks

by John L. Bledsoe

Have you sometimes wondered why it seems so difficult to communicate with some people? And why at other times you instantaneously hit it off with someone you have just met? There seems to be a basis of understanding that is more than could be explained by a common background or related profession.

Or perhaps you've been surprised by an abrupt breakthrough in understanding when talking to a friend or business associate. You may have spent several minutes presenting what you see as relevant information — background material, pertinent facts, logical options. Your friend or associate has been growing progressively more restless. Then you decide to tell him how it *feels,* and, suddenly, you have instant communication.

What accounts for this change? And why do we seem to relate better with some people than with others?

The secret was unlocked by Carl Jung, a Swiss psychoanalyst. In a monumental work, *Psychological Types,* written in the 1920's but not translated in its entirety and

published in the U.S. until 1974, Jung articulated a theory of personality so revolutionary in its divergence from so-called modern psychology that most personality theoreticians have, at this writing, refused to rebut it, much less assimilate it. To do so would involve nothing less than scrapping fifty years' worth of accumulated "psychological laws and truth."

What really accounts for personality differences, Jung said, is that every individual develops a primacy in one of four major behavioral functions:

*Intuiting:* speculating, imagining, envisioning, daydreaming, creating, innovating.
*Thinking:* rationally deducting, analyzing, ordering facts, identifying and weighing options, reflecting.
*Feeling:* empathizing, perceiving, associating, remembering, relating.
*Sensing:* acting — doing, relying on sensory data, combating-competing, striving for results, living in the here and now.

Behavior patterns, Jung claimed, are genetically determined and are reflected by infants during their first day of life. Study young children, he said, truly observe

them and you must discover that they process experience on different primary channels. The truth is that children in elementary school can be validly classified as intuitors, thinkers, feelers, and sensors.

The *intuitor* child sits alone, apparently daydreaming. In reality, he is forming global concepts, integrating experience in a constant quest to determine the *why* of things. Knowing something because the teacher says it's true is not sufficient. He must discover why a thing is true. In the absence of such discovery, he will summarily reject your premise.

The *thinker* child prides himself

on being correct. He demonstrates a structured and systematic approach to learning. He gathers facts, not ideas. His concern is to systematize, to collect and infer but not to dream. His approach is information-centered.

The *feeler* child responds to mood, to affect — his own as well as the emotions of others. He learns through his emotions, his visceral responses. He is empathetic, sentimental. He demonstrates keen interpersonal radar. Whether or not he engages in an activity with true commitment depends upon its perceived meaning in terms of past experience — not future possibilities or book-learned facts. His touchstone of reality is meaningful memories.

The *sensor* child is the doer, the fast-mover, the restless jack-in-the-box, the learner who must grab the rock or the frog in his own hands to know its reality; the child who is sent to the principal's office today and who emerges as the corporate president of one of Fortune's 500 tomorrow. He dissipates anxiety through action, he knows by *doing* — not by imagining, thinking, or feeling. As a man, he becomes a Vince Lombardi; as a woman, the type of mother who completes her housecleaning by 9:30 a.m. in order to get to her "own thing" before 10 a.m.

So what does this have to do with training in U.S. corporations today? Perhaps a great deal more than you may imagine.

Consider these concepts:

1. Every one of us, trainer and trainee (yes, even you), uses a blend of the four behavioral styles. No one is a walking "pure style" or cardboard creature.

2. Despite using a blend or style-mix, each person relies most heavily on a primary or dominant style.

3. An individual's weaknesses — or areas of key behavioral difficulty — often represent an over-extension of his strengths.

4. An individual's style is reflected in his behavior and is therefore *observable* and *identifiable*.

Psychologist Paul Mok saw the need to translate Jung's theories into *action* terms, to make the theory "see-able" and "do-able." Mok figured that if people do use these four main styles to process data (receive) and to broadcast data (send), then it follows that one of their primary functions is to serve as communication channels.

No style should be considered good or bad. No one style is more "right" or "wrong" than another. The communicating styles we have developed over the years have little to do with intellectual abilities, aptitudes, performance, or concerns about mental health or illness. You use four main channels of communication; so do I. So does every boss and every subordinate, every salesman and every customer, every husband and every wife, every teacher and every pupil.

Transactional analysis, based on the Freudian model of personality, suggests that if you and I are communicating in our adult ego states, we will be engaged in adult-adult communication, ergo a parallel transaction. Not necessarily so.

Why? If you are a primary sensor functioning in your adult ego state, you want to know *immediately* what

| Primary Communicating Style | TYPICAL TELEPHONE BEHAVIOR | TYPICAL OFFICE DECOR OR SURROUNDINGS |
|---|---|---|
| INTUITOR | Wordy but aloof. Impersonal. Goes off on tangents. Not mindful of your time or his. | Intuitors are likely to demonstrate their imagination in their selection of new-wave furnishings and decor. Those in "think" occupations and professions have offices resembling mini think-tanks: round conference tables, inspiration-pads on walls, offbeat periodicals. Add citations for idealistic work, community service and pet causes. |
| THINKER | "Business like" but lackluster. Little voice inflection. Ticks off specifics. Ordered, measured manner. Sometimes suggests ground-rules for phone conversation, i.e., "Shall we begin with your agenda or mine?" | Thinkers like their work surroundings to be correct and non-distracting. They select furnishings that are tasteful but conventional. Likely to have charts for business use, reports, and reference works nearby. Few touches of informality and color. |
| FEELER | Warm and friendly, sometimes seemingly too much so. Doesn't seem to distinguish between business and personal calls in the sense that he's likely to be quite informal. Interjects humor, personal associations, questions about one's well-being, etc. Likes to "gossip." Talks incessantly. Feels rude if hangs up fast. | Feelers tend to personalize their surroundings, make their offices informal and somewhat "homey." They like warm colors, antiques; big, live plants, mementos, snapshots rather than formal photographs of family. Papers and files, etc., are likely to be messy on the surface, "organized" underneath in a personal way only they can understand. |
| SENSOR | Abrupt. Staccato. Gets to the point, expects others to do the same. Interrupts. Needs to control the conversation. | Sensors generate atmosphere of hard-charging clutter. Mementos, if any, connote action: heads of animals hunted, golf trophies, mounted fish, racing prints. Desk is likely to be big, messy. Sensor is too busy to be neat, too action-oriented to be concerned with image unless he has a strong thinker back-up style. |

I'm proposing, what the *upshot* or *bottom line* is that I'm suggesting.

If I'm a primary thinker functioning in my adult ego state, and I want you to *know all the facts* and insist on giving you a *long-detailed rundown* on my *fact-finding* and *historical review* of the situation, we are not effectively interacting, not communicating in parallel!

Certainly, there are applications for the teacher. It's very hard to have a successful education experience if the trainee is trying to learn on one wavelength and the trainer is trying to teach on another.

Mok designed a Communicating Styles Survey which, in a few minutes, can give an individual valid data on his primary communicating style, his back-up style, and his short-suit (or less typically relied upon) styles which he uses under everyday normal conditions. The same instrument also provides data feedback on the individual's *style-shifts* under stress (e.g., the normally fast-moving, hard-charging sensor who becomes, under stress, a conservative, cautious, weighing thinker).

The accompanying tables will demonstrate. First, try to pinpoint the positive characteristics associated with your primary style. Then, imagine situations in which you would be apt to over-extend these positive characteristics (see table of characteristics). Do you realize how your positive characteristics can, as a result of over-reliance and a lack of self-monitoring, become negative or dysfunctional?

For example, if you are a primary thinker, you probably tend to be analytical. But you must be careful not to over-extend this characteristic and become rigid and overly serious.

The point is, individuals *can* learn to read their communicating styles more accurately, and to read and assess the styles of other individuals with whom they do business on a daily basis.

Once they accept this concept and relate it to increased personal awareness, it's time to learn to *style-flex*. Style-flexing means communicating with another individual on *his* primary channel rather than communicating with all people as though they were all, say, primary thinkers. Is this really possible?

Absolutely.

Is it easy?

Certainly not.

Jung indicated that individuals rarely outgrow or discard their primary styles. In other words, a person's communicating style tends to be very stable through time.

It would be difficult, if not impossible, for you or me, even as professional trainers, to style-flex continuously over a 24-hour period. That is, if you're a primary thinker, it would be unrealistic to expect you to be able to communicate effectively as a feeler for an entire day. But most transactions are much shorter in duration. How long is an average sales call — 45 minutes to an hour and a half? How long is a

| TYPICAL STYLE OF DRESS | CHARACTERISTICS ASSOCIATED WITH THE COMMUNICATING STYLES | |
|---|---|---|
| | **Effective Application** | **Ineffective Application** |
| Hard to predict. May be like "absent-minded professor," more into ideas than image, a la Howard Hughes. May be too wrapped up in future goals to think about daily appearance. Alternatively may have imaginative self-concept that may reflect in clothes from stunning to outlandish. | original<br>imaginative<br>creative<br>broad-gauged<br>charismatic<br>idealistic<br>intellectually tenacious<br>ideological | unrealistic<br>"far-out"<br>fantasy-bound<br>scattered<br>devious<br>out-of-touch<br>dogmatic<br>impractical |
| Conservative, "proper." Unassuming, understated. Dress invariably appropriate to circumstance. Business-like in office; well tailored, "correct" in non-work atmosphere. Color-coordinated, but not colorful. | effective communicator<br>deliberative<br>prudent<br>weighs alternatives<br>stabilizing<br>objective<br>rational<br>analytical | verbose<br>indecisive<br>over-cautious<br>over-analyzes<br>unemotional<br>non-dynamic<br>controlled and controlling<br>over-serious, rigid |
| Dress is more according to own mood than to suit others' expectations. Likes colorful, informal clothes. Often has sentimental, favorite articles of clothing. Sometimes shows a hankering for old-fashioned touches or "costume" effects. | spontaneous<br>persuasive<br>empathetic<br>grasps traditional values<br>probing<br>introspective<br>draws out feelings of others<br>loyal | impulsive<br>manipulative<br>over-personalizes<br>sentimental<br>postponing<br>guilt-ridden<br>stirs up conflict<br>subjective |
| Informal, simple, functional clothes are the order of the day. Wants to be neat but not fancy. Tends to categorize: everyday or dress-up. If sensors see the occasion as being "special," they throw simplicity to the winds; their competitive zeal then rises to the surface and they may "outclass" everyone. | pragmatic<br>assertive, directional<br>results-oriented<br>objective — bases opinions on what he actually **sees**<br>competitive<br>confident | doesn't see long-range<br>status seeking, self-involved<br>acts first then thinks<br>lacks trust in others<br><br>domineering<br>arrogant |

typical boss-subordinate performance review session — an hour or two? Most people can, with practice, learn to style-flex for limited periods of time.

And style-flexing is, in itself, not the only key. Sometimes just asking a person the "right question" can thaw a difficult communication transaction. For example, if you're dealing with a primary intuitor, ask him, "How do you feel about the basic *concept* underlying this proposal?"

To a thinker, ask: "Based on your own *analysis,* how would you evaluate the relevance of the facts I've presented?"

To a feeler: "I've given this a lot of consideration but I'd like to know *how you feel we're tracking.*"

To a sensor: "I hope I haven't bored you; what's your reaction to the *main point* here?"

If you take the time and trouble to learn the technology presented here and to apply it by style-flexing, will people regard you as a phony? That's a common fear, but experience by thousands in industry proves quite the contrary. People will say, "Now you're on *my* wavelength!" Or, "I appreciate your being open enough to share some of your doubts and apprehensions." Or, "Thanks for boiling it down and respecting the fact that I really don't have a hell of a lot of time!"

A few weeks ago, Bob Baker, regional administrator of a Fortune 500 listed corporation and a very hard-nosed, competitive person, made this comment: "I've seen it all — sensitivity training, TA workshops, team-building, you name it. But in the three months since I learned style-flexing and began applying it, I've realized for

the first time that I'd been treating certain types of subordinates like dirt under my shoe. One subordinate whom I was convinced had to be terminated has now emerged as my most promotable assistant."

Eighteen hundred miles away in Atlanta, a 44-year-old Coca Cola account executive wrote: "Yesterday I approached a new prospect, a VP of purchasing for 300 fast-food chain stores, about Coke syrup. In eight minutes, I read him as a primary feeler, so I style-flexed, shifting my presentation from my natural thinker style to his major receptivity channel. He placed an initial order of $150,000 and thanked *me!* Why? I spoke *his* language!"

Are you a doubting Thomas?
You might be missing the best bet of your life! **T**

Studies of human behavior bring to light a startling gap between attitude and action

# Changing what trainees say doesn't always change what they do

by Joe Seacrist

Fire-and-brimstone preachers exhort their flocks to repent. Feminists hold consciousness-raising rap sessions. Training directors conduct training programs. Does all this organized brainwashing work? Can attitudes and beliefs be changed? In adults? A growing body of scientific research indicates that the preachers, feminists and training directors are right. Attitudes and beliefs can be changed. And in a relatively short time. Since it's also been proved that existing attitudes determine behavior, it's logical to assume that if you change a person's attitude, you'll change his behavior. It's logical, but it isn't true.

New scientific studies of human behavior bring to light a startling gap between attitude and action, behavior and belief. One of the most interesting of these studies was done in an industrial setting by a team of Ohio State University researchers. They set out to measure the behavior changes in a group of plant foremen who were about to undertake a two-week course in human relations. The course emphasized ways and means of dealing with subordinates. The plant foremen were exposed to lectures, group discussions, visual aids and role plays—all the techniques used in highly sophisticated training programs. The general purpose of the program was to persuade foremen that mutual trust, warmth and consideration are desirable in dealing with subordinates.

The foremen filled out questionnaires before taking the course, and afterwards. The results of the questionnaires indicated that after taking the course, foremen were sold on mutual trust, warmth and consideration.

Had the study stopped here as most studies do, it would not have turned up a surprising fact. When the researchers went into the plant and measured the behavior change of the trained foremen against a group of untrained foremen—a control group that had not taken the course—they found *no discernable difference in behavior*. In other words, attitudes which were changed in the training sessions did not cause changes in behavior in the factory. Why? This is a question which is probably not asked often enough.

Arthur R. Cohen, renowned researcher and author of social psychology texts, points out this disinclination in his book, ATTITUDE CHANGE AND SOCIAL INFLUENCE. He says, "Attitudes are always seen to be a precursor to behavior, a determinant of what behaviors the individual will actually go about doing in his daily affairs. However, though most psychologists assume such a state of affairs, very little work on attitude change has explicitly dealt with the behavior that may follow upon a change of attitudes. Most researchers in the field are content to demonstrate that there are factors which affect attitude change

Reprinted from TRAINING, February 1976

and that these factors are open to orderly exploration, without actually carrying through to the point where they examine the links between changed attitudes and changes in learning performance, perception and interaction."

Attempting to examine these links, let's go back to the plant foremen. Whatever happened to them in the training program aimed at changing attitudes evidently worked. It changed their beliefs and attitudes. Then they left the training environment and went back to the factory, where a different set of stimuli worked on them. Instead of a training director, there was a boss and a quota. Instead of lectures and films there was work to get out. Instead of an approving peer group, there was derision. In short, whatever pressures had formed their original opinions—before training—were alive and well and operative.

Another example can be seen in the salesman who believes in high-pressure closes as the best way to make sales. He's developed the opinion over the years. He's been successful with the technique. He's seen other salesmen succeed with it. After hours, he's heard fellow salesmen brag about their ability to make high-pressure closes and the benefits they've reaped because of this ability. When he manages a high-pressure close himself, he gets a lot of satisfaction out of it. Nobody has ever complained, and once when he used a high-pressure close, two people came up to him afterwards and commented on how forceful he was in the final minutes of his presentation. Surely, this man feels, high-pressure closes must be desirable.

At this point, the salesman has a discussion with his newly-appointed sales manager who tells him that he does not approve of high-pressure closes, that he, himself, has never needed them. The sales manager tells many success stories proving that soft sell works better. The salesman knows many of the stories are true. He respects the sales manager and is impressed by his sales record and actually begins to believe that high-pressure closes aren't desirable. Now, if the salesman were asked on a questionnaire if high-pressure closes were desira-ble, he would probably answer no. He might even decide that on his next sales call, he would try a different approach. However, when he actually makes the call, what happens? The salesman remembers how important this sale is, to his record, income, ego. He finds it easy to go back to his tried-and-true high-pressure tactic. Some other time, he tells himself, he will try soft sell. But now, because he really needs this sale, he'd better nail it down the best way he knows. So he uses his usual high-pressure close. He is still not convinced it's the best way, but the environment makes it too convenient for him to use it.

As these examples demonstrate, psychologists are coming to see that when opinions and attitudes are changed through the impact of a persuasive communication, the change is likely to disappear unless it is supported by an environmental change as well. Before we

---

**Even though attitudes are changed through persuasive communication, the change is likely to disappear unless supported by a change in the environment. We are not that easy to manipulate.**

---

can provide these changes, we need to know what they should be and we need to know more about how people receive and maintain attitudes and beliefs and translate them into behavior. Currently, there are a number of intriguing pieces to this puzzle.

1. Attitudes frequently function to meet psychological needs. It's useless to try and change an attitude without knowing the psychological need it is meeting.

2. The old punishment-reward idea is still valid. People do develop favorable attitudes towards objects associated with satisfaction of needs and react unfavorably toward objects or events which thwart.

3. The clarity, consistency and nearness of rewards and punishments as they relate to the individual's activities and goals are im-portant factors in the development of attitudes. For example, management seeks to increase production by convincing workers that the plant is a good place to work, assuming that production will correspondingly rise. Management succeeds in convincing the workers that the plant is a good place to work. But production rates do not climb.

4. A hard-to-fit piece of the puzzle is the fact that when human subjects in research are invariably rewarded for correct responses, they do not tend to retain their learned responses as well as when the reward is sometimes skipped.

5. Many attitudes function to protect self-image. In these instances, external rewards and punishments are less important than the subject's own deep feelings. Satisfactions also accrue from the expression of attitudes which reflect cherished beliefs. The reward in these instances is not so much a matter of gaining social recognition or money as of confirming the subject's notion of the sort of person he seems to be.

6. People acquire attitudes and beliefs not only to satisfy needs, but also to give meaning to what would otherwise be an unorganized chaotic universe. To the educator's dismay, people are not too often seekers-after-knowledge-in-general. They *do* want to understand the events which impinge on their lives. Developing attitudes and beliefs about these events gives them order and clarity. Giving up these attitudes and beliefs threatens what Walter Lippman has called "the ordered more or less consistent picture of the world to which our habits, our tastes, our capacities, our comforts and our hopes have adjusted themselves."

One thing is clear. What Arthur Cohen has called "the links between changed attitudes and changes in learning performance, perception and interaction" need a lot more study. When it comes to training programs, the hard fact is: training programs which change attitudes and beliefs without forcing changes in the environment will result in workers talking a better game but doing the same old thing. Is that what we want? **T**

The basic laws of human behavior and learning are deceptively simple. Here's how to make sure you don't forget them

# Behavior modification principles for trainers

by Charles F. Schuler

As far as I'm concerned, the basic laws of human behavior are deceptively simple. So simple, in fact, and so deceptive in their simplicity, that it's possible to lose the flavor of their simplicity in the morass of overly complex academic explanation that characterizes much of the behavioral sciences. My own technique for keeping learning theory straight in my mind is, well, pretty simple. When in doubt about what I'm listening to or reading, I simply reflect on three little sentences:

- 99-44/100% of all behavior is learned.
- S.O.C. it to 'em.
- Behavior is a result of its consequences.

No matter how cloudy the writing or obscure the speaker, I can sort out what's being said using these three simple sentences.

The first of the three sentences says 99-44/100% of all behavior is learned. Yes, I stole my numbers from a box of Ivory soap; and, of course, I don't know if the figure is actually correct but I don't care. The point is that *almost* all behavior is learned behavior and the over-statement helps me remember that we learn to do most of the things we do; behavioral genetics be damned! The "almost but not quite" figure of 99-44/100 cues me to remember that in fact.

There are two categories of behavior; operant and respondent. Respondent behaviors are those few that we are born with. Nobody has to teach a baby to cry. No one needs to train us to quickly pull our hand away when we touch a hot burner on a stove. These behaviors are respondent, or reflex behaviors. We are born with them but they represent only a very small portion of the total number of things that we know how to do.

The other category, the operant behaviors, contains all of the things that we do when we operate within our environment. These are learned behaviors. No one necessarily taught them to us, but we did learn them and we learned them because of the natural laws of behavior. For all intents and purposes, almost all behavior is learned behavior. Certainly the behaviors that trainers deal with are operant, or learned, behaviors.

## S.O.C. it to 'em!

S.O.C. is actually an acronym for *specification, observation* and *consequation*. These are the three steps one performs to produce a behavior change.

**The specification step** sometimes takes place on paper in the form of writing goals or objectives for a formal training program. It also may take place in the mind of the trainer, supervisor or manager in working directly with an employee. If you're going to cause someone to be able to do something new, then you must be able to clearly specify exactly what that new behavior is to be. Our purpose here is not to go into an essay on behavioral objectives, but if you can't clearly define the new behavior, how are you going to know when the trainee has learned it? The first step is the precise specification of what you want the trainee to be able to do. Oh yes, sharing that expectation with the performer is part of the system. Both trainer and trainee must know what the expected behavior is.

**Observation is the second step.** The effective trainer, or manager or supervisor, must be able to determine what the employee is doing now in order to be able to tell when the behavior is changing. Researchers call this gathering baseline data. I just call it a part of good common sense. Suppose that you are a sales manager and you want each of your salespeople to get at least one new referral from each existing client. It's only logical that you have to know how many referrals they're getting now, in order to be able to measure any change or improvement. There are lots of ways of gathering this information and, of course, that depends upon what business or industry you're in and what new behaviors you're trying to teach.

**Consequation step is the final one.** It's the payoff that will actually cause the change to occur. As a trainer, you must arrange the consequences of what the employee is presently doing so that the desired change, that is, the new behavior that you have specified, begins to replace the present, or old behavior, that is taking place. In the case of the sales referrals, a positive consequence might be extra commissions, a bonus, a day off or just some highly complementary recognition from the regional manager. Start with the latter, interpersonal stroking; it's cheap and often effective. Best bet of all is to *ask* the performer what he or she would *like* as a payoff. Different strokes for different folks and all that.

## Behavior is the result of its consequences

This particular principle is really the only one that ever confuses anyone. The consequence of a behavior is that event which happens after you do something. Most behaviors have rather immediate consequences. Sometimes, however, the consequence, or payoff, doesn't come until sometime later. We are most influenced by that which happens to us after we perform the desired behavior. If good things happen to us after we exhibit some behavior, then we will be likely to exhibit that behavior again. Likewise, if bad things happen, then we probably won't exhibit that behavior again in the near future. For example, if a restaurant owner switches to a new brand of coffee and he finds that coffee sales increase, then he will probably continue to serve that type of coffee. On the other hand, if sales dropped, he would be likely to stop serving the new coffee and change back to the old brand.

In general, there are two major categories of consequences, good things and bad things. In more sophisticated terms, the good things are called reinforcers, and bad things are called punishers. By definition, a reinforcer is any event, or consequence, that increases the frequency or duration of the behavior that it follows. A punisher is any event, or consequence, that decreases the frequency or duration of the behavior that it follows. Remember, it is the *function* of the event, not the intent, that determines whether it is a reinforcer or a punisher. To determine if a consequence has reinforced or punished a behavior, you must look at what happened *after* it was applied.

Now comes the twist that sometimes confuses. There are two subcategories of reinforcement and two of punishment, giving us a total of four techniques that can be used to effectively change behavior. It is within these subcategories that misunderstandings and misuses are generally found. In designing training programs or materials, all four techniques can be effectively used under the appropriate circumstances. It is important that we understand the differences in the four processes.

## Reinforcement

The two types of reinforcement are positive reinforcement and negative reinforcement. Remember that by definition *all* reinforcers *increase* the behaviors that they follow. Positive reinforcers are those events that add something good to the employee's life. A pat on the back, a smile, a bonus, an extra commission or a prize for selling the most widgits could all be examples of positive reinforcers. Most company incentive programs try to deal in positive reinforcement.

Negative reinforcement is the process of removing something bad from the employee's life. Suppose that your labor crew was told that all of those who had perfect on-time attendance for 30 days would be excused from some particularly distasteful job that is usually done on the last day of the month; for instance, shoveling grindings in a steel mill. You would be negatively reinforcing good "on-time" attendance by removing a distasteful event. This is still a *reinforcer* because it will *increase* the frequency of the target behavior, on-time attendance.

Punishers also fall into two subgroups. Although it sounds rather unusual, the two types are positive punishment and negative punishment. Both types of punishers are designed to *decrease* the behavior that they follow. Positive punishment is the process of adding something bad to the employee's environment. Examples of positive punishment might include a negative comment or harsh words from the boss, a poor employee rating, or extra work to do (such as doing a job over if it wasn't done correctly the first time).

Negative punishment decreases the target behavior by removing something good from the employee's environment. A fine (i.e., removal of some portion of your wages), or the loss of a privilege might be examples of negative punishment.

In almost all instances, reinforcement techniques are far superior to punishment techniques in producing lasting changes in behavior. Research supports this feeling and also substantiates some other negative results of the use of punishment.

Well, that's it in a nutshell. And, as promised, these underlying principles of human behavior, principles I believe need to be in the professional trainer's toolbox, are indeed fairly simple—at least in concept. Application is another "horse," so to speak. The best way to learn application is from the experiences of others. Read TRAINING and other professional magazines. Whatever you read, ask yourself, "How do the principles apply here? What little things did the writer have to do to apply the principles effectively?"

And talk to people. Talk to people who are trying to apply sound learning principles to their training. Talk to people who are applying the principles of learning to the management of people. Find out what they learned, where they made mistakes, what they would do differently next time.

Finally, look about yourself for opportunities to apply these simple but powerful concepts systematically. Start small, but think big. Apply them in your own office with your own staff. Then find a situation, a good win-win situation with a supervisor or manager who is doing well and who wants to do better. Help him or her use these simple learning principles to enhance the organization's operation.

Behavioral psychology has brought us a set of very simple but very powerful tools we can use in the human resources development effort. Conceptually they are pretty easy to understand. But like any other "deceptively simple" set of ideas, they are worthless unless they are used. We must not only understand these principles but we must be prepared to apply them and apply them well. For that part of the story to have a happy ending, we must continually be looking for opportunities to succeed. And we must be willing to share our successes—and failures—with others. **T**

Helping trainees behave like high achievers has another payoff: Trainees learn complex technical skills faster—and better

# Enhancing skills acquisition through achievement motivation

by Lawrence Holpp

Skills training, whether it involves complex or routine tasks, can become boring and arduous work both for trainee and trainer. Seldom is all the information you teach in the classroom used on the job, and the excitement and urgency of the actual work environment is rarely present in training seminars.

Some of the reinforcing properties of on-the-job learning can, however, be built into skills training. One way is to base training on a theoretical model that has been shown to produce trainees motivated by a need for high achievement. That need—a powerful psychological drive—causes people to work harder at doing things better. Research by David C. McClelland and his associates indicates that individuals who have a high need to achieve (n Achievement) approach goal setting, problem solving, planning and organizing— all key management processes— with a degree of creativity and energy significantly greater than that of their peers. Direct training for n Achievement is effective in motivating owners of small businesses, corporate executives and students to behave in a more aggressive, entrepreneurial manner in their work. Can an approach to skills training that uses an achievement-motivation design have a similar effect?

Work in training underwriters to be better negotiators suggests that it can. Experience also suggests that n Achievement training can help them master, on the job, many complex technical areas with minimum cost to the organization. An n Achievement design can also produce measurable changes in the climate of an organization, resulting in higher morale, lower turnover rates, increased confidence and specific, quantifiable improvements in sales-related activities.

The need for achievement is a drive. Henry Murry, who first named n Achievement, described it in the following way: "To accomplish something difficult. To master, manipulate, or organize physical objects, human beings or ideas. To do this as rapidly and as independently as possible. To excel oneself." (From *Explorations in Personality*, 1938.)

Overall, this drive produces highly efficient, goal-directed people. However, the nature and strength of drives are variable and subject to competing psychological interpretations. To be measurable, a drive must activate behavior—it must cause the individual to operate on the environment, not merely respond when conditions call it forth. An individual who has operant n Achievement characteristics thinks about achievement and structures his life accordingly. The *respondent* individual may show an interest in achievement, but only when prompted from outside. This is a key difference. The individual high in n Achievement scans the environment for opportunities; the respondent individual waits for opportunity to knock.

We measure this characteristic by qualitative, not merely quantitative, behavior. High n Achievers may or may not contemplate achievement more often than those low in n Achievement, but they will more frequently focus their achievement-related imagery *toward goals*.

McClelland and his colleagues used Murry's Thematic Apperception Test (T.A.T.) to measure the degree to which n Achievement thinking was present in their subjects. By comparing pre-training and post-training T.A.T. scores of latent n Achievement, McClelland showed that it was possible to increase the number of operant verbal responses indicating n Achievement through training his subjects to think and act in more goal-directed ways. This is important because such increases lead directly to better performance on a variety of tasks. Since organizations are interested in performance, not "operant verbal responses," let us focus on the specific behaviors and conditions research has indicated will increase performance.

N Achievement skills training is based on observed behaviors of individuals high in n Achievement. These behaviors show interest in goal setting, responsibility, feedback and activity— all of which indicate that an n-Achievement design is well suited to organizational development.

• **Goal setting:** N Achievers set goals of moderate difficulty that are challenging but attainable. Moderate goals tell the n Achiever more about how he or she is doing than goals that are either too hard or too easy.

• **Responsibility:** Individuals high in n Achievement like to take responsibility for their actions. They gravitate to jobs that allow them maximum control over the means of attaining their goals.

• **Feedback:** N Achievers select goals and milestones which are concrete and readily measurable. Because profit and loss statements tend to fall in this category, business people often show considerable n Achievement.

• **Activity:** N Achievers are very active. They have high energy levels, and they apply their energy to solving business problems, bringing them closer to their goals.

Training designed around these four characteristics will promote frequent goal setting, encourage and reward people to take responsibility for new ideas, provide a mechanism for

## Figure 1. How to get started

If you decide to go with this approach to skills training, here are a few things you will need to do to help make it work.

1. **Technical information:** Any information which can be learned individually or in small groups can be taught with this approach. Be sure to divide your material into half-hour to four-hour study blocks, even if it means tearing apart your regular binders and repackaging the material. This will allow your trainees to set *moderate* learning goals.

2. **Activity:** Be sure each study session is followed by some sort of practice with the material. Activity with the new ideas is vital for any learning, particularly for achievement learning. Our example in this paper is role playing, which is learning by doing. If you should go with role playing, don't try to script dozens of role plays but let your people work them out from your clear directions. Be sure to include goal milestones, control and responsibility, feedback and opportunities for expanded enterprise.

3. **Climate:** Since you probably won't have the chief executive officer in your first group, you'll have to promote a good climate from the bottom up. We suggest some sort of coaching model. This lets you turn a staff function into a line function. Once strong line people buy in, climate creates itself.

4. **Following up:** Once you have run a briefing, move out of center field. If the reporting structure is clear, the system will move without you.

5. **Planning:** Most foes of this kind of approach don't try new things and fail, they fail to try at all. Plans for on-the-job application of skills must be made following each study segment and shared with peers and superiors.

## Figure 2. Is achievement motivation training for your organization?

Use the following questions to determine whether or not your training program can use the *n* Achievement approach.

1. Does the training emphasize goal setting?
2. Does training distinguish between goals of moderate, high and low difficulty?
3. Can goals be made challenging?
4. Will participants have input into how goals are met?
5. Is the responsibility for success or failure of goals in the participants' hands?
6. Can participants set training objectives?
7. Is the participant's role clear?
8. Is the boss's role clear?
9. Are channels of communication open to facilitate concrete feedback?
10. Is "good performance" an objective measure?
11. Is the climate of your organization conducive to displays of individual initiative?
12. Is there an organizational support system for planning and goal setting?

5 = Substantially
4 = Somewhat
3 = A little
2 = Not much
1 = Not at all

feedback and create organizational channels so that activity in new areas is encouraged.

In a program to train underwriters, technical material was structured in a series of cases, or practice sessions, ollowed lby role plays. Scripts were not written for the role plays, but careful directions were given. After every practice session, each participant developed a personal plan for the role play, going back to the technical information presented in the practice session to retrieve needed facts and figures. How well a person did this depended, in part, upon his or her level of *n* Achievement.

In order to develop a plan for the role play, an individual must set moderate but challenging goals, devise his or her own way of reaching those goals, assume responsibility for success or failure (saying "the boss told me so" is not allowed), devise a system for obtaining feedback and engage in systematic planning that includes anticipating problems and developing flexibility to accommodate changing situations. The effects of this kind of training are significant. Participants' confidence and energy levels increase, along with sales calls.

## Using coaches

In the underwriter training program, line managers were designated coaches, and the responsibility for creating a positive climate was put in their hands. Their jobs were carefully spelled out to include helping employees set goals and get feedback for their efforts, maintaining an organizational climate conducive to testing new ideas at a line level, facilitating the acquisition of vital skills in product areas and cross-training between departments.

To ensure that the coaches (first- or second-level supervisory managers) kept their people on track, they were in turn supervised by a business development manager who reported directly to the branch manager. Overall team success became an element in measuring the coaches' performance, making it worth their while to give feedback and keep things going.

## Climate

Changing the climate in an organization to facilitate high achievement is usually an expensive and complex organizational development effort conducted from the top down. When line managers are used as coaches in skills training and given clear authority to keep organizational channels open, their team members gain access to new challenges and opportunities for growth and experimentation. This produces an organizational climate conducive to *n* Achievement from the bottom up. Not only is the coach responsible for advocating or running interference for team members, he or she is able to get a payoff at appraisal time for doing so.

## Cross-training

In any industry, the more people trained to do several different jobs, the more useful they are and the better they are able to represent their organization. This can be accomplished by forming coaching groups across departmental lines. Any skill which is common to most of the members of an organization can be taught interdepartmentally, with cross-training results.

## Summary

Strong evidence suggests that organizations that demonstrate a favorable climate to *n* Achievement are more productive, show increases in sales, decreased turnover, lower rates of absenteeism, healthier employees, greater geographic growth— even more suggestions in the suggestion box. By using a training design shown to be effective in getting employees to behave like high achievers, and by creating a climate that will encourage their efforts, the human-resource professional can help carry the motivating influence of the bench, shop or work unit into the classroom and back again.

This system is good for the organization because it minimizes time off for centralized training and because it has many characteristics of on-the-job learning. In the long run, the success of this approach will earn the trainer valuable support within the organization for infusing new and different ideas— which is, after all, the final purpose of education. And the trainee, to paraphrase a very old saying, has been given not a fish, but a fishing rod and a clear map to a well stocked stream. **T**

### References

Litwin, G.H. & Stringer, R.A. *Motivation and Organizational Climate*. Boston. Division of Research, Graduate School of Business Administration, Harvard University, 1968.

McClelland, D.C. (1962) "Business Drive and National Achievement," *Harvard Business Review*, 40:July-August, 99-112.

McClelland, D.C. & Winter, D. *Motivating Economic Achievement*. New York, N.Y. The Free Press, 1969.

McClelland, D.C. (Ed.) *Human Motivation*. Morristown, N.J. General Learning Press, 1973.